KAVOUSI

The Results of the Excavations at Kavousi in Eastern Crete

Directed by
Geraldine C. Gesell, Leslie Preston Day,
and William D.E. Coulson

Sponsored by
The University of Tennessee

Under the auspices of
The American School of Classical Studies at Athens

Frontispiece. Large pedestaled krater (**GR27 P4**), Early Orientalizing. Watercolor D. Faulmann.

KAVOUSI IV

The Early Iron Age Cemeteries at Vronda

Part 2

TABLES, CHARTS, FIGURES, AND PLATES

By

Leslie Preston Day and Maria A. Liston

Contributions by

Kimberly Flint-Hamilton, Kevin T. Glowacki, Eleni Nodarou,
Effie Photos-Jones, David S. Reese, Lynn M. Snyder, and Julie Unruh

Edited by

Geraldine C. Gesell and Leslie Preston Day

Published by
INSTAP Academic Press
Philadelphia, Pennsylvania
2023

Design and Production
INSTAP Academic Press, Philadelphia, PA

Printing and Binding
HF Group – Acmebinding, Charlestown, MA

INSTAP Academic Press, a part of the Institute for Aegean Prehistory (INSTAP), was established to publish projects relevant to the history of the Aegean world, in particular from the Paleolithic to the 8th century B.C. It is a scholarly nonprofit publisher specializing in high-quality publications of primary source material from archaeological excavations as well as individual studies dealing with material from the prehistoric periods—exemplified by its *Prehistory Monographs* series of volumes. INSTAP is committed to engaging a variety of audiences by disseminating knowledge through its scholarly publishing program, which produces award-winning monographs at reasonable prices that are both academically and popularly acclaimed.

Library of Congress Cataloging-in-Publication Data

Names: Day, Leslie Preston, author, editor. | Liston, Maria A., author. | Flint-Hamilton, Kimberly, contributor. | Glowacki, Kevin T. (Kevin Thomas), 1961- contributor | Nodarou, Eleni, contributor | Photos-Jones, Effie, contributor | Reese, David S., 1954- contributor | Snyder, Lynn M., contributor | Unruh, Julie contributor. | Gesell, Geraldine Cornelia, editor. Title: Kavousi IV : the early Iron Age cemetaries at Vronda / by Leslie Preston Day and Maria A. Liston ; contributions by Kimberly Flint-Hamilton, Kevin T. Glowacki, Eleni Nodarou, Effie Photos-Jones, David S. Reese, Lynn M. Snyder, and Julie Unruh ; edited by Geraldine C. Gesell and Leslie Preston Day.

Description: Philadelphia, Pennsylvania : INSTAP Academic Press, 2023. | Series: Prehistory monographs ; 71 | Includes bibliographical references and index. | Contents: Introduction / Leslie Preston Day -- Tholos tombs at Vronda / Leslie Preston Day and Maria A. Liston -- Enclosure burials at Vronda / Leslie Preston Day, Maria A. Liston, Kimberly Flint-Hamilton, David S. Reese, and Lynn M. Snyder -- Cremation process / Maria A. Liston -- Human remains / Maria A. Liston -- Faunal and botanical remains / Lynn M. Snyder, David S. Reese, and Kimberly Flint-Hamilton -- Funerary architecture / Leslie Preston Day -- Early Iron Age pottery / Leslie Preston Day -- Petrographic analysis of the grave ceramic assemblage / Eleni Nodarou -- Finds other than pottery / Leslie Preston Day, with a contribution by Julie Unruh -- Burial customs / Leslie Preston Day -- History and society in the Vronda graves / Leslie Preston Day. | Summary: "This volume presents the results of the excavation of two cemeteries at the site of Vronda Kavousi in East Crete: the cemetery of tholos tombs belong to the Subminoan to Protogeometric periods (with some use in the eighth century B.C.) and the cemetery of enclosure graves with cremation burials belonging to the Late Geometric to Late Orientalizing periods. A discussion of individual graves (including the stratigraphy, architecture, human remains, faunal and botanical remains, pottery, and other finds) is followed by the analysis of the cremation process and human remains, the faunal and botanical remains, the pottery, the petrographic analysis of the pottery, the metalsand other finds, the burial customs, and the history and society of the burying population. A study of the capacities of some of the pottery vessels and a metallurgical analysis of the iron objects appear in appendices"-- Provided by publisher.

Identifiers: LCCN 2022055543 (print) | LCCN 2022055544 (ebook) | ISBN 9781931534369 (v. 1 ; hardback) | ISBN 9781931534369 (v. 2 ; hardback) | ISBN 9781623034412 (pdf)

Subjects: LCSH: Excavations (Archaeology)--Greece--Kavousi Region. | Cemeteries--Greece--Kavousi Region. | Grave goods--Greece--Kavousi Region. | Human remains--Greece--Kavousi Region. | Tombs--Greece--Kavousi Region. | Iron Age--Greece--Kavousi Region. | Kavousi Region (Greece)--Antiquities.

Classification: LCC DF261.K4 D397 2023 (print) | LCC DF261.K4 (ebook) | DDC 938--dc23/eng/20230505

LC record available at https://lccn.loc.gov/2022055543

LC ebook record available at https://lccn.loc.gov/202205554

Table of Contents

Tables

Charts

Figures

Plates

List of Tables

List of Charts

List of Figures

List of Plates

Tables

Approximate Date (B.C.)	Knossos	Eleutherna	East Crete	Kavousi Kastro	Kavousi Vronda	Athens
1050	SM					EPG, MPG
1000			SM	Transitional LM IIIC–PG	SM	
970	EPG					LPG
950						
920						
900	MPG	MPG	PG	PG		EG I
875	LPG	LPG			PG	EG II
850		PGB				
840	PGB			SubPG		MG I
810		EG	PGB			
800	EG					MG II
790	MG	MG		G	G	
760			G/LG			LG I
745	LG	LG		LG	LG	LG II
700	EO	EPAR	EO	EO	EO	
670	MO				LO	ProtoAttic/ SubG
630	End of North Cemetery, LO	LPAR				
600			O	O	End of Vronda Cemetery	
570–480	Archaic	Archaic	Archaic	Archaic		Archaic

Table 1. Comparative Late Bronze Age and Early Iron Age chronologies. After Coldstream 2001, 22 (Knossos, Athens); Mook 2004, 164–173 (Kavousi Kastro); Tsipopoulou 2005, 345–348 (East Crete); Kotsonas 2008, 32–36 (Eleutherna); and Day 2016, 197–199 (Kavousi Vronda). Wavy lines indicate that boundaries between periods are not secure.

Tomb	Fauna	Number of Specimens	Context
I total: 1	*Ovis aries* or *Capra hircus*	1	Dromos
II total: 4	*Ovis aries* or *Capra hircus*	3	Cleaning
	Unidentifiable	1	Cleaning
IV total: 1	*Ovis aries* or *Capra hircus*	1	Cleaning
V total: 2	*Ovis aries* or *Capra hircus*	2	Dromos

Table 2. Tholos tombs: summary of faunal remains. Common names include: *Bos taurus* = cattle, *Canis familiaris* = dog, *Capra hircus* = goat, *Lepus* = rabbit or hare, *Ovis aries* = sheep, *Sus scrofa* = pig.

Tomb	Fauna	Number of Specimens	Context
VI total: 20	*Lepus* sp.	1	Cleaning
	Capra hircus	4	Cleaning
	Ovis aries or *Capra hircus*	13	Cleaning
	Canis familiaris	2	Cleaning
VIII total: 8	*Capra hircus*	1	Hard soil at bottom
	Ovis aries or *Capra hircus*	5	Hard soil at bottom
	Rattus rattus	2	Hard soil at bottom
X total: ca. 7,500, including bone fragments	*Canis familiaris*	2,942 (MNI = 12) + fragments	Pit below tomb
	Felis sylvestris	256 (MNI = 4) + fragments	Pit below tomb
	Ovis aries or *Capra hircus*	few	Pit below tomb
	Sus scrofa	few	Pit below tomb
	Bos taurus	few	Pit below tomb
XI total: 4	*Ovis aries* or *Capra hircus*	1	Pit in front of stomion
	Bos taurus?	1	Stones over pit
	Ovis aries or *Capra hircus*	2	Stones over pit

Table 2, cont. Tholos tombs: summary of faunal remains. Common names include: *Bos taurus* = cattle, *Canis familiaris* = dog, *Capra hircus* = goat, *Felis sylvestris* = cat, *Lepus* = rabbit or hare, *Ovis aries* = sheep, *Rattus rattus* = rat, *Sus scrofa* = pig.

Tomb	Species	Complete	Fragments	Comments	Location
IV	*Glycymeris*	1?	—	Very waterworn, upper part and side, ancient breaks	Cleaning
VIII	*Mactra*	—	1	Side fragment, medium	V 7102.2
	Phorcus	—	Several	1 MNI	V 7606.1
	Patella	—	2	1 center, 1 edge, 1 MNI (medium/large)	V 7613.1
	Patella	—	1	Center, large	V 7613.3
	Patella	1	—	Open center, L. 41.00 mm	V 7617.2 (pseudo-dromos)
IX	*Glycymeris*	1		Waterworn, no distal (ancient break) (h. 50.00+ mm; w. 59.75 mm; hole at umbo 5.25 x 3.25 mm)	Dump
	Glycymeris	—	1	Hinge, waterworn (w. ca. 37.00+ mm), ancient break	Dump
X	*Hexaplex*	1?	—	Waterworn, small (L. 33.00 mm; w. 22.75 mm)	Interior, northeast corner
XI	*Glycymeris*	1?	—	Waterworn, no hinge/distal/sides, rather large	Consolidation

Table 3. Tholos tombs: summary of marine shells. Common names include: *Glycymeris pilosa* = dog cockle, *Hexaplex* = murex, *Mactra corallina* = trough shell, *Phorcus* = *Monodonta turbinata* = topshell, *Patella* = limpet.

Grave	Fauna	Number of Specimens	Context
1 total: 222 (209 calcined)	Ovis aries or Capra hircus	9 (8 calcined)	V 310.2, V 337.4
	Cf. Ovis aries or Capra hircus	184 (all calcined)	V 302.1, V 310.2
	Cf. Cervidae sp.	6 (all calcined)	V 805.2, V 805.3
	Unidentifiable	23 (11 calcined)	V 337.4, V 805.2, V 805.3
2 total: 31 (4 burned)	Cf. Ovis aries or Capra hircus	11	V 12402.4
	Canis familiaris	4 (all burned)	V 12400.1
	Unidentifiable	16	V 12400.1, V 12402.4, V 12452.1
4 total: 30 (4 calcined)	Sus scrofa	1	V 4004.1
	Ovis aries or Capra hircus	5	V 4004..4, V 4009.1
	Cf. Ovis aries or Capra hircus	1 (calcined)	V 4009.1 and .2
	Lepus	2	V 4009.1, V 4009.2
	Unidentifiable	21 (3 calcined)	V 4003.2, V 4004.1, V 4004.4, V 4009.1, V 4009.2
5 total: 167 (2 burned, 13 calcined)	Bos taurus?	1	V 4012.4
	Sus scrofa	4	V 4017.2, V 4017.3
	Ovis aries or Capra hircus	18 (1 burned)	V 4007 ext., V 4012, V 4012.4, V 4012.6, V 4016, V 4016.2, V 4017.2, V 4017.3, V 3509.1, V 3509.5
	Cf. Ovis aries or Capra hircus	9, plus additional tooth fragments	V 4007 ext., V 4012.4, V 4012.6, V 3509.5
	Ovis aries, Capra hircus or Sus scrofa	1	V 3506.2
	Canis familiaris	1	V 4016.1
	Unidentifiable	133 (1 burned, 13 calcined)	V 4012.4, V 4012.1, V 4012.4, V 4012.6, V 4016, V 4016.1, V 4017.2, V 4017.3, V 3505.2, V 3506.2, V 3509.1, V 3509.2

Table 4. Graves 1, 2, 4, and 5: summary of faunal remains. *Cervidae* = deer; for other common names, see Table 2.

Grave(s)	Species	Complete	Fragments	Comments	Location
1	Vermetid	1	—	Max. ext. d. 14.0 mm; large, L. 34.5 cm; could be strung, broken at either end	V 302.1
4	Patella	—	1	—	V 4011.1
15	Phorcus	—	2	1 MNI	VW 10012.1
28	Hexaplex	1	—	Worn, open body	VW 11108
30, 7, 33	Patella	1	—	1 MNI	VW 9008.1
36	Patella	—	2	1 small–medium MNI	V 12802.3

Table 5. Enclosure burials: summary of marine shells. For common names, see Table 3.

Grave	Fauna	Number of Specimens	Context
6 total: 21 (5 calcined, 2 partially burned)	*Bos taurus*	1	V 10801.1
	Sus scrofa	1 (partially burned)	V 10818.2
	Ovis aries or *Capra hircus*	8	V 10812.1, V 10817.1, V 10820, V 10821.2
	Cf. *Ovis aries* or *Capra hircus*	6 (2 calcined)	V 10802.1, V 10807.2, V 10815.1
	Cervidae sp.	3 (all calcined)	V 10819.4, V 10821.1
	Unidentifiable	2 (1 partially burned)	V 10812.3, V 10818.2
8 total: 5	Unidentifiable	5	VW 9014.3, VW 9014.4
9 total: 503 (25 burned, 29 calcined)	*Sus scrofa*	1	V 5302.1
	Ovis aries	2 (1 burned, 1 calcined)	V 5312.4, V 5313.2
	Ovis aries or *Capra hircus*	12 (5 burned, 6 calcined)	V 5312.1, V 5312.4, V 5313.3, V 5314.2, V 5314.6, V 5314.7, V 5319.1, V 5324.1
	Cf. *Ovis aries* or *Capra hircus*	17, plus additional fragments (calcined)	V 5311.1, V 5314.3, V 5314.5–7, V 5324.1
	Lepus sp.	4	V 5302.2, V 5310.1, V 5312.2, V 5324.1
	Snake sp.	6 (all burned)	V 5312.3, V 5319.2, V 5319.4/5
	Unidentifiable small rodent or insectivore	420 (1 burned, 14 calcined)	V 5310.3, V 5312.1, V 5312.3, V 5312.4/5, V 5319.2
	Unidentifiable small mammal	6 (1 burned, 5 calcined)	V 5312.3, V 5319.2
	Unidentifiable	35 (11 burned, 3 calcined)	V 5302.1, V 5302.2, V 5311.1, V 5312.2, V 5314.3

Table 6. Graves 6, 8, and 9: summary of faunal remains. For common names, see Tables 2 and 4.

Grave	Fauna	Number of Specimens	Context
10 total: 578 (1 calcined)	*Ovis aries* or *Capra hircus*	2	V 4800.4
	Lepus sp.	8	V 4804.2
	Unidentifiable: small, probably *Lepus*	568 (1 calcined)	V 4800.4, V 4804.2, V 4804.3
12 total: 649 (100+ burned, 28 calcined, 1 with cut marks)	*Sus scrofa*	7 (1 burned, 1 calcined)	V 4805.3, V 4805.5, V 4805.6
	Cf. *Sus scrofa*	1	V 4805.3
	Ovis aries or *Capra hircus*	47 (some burned, 1 calcined)	V 4805, V 4805.3, V 4805.4, V 4805.5

Table 7. Graves 10, 12, 13, and 15–17: summary of faunal remains. *Aves* = bird; for other common names, see Table 4.

Grave	Fauna	Number of Specimens	Context
12, cont. total: 649 (100+ burned, 28 calcined, 1 with cut marks)	Cervidae sp.	8 (3 calcined; 1 with cut marks)	V 4805.2, V 4805.3, V 4805.4
	Mouse sp.	1	V 4805.3
	Aves sp.	1	V 4805.5
	Unidentifiable	584 (99 plus many others burned, 23 calcined)	V 4805, V 4805.2, V 4805.3, V 4805.4, V 4805.5, V 4805.6
13 total: 24 (5 calcined)	*Ovis aries* or *Capra hircus*	3	VN 201.1–4, VN 202.3, VN 210.1
	Canis familiaris	1	VN 205.10
	Unidentifiable	20 (5 calcined)	VN 201.1–4, VN 202.3, VN 205.10, VN 206.4, VN 206.7, VN 210.1
15 total: 26 (3 calcined)	*Ovis aries* or *Capra hircus*	4	VW 10012.1, VW 10012.2, VW 10102.1
	Unidentifiable	22 (3 calcined)	VW 10012.1, VW 10012.2, VW 10102.1
16 total: 44 (9 calcined, 7 partially burned)	*Lepus* sp.	1	V 6204.1
	Unidentifiable	43 (9 calcined, 7 partially burned)	V 6204.1, V 6205.2
17 total: 30	*Sus scrofa*	1	V 4809.2
	Unidentifiable	29	V 4809.1, V 4809.2

Table 7, cont. Graves 10, 12, 13, and 15–17: summary of faunal remains. *Aves* = bird; for other common names, see Table 4.

Grave	Fauna	Number of Specimens	Context
20 total: 363 (37 burned, 19 calcined, 6 burned or calcined, 4 heated)	*Sus scrofa*	1	V 4709.2
	Cf. *Sus scrofa*	1 (burned)	V 4709.2
	Ovis aries or *Capra hircus*	13 (5 burned, 1 calcined)	V 4701.1, V 4703.1, V 4703.2, V 4704.2, V 4709.2, V 4709.3,
	Lepus sp.	1	V 4701.2,
	Cf. *Lepus* sp.	1	V 4709.2
	Unidentifiable	346 (32 burned, 18 calcined, 6 burned or calcined, 4 heated)	V 4701.1, V 4701.2, V 4703.1, V 4704.2, V 4704.4, V 4705.2, V 4705.3, V 4707.1, V 4708.3, V 4709.2, V 4709.3
21 total: 146 (2 burned, 4 calcined, 2 burned or calcined)	*Sus scrofa*	5 (1 burned)	V 5349.1, V 5349.2, V 5351.2
	Ovis aries or *Capra hircus*	4 (1 calcined)	V 5348.3, V 5349.1, V 5349.2

Table 8. Graves 20, 21, 23, and 24: summary of faunal remains. For common names, see Tables 2 and 4.

Grave	Fauna	Number of Specimens	Context
21, cont. total: 146 (2 burned, 4 calcined, 2 burned or calcined)	Cf. *Ovis aries* or *Capra hircus*	1	V 5347.1
	Canis familiaris	6	V 5348.4, V 5349.2, V 5351.2
	Cervidae sp.	1 (burned or calcined)	V 5348.3
	Cervidae sp. or *Bos taurus*	1 (burned or calcined)	V 5351.1
	Ovis aries, Capra hircus, or *Sus scrofa*	1	V 5351.2
	Unidentifiable	127 (1 burned, 3 calcined)	V 5347.1, V 5348.2, V 5348.3, V 5348.4, V 5349.1, V 5349.2, V 5350.4, V 5351.2
23 total: 7 (1 burned, 1 calcined)	*Ovis aries* or *Capra hircus*	1	VW 8101.2
	Cf. *Ovis aries* or *Capra hircus*	1	VW 8104.3
	Unidentifiable	5 (1 burned, 1 calcined)	VW 8101.4
24 total: 72 (1 burned, 1 calcined)	*Bos taurus*	1	VW 9208.4
	Sus scrofa	7	VW 9208.1, VW 9208.4
	Ovis aries or *Capra hircus*	5	VW 9208.2, VW 9208.4
	Unidentifiable	59 (1 burned, 1 calcined)	VW 9205.1, VW 9208.1, VW 9208.2, VW 9208.4

Table 8, cont. Graves 20, 21, 23, and 24: summary of faunal remains. For common names, see Tables 2 and 4.

Grave	Fauna	Number of Specimens	Context
26 total: 413 (66 burned, 31 calcined, 196 burned or calcined, 2 heated or burned)	*Ovis aries* or *Capra hircus*	40 (21 burned, 9 calcined, 3 burned or calcined)	V 8732.1, V 8732.2, V 8732.3, V 8732.4, V 8732.1–5
	Unidentifiable	373 (45 burned, 22 calcined, 193 burned or calcined, 2 heated or burned)	V 8730.1, V 8732.1, V 8732.2, V 8732.3, V 8732.4, V 8732.5
27 total: 24 (2 burned, 1 burned or calcined)	*Ovis aries* or *Capra hircus*	1 (burned or calcined)	V 9255.1
	Cervidae sp.	1	V 9254.1
	Unidentifiable	22 (2 burned)	V 9255.1, V 9261.2
29 total: 139 (2 heated or burned, 11 calcined)	*Bos* sp.	1	V 14408.2
	Sus	2	V 14404.1, V 14408.2

Table 9. Graves 26, 27, and 29–32: summary of faunal remains. For common names, see Tables 2 and 4.

Grave	Fauna	Number of Specimens	Context
29, cont. total: 139 (2 heated or burned, 11 calcined)	*Ovis aries* or *Capra hircus*	8	V 14404.1, V 14408.1, V 14408.2
	Cf. *Ovis aries* or *Capra hircus*	1 (calcined)	V 14408.1
	Unidentifiable	127 (2 heated or burned, 10 calcined)	V 14404.1, V 14408.1, V 14408.2
30 total: 48 (18 burned, 16 calcined, 4 burned or calcined)	*Bos?*	1 (calcined)	VW 8010.2
	Sus scrofa	1 (calcined)	VW 8011.3
	Sus or *Bos*	1 (calcined)	VW 8010.2
	Ovis aries or *Capra hircus*	11 (3 calcined)	VW 8001.1, VW 8010.2, VW 8011.2, VW 8011.3, VW 9008.1
	Cf. *Ovis aries* or *Capra hircus*	8 (5 burned)	VW 8011.2/3, VW 9008.1
	Unidentifiable	26 (13 burned, 10 calcined, 4 burned or calcined)	VW 8010.2, VW 8011.2, VW 8011.3, VW 9001.2, VW 9007.1, VW 9008.1
31 total: 6 (2 burned, 5 calcined)	Cf. *Bos* or Cervidae	1 (burned)	V 4524.1
	Unidentifiable	5 (all calcined)	V 4524.1
32 total: 16 (4 burned, 3 calcined, 7 burned or calcined)	*Sus scrofa*	1 (burned)	V 8805.1
	Ovis aries or *Capra hircus*	1	V 8305.3
	Unidentifiable	14 (3 burned, 3 calcined, 7 burned or calcined)	V 8209.1, V 8209.2, V 8802.3, V8805.1

Table 9, cont. Graves 26, 27, and 29–32: summary of faunal remains. For common names, see Tables 2 and 4.

Grave	Fauna	Number of Specimens	Context
34 total: 48 (17 calcined)	*Ovis aries* or *Capra hircus*	5, plus additional tooth fragments	VW 12014.1, VW 12014.2, VW 12015.1, VW 12015.3
	Cf. *Ovis aries*, *Capra hircus*, or Cervidae	1 (calcined)	VW 12012.1
	Unidentifiable	42 (16 calcined)	VW 12014.1, VW 12014.2, VW 12015.1, VW 12015.3
36 total: 131 (101 calcined)	*Sus scrofa*	2	V 12803.3
	Mouse or shrew	1	V 12807.2
	Unidentifiable	128 (101 calcined)	V 12803.3, V 12805.1, V 12805.2, V 12806.1, V 12806.2, V 12807.2

Table 10. Graves 34 and 36: summary of faunal remains. For common names, see Tables 2 and 4.

TABLE 11

Grave	Burial	Age Category	Age (Years)	Sex	Type	Deposition	Structure	Total Wt. (g)/ Number of Burials Included	Comments
1	1	Adult	20–40	Male	Cremation	Disturbed	Enclosure	1,572/2	n/a
	2	Adult	n/a	Unknown	Cremation	Disturbed	Enclosure	1,572/2	n/a
2	1	Adult	n/a	Female	Cremation	Disturbed	Rock tumble	667	Possibly from Grave 5
3	1	Adult	20–40	Male	Cremation	Disturbed	Enclosure	550	n/a
	2	Juvenile	16–20	Female	Cremation	Disturbed	Enclosure	617	n/a
4	1	Juvenile	15–20	Female	Cremation	Disturbed	Enclosure	606	n/a
	2	Fetus	20 weeks	Unknown	Cremation	Disturbed	Enclosure	8	n/a
	3	Infant	12–14 months	Unknown	Cremation	Disturbed	Enclosure	91	n/a
5	1	Adult	25–40	Male	Cremation	Disturbed	Enclosure	1,264	With Grave 11 added
	2	Adult	40–60	Male	Cremation	Disturbed	Enclosure	1,278/2	n/a
	3	Juvenile	18–20	Female?	Cremation	Disturbed	Enclosure	1,278/2	n/a
	4	Infant	40 weeks	Unknown	Cremation	Disturbed	Enclosure	367	n/a
	5	Juvenile	9–12	Unknown	Cremation	Disturbed	Enclosure	596	n/a
	6	Infant	3–9 months	Unknown	Cremation	Disturbed	Enclosure	108	n/a
	7	Adult	60+	Male	Inhumation	Primary	Enclosure	Not recorded	n/a
6	1	Adult	20–40	Unknown	Cremation	Disturbed	Enclosure	791	n/a
	2	Infant	40 weeks	Unknown	Cremation	Disturbed	Enclosure	35	n/a
	3	Adult	20–40	Unknown	Cremation	Disturbed	Enclosure	1,102	n/a
	4	Adult	50–60	Male	Cremation	Primary	Enclosure	2,523	n/a
	5	Adult	60+	Unknown	Inhumation	Disturbed	Enclosure	194	n/a
7*	See Grave 30	n/a	n/a	n/a	n/a	n/a	n/a	n/a	n/a
8	1	Adult	20–40?	Female?	Cremation	Secondary	Pit	346	n/a
	2	Fetus	16–20 weeks	Unknown	Cremation	Secondary	Pit	5	n/a
9	1	Adult	40–60	Male?	Cremation	Disturbed	Enclosure	504	With Grave 14 added
	2	Adult	35–39	Female?	Cremation	Disturbed	Enclosure	2,454	n/a
	3	Fetus	20–24 weeks	Unknown	Cremation	Disturbed	Enclosure	17	n/a
	4	Adult	40–60	Male	Cremation	Disturbed	Enclosure	2,407	n/a

Table 11. Skeletal remains from Vronda enclosure graves and tholos tombs. *Grave number originally assigned, but later found be discard deposit.

TABLE 11

Grave	Burial	Age Category	Age (Years)	Sex	Type	Deposition	Structure	Total Wt. (g)/ Number of Burials Included	Comments
9	5	Adult	n/a	Unknown	Cremation	Disturbed	Enclosure	2,063/2	n/a
	6	Adult	n/a	Unknown	Cremation	Disturbed	Enclosure	2,063/2	n/a
	7	Infant	0.5–2.0	Unknown	Cremation	Disturbed	Enclosure	144	n/a
10	1	Juvenile	5–6	Unknown	Inhumation	Primary	Pithos in enclosure	Not recorded	n/a
11*	See Grave 5	n/a	n/a	n/a	n/a	n/a	n/a	n/a	n/a
12	1	Adult	n/a	Unknown	Cremation	Disturbed	Enclosure	18	n/a
	2	Adult	n/a	Unknown	Cremation	Disturbed	Enclosure	159/2	n/a
	3	Adult	n/a	Unknown	Cremation	Disturbed	Enclosure	159/2	n/a
	4	Adult	20–40	Unknown	Cremation	Primary?	Enclosure	2,921/2	n/a
	5	Adult	40–60	Male	Cremation	Disturbed	Enclosure	2,921/2	n/a
	6	Adult	22–24	Female	Cremation	Primary	Enclosure	1,767	n/a
	7	Fetus	22–34 weeks	Unknown	Cremation	Disturbed	Enclosure	29	n/a
	8	Juvenile	5–6	Unknown	Cremation	Disturbed	Enclosure	167	n/a
13	1	Adult	n/a	Unknown	Cremation	Disturbed	Pyre	198/2	n/a
	2	Adult	n/a	Unknown	Cremation	Disturbed	Pyre	198/2	n/a
14*	See Grave 9	n/a	n/a	n/a	n/a	n/a	n/a	n/a	n/a
15	1	Adult	40–60	Unknown	Cremation	Disturbed	Enclosure	1,424/2	n/a
	2	Adult	n/a	Female	Cremation	Disturbed	Enclosure	1,424/2	n/a
	3	Fetus	16–32 weeks	Unknown	Cremation	Disturbed	Enclosure	13	n/a
	4	Adult	n/a	Unknown	Cremation	Disturbed	Enclosure	623	n/a
16	1	Juvenile	13–20	Unknown	Cremation	Disturbed	Enclosure	839/2	n/a
	2	Adult	30–40	Unknown	Cremation	Disturbed	Enclosure	839/2	n/a
17	1	Adult	40–60	Male	Cremation	Disturbed	Enclosure	2,065	n/a
	2	Juvenile	15–17	Unknown	Cremation	Disturbed	Enclosure	138	n/a
	3	Infant	40 weeks	Unknown	Cremation	Disturbed	Enclosure	20	n/a
18*	See Tholos VIII	n/a	n/a	n/a	n/a	n/a	n/a	n/a	n/a
19	1	Adult	20–40?	Unknown	Cremation	Disturbed	Enclosure	1,833/2	n/a

Table 11, cont. Skeletal remains from Vronda enclosure graves and tholos tombs.*Grave number originally assigned but later found be discard deposit.

TABLE 11

Grave	Burial	Age Category	Age (Years)	Sex	Type	Deposition	Structure	Total Wt. (g)/ Number of Burials Included	Comments
19, cont.	2	Adult	n/a	Female	Cremation	Disturbed	Enclosure	1,833/2	n/a
	3	Fetus	22–36 weeks	Unknown	Cremation	Disturbed	Enclosure	10	n/a
	4	Adult	60+	Male	Cremation	Disturbed	Enclosure	1,218	n/a
20	1	Adult	60+	Male	Cremation	Disturbed	Enclosure	1,461/3	n/a
	2	Adult	n/a	Male?	Cremation	Disturbed	Enclosure	1,461/3	n/a
	3	Adult	n/a	Female	Cremation	Disturbed	Enclosure	1,461/3	n/a
	4	Fetus	18–22 weeks	Unknown	Cremation	Disturbed	Enclosure	14	n/a
	5	Adult	60+	Male	Cremation	Disturbed	Enclosure	376	n/a
	6	Adult	n/a	Male	Cremation	Disturbed	Enclosure	1,715	n/a
	7	Adult	45–50	Male	Cremation	Disturbed	Enclosure	1,855	n/a
21	1	Juvenile	3–4	Unknown	Inhumation	Primary?	Pithos	29	n/a
	2	Adult	45–55	Female	Cremation	Secondary	Pithos	2,284/2	n/a
	3	Adult	50+	Male	Cremation	Secondary	Pithos	2,284/2	n/a
	4	Adult	n/a	Female	Cremation	Primary	Enclosure	2,877/3	n/a
	5	Adult	40–60	Male	Cremation	Primary	Enclosure	2,877/3	n/a
	6	Adult	n/a	Male?	Cremation	Primary	Enclosure	2,877/3	n/a
	7	Fetus	20–24 weeks	Unknown	Cremation	Disturbed	Enclosure	11	n/a
22*	See Grave 21	n/a	n/a	n/a	n/a	n/a	n/a	n/a	n/a
23	1	Infant	40 weeks	Unknown	Cremation	Disturbed	Enclosure	186	n/a
	2	Adult	n/a	Unknown	Cremation	Disturbed	Enclosure	852/2	n/a
	3	Adult	n/a	Unknown	Cremation	Disturbed	Enclosure	852/2	n/a
	4	Adult	40–60	Unknown	Inhumation	Primary	Enclosure	148	n/a
24	1	Juvenile	6–7	Unknown	Inhumation	Primary	Rock tumble	174	n/a
25*	See Grave 32	n/a	n/a	n/a	n/a	n/a	n/a	n/a	n/a
26	1	Adult	n/a	Unknown	Cremation	Disturbed	Enclosure	1,632/2	n/a
	2	Juvenile	16–18	Unknown	Cremation	Disturbed	Enclosure	1,632/2	n/a
	3	Adult	n/a	Unknown	Cremation	Secondary	Amphora	9	n/a
27	1	Adult?	n/a	Unknown	Cremation	Disturbed	Enclosure	66	n/a

Table 11, cont. Skeletal remains from Vronda enclosure graves and tholos tombs.*Grave number originally assigned but later found be discard deposit.

TABLE 11

Grave	Burial	Age Category	Age (Years)	Sex	Type	Deposition	Structure	Total Wt. (g)/ Number of Burials Included	Comments
28	1	Adult	40–60	Male	Cremation	Disturbed	Enclosure	1,350	n/a
	2	Juvenile	7–14	Unknown	Cremation	Disturbed	Enclosure	487	n/a
	3	Adult	20–40	Female?	Cremation	Primary	Enclosure	1,351	n/a
	4	Adult	60+	Male?	Cremation	Disturbed	Enclosure	302	n/a
	5	Adult	20–40	Unknown	Cremation	Disturbed	Enclosure	242	n/a
	6	Adult	n/a	Unknown	Cremation	Secondary	Amphora	19	n/a
	7	Adult	n/a	Unknown	Crematon	Secondary	Jar	14	n/a
	8	Adult	60+	Male	Cremation	Primary	Enclosure	2,134	n/a
29	1	Adult?	n/a	Unknown	Cremation	Disturbed	Enclosure	94	n/a
30	1	Adult	20–40	Male?	Cremation	Disturbed	Enclosure	597	n/a
	2	Adult	40–60	Male	Cremation	Disturbed	Enclosure	1,128	Includes bone from Graves 7 and 33
	3	Adult	20–40	Unknown	Cremation	Disturbed	Enclosure	772	n/a
	4	Infant	0–12 months	Unknown	Cremation	Primary	Enclosure	116	n/a
	5	Adult	35–39	Female	Cremation	Primary	Enclosure	1,918	n/a
31	1	Adult	n/a	Female	Cremation	Disturbed	Pyre	424	n/a
32	1	Adult	40–60	Female	Cremation	Disturbed	Enclosure	1,157/2	Includes bone from Grave 25
	2	Adult	20–40	Female	Cremation	Disturbed	Enclosure	1,157/2	Includes bone from Grave 25
	3	Infant	36–40 weeks	Unknown	Cremation	Disturbed	Enclosure	7	n/a
33*	See Grave 30	n/a	n/a	n/a	n/a	n/a	n/a	n/a	n/a
34	1	Adult	35–40	Female	Cremation	Primary	Enclosure	1,639	n/a
	2	Juvenile	2–8	Unknown	Cremation	Primary	Enclosure	139	n/a
35	1	Adult	20–40	Unknown	Inhumation	Secondary	Dump	26	n/a
36	1	Infant	0.5–1.0	Unknown	Cremation	Disturbed	Enclosure	26/2	n/a
	2	Infant	0.5–1.0	Unknown	Cremation	Disturbed	Enclosure	26/2	n/a
	3	Adult	20–40	Unknown	Cremation	Disturbed	Enclosure	1,207/2	n/a
	4	Juvenile	18–20	Unknown	Cremation	Disturbed	Enclosure	1,207/2	n/a

Table 11, cont. Skeletal remains from Vronda enclosure graves and tholos tombs. *Grave number originally assigned but later found be discard deposit.

TABLE 11

Grave/ Tomb	Burial	Age Category	Age (Years)	Sex	Type	Deposition	Structure	Total Wt. (g)/ Number of Burials Included	Comments
36, cont.	5	Juvenile	3–6	Unknown	Cremation	Disturbed	Enclosure	55	n/a
	6	Adult	20–40	Unknown	Cremation	Disturbed	Enclosure	1,775/2	n/a
	7	Adult	40–60	Male	Cremation	Primary	Enclosure	1,775/2	n/a
37	1	Adult	n/a	Unknown	Cremation	Surface cleaning	n/a	Not recorded	n/a
I	1	Adult	n/a	Unknown	Inhumation	Cleaning	Tholos	n/a	n/a
II	1	Adult	n/a	Unknown	Inhumation	Cleaning	Tholos	n/a	n/a
III	n/a	n/a	n/a	n/a	n/a	n/a	n/a	n/a	Not found**
IV	1	Adult	Mature	Male	Inhumation	Dump	Tholos	n/a	n/a
	2	Adult	n/a	Unknown	Inhumation	Dump	Tholos	n/a	n/a
	3	Adult	n/a	Unknown	Inhumation	Dump	Tholos	n/a	n/a
	4	Juvenile	6–12	Unknown	Inhumation	Dump	Tholos	n/a	n/a
	5	Adult	n/a	Unknown	Inhumation	Area in front	Tholos	n/a	n/a
	6	Adult	n/a	Unknown	Inhumation	Area in front	Tholos	n/a	n/a
V	n/a	n/a	n/a	n/a	n/a	n/a	n/a	n/a	No human remains
VI	n/a	n/a	n/a	n/a	n/a	n/a	n/a	n/a	No human remains
VII	n/a	n/a	n/a	n/a	n/a	n/a	n/a	n/a	No human remains
VIII	1	Juvenile	1–2	Unknown	Inhumation	Cleaning	Tholos	n/a	n/a
	2	Juvenile	10–16	Unknown	Inhumation	Cleaning	Tholos	n/a	n/a
	3	Adult	n/a	Male	Inhumation	Cleaning	Tholos	n/a	n/a
	4	Adult	n/a	Unknown	Inhumation	Cleaning	Tholos	n/a	n/a
IX	1	Juvenile	n/a	Unknown	Inhumation	Cleaning	Tholos	n/a	n/a
	2	Adult	n/a	Male	Inhumation	Cleaning	Tholos	n/a	n/a
	3	Adult	40–49	Male	Inhumation	Cleaning	Tholos	n/a	n/a
X	1	Juvenile	5–7	Unknown	Inhumation	Cleaning	Tholos	n/a	n/a
XI	1	Adult	n/a	Male?	Inhumation	Floor	Tholos	n/a	n/a
	2	Adult	n/a	Female?	Inhumation	Floor	Tholos	n/a	n/a

Table 11, cont. Skeletal remains from Vronda enclosure graves and tholos tombs. *Grave number originally assigned, but later found be discard deposit. ** Boyd originally excavated this grave but the Kavousi Project could not find it.

TABLE 12

Grave	Burial	Age Category	Age (Years)	Sex	Bone Pathology	Dental Pathology	Anomalies
1	1	Adult	20–40	Male	n/a	n/a	n/a
	2	Adult	n/a	Unknown	n/a	Heavy anterior dental wear	n/a
2	1	Adult	n/a	Female	Endocranial porosity (infection?)	n/a	n/a
3	1	Adult	20–40	Male	Hyperostosis frontalis interna remodeled, porotic hyperostosis	n/a	n/a
	2	Juvenile	16–20	Female	Moderate diffuse periosteal bone on tibia and unidentified leg bone fragments	n/a	n/a
4	1	Juvenile	15–20	Female	Remodeled cribra orbitalia	n/a	n/a
	2	Fetus	20 weeks	Unknown	n/a	n/a	n/a
	3	Infant	12–14 months	Unknown	n/a	n/a	n/a
5	1	Adult	25–40	Male	Right parietal trepanation, possible hyperostosis frontalis interna, cribra orbitalia, osteoarthritis, healed fractures on humerus and patella	n/a	n/a
	2	Adult	40–60	Male	Healed fracture of left orbit margin; two actively healing rib fractures	n/a	n/a
	3	Juvenile	18–20	Female?	n/a	n/a	n/a
	4	Infant	40 weeks	Unknown	Ossification lacuna on right sphenoid greater wing	n/a	n/a
	5	Juvenile	9–12	Unknown	n/a	n/a	n/a
	6	Infant	3–9 months	Unknown	n/a	n/a	n/a
	7	Adult	60+	Male	Remodeled osteomyelitis with cloaca on right ulna with associated remodeled periosteal bone on right radius; healed fracture of right-hand distal phalanx; osteoarthritis, right and left shoulders (glenoid fossa), osteoporosis	n/a	n/a
6	1	Adult	20–40	Unknown	Proximal linea aspera enthesopathy with pitting and osteophytes; bilateral pitting and enthesophytes on ulna tuberosities (insertion of brachialis muscle)	n/a	n/a
	2	Infant	40 weeks	Unknown	n/a	n/a	n/a
	3	Adult	20–40	Unknown	n/a	n/a	n/a

Table 12. Pathologies and anomalies on skeletons from the Vronda enclosure graves.

TABLE 12

Grave	Burial	Age Category	Age (Years)	Sex	Bone Pathology	Dental Pathology	Anomalies
6	4	Adult	50–60	Male	Porotic hyperostosis	n/a	n/a
	5	Adult	60+	Unknown	Osteoarthritis of ankle joints (distal tibia, talus, calcaneus); periosteal bone on anterior tibia shaft indicating generalized infection; lytic foci on interior parietal and frontal bone fragments; cribra orbitalia	Tooth wear	n/a
7	See Grave 30	n/a	n/a	n/a	n/a	n/a	n/a
8	1	Adult	20–40?	Female?	Very thin cortical bone on humerus; osteoporosis?	n/a	n/a
	2	Fetus	16–20 weeks	Unknown	n/a	n/a	n/a
9	1	Adult	40–60	Male?	Remodeled porotic hyperostosis, vertebral facet osteoarthritis, osteoporosis/osteopenia	n/a	n/a
	2	Adult	35–39	Female?	Remodeled porotic hyperostosis, cribra orbitalia	n/a	n/a
	3	Fetus	20–24 weeks	Unknown	n/a	n/a	n/a
	4	Adult	40–60	Male	Remodeled porotic hyperostosis, cribra orbitalia, vertebral facet osteoarthritis, fractured toe	Extreme wear on anterior teeth	n/a
	5	Adult	n/a	Unknown	Osteoarthritis of right elbow, right knee, vertebrae	n/a	n/a
	6	Adult	n/a	Unknown	Cribra oribitalia	n/a	n/a
	7	Infant	0.5–2.0	Unknown	n/a	n/a	n/a
10	1	Juvenile	5–6	Unknown	n/a	Linear enamel hypoplasias on forming adult incisors and canines	n/a
11	See Grave 5	n/a	n/a	n/a	n/a	n/a	n/a
12	1	Adult	n/a	Unknown	n/a	n/a	n/a
	2	Adult	n/a	Unknown	n/a	n/a	Trace metopic
	3	Adult	n/a	Unknown	n/a	n/a	n/a
	4	Adult	20–40	Unknown	Arthritis in left temporomandibular joint	Interproximal caries at cemento-enamel junction	Metopic suture
	5	Adult	40–60	Male	Porotic hyperostosis	n/a	Trace metopic
	6	Adult	22–24	Female	Fractured toe	n/a	Metopic suture

Table 12, cont. Pathologies and anomalies on skeletons from the Vronda enclosure graves.

TABLE 12

Grave	Burial	Age Category	Age (Years)	Sex	Bone Pathology	Dental Pathology	Anomalies
12	7	Fetus	22–34 weeks	Unknown	n/a	n/a	n/a
	8	Juvenile	5–6	Unknown	n/a	n/a	Metopic suture
13	1	Adult	n/a	Unknown	n/a	n/a	n/a
	2	Adult	n/a	Unknown	n/a	n/a	n/a
14	See Grave 9	n/a	n/a	n/a	n/a	n/a	n/a
15	1	Adult	40–60	Unknown	Remodeled porotic hyperostosis	Extreme anterior dental wear	n/a
	2	Adult	n/a	Female	n/a	n/a	n/a
	3	Fetus	16–32 weeks	Unknown	n/a	n/a	n/a
	4	Adult	n/a	Unknown	n/a	n/a	n/a
16	1	Juvenile	13–20	Unknown	n/a	n/a	n/a
	2	Adult	30–40	Unknown	Periosteal bone on tibiae, osteoarthritis	Wear on anterior teeth	n/a
17	1	Adult	40–60	Male	Cribra orbitalia, porotic hyperostosis	n/a	n/a
	2	Juvenile	15–17	Unknown	n/a	n/a	n/a
	3	Infant	40 weeks	Unknown	n/a	n/a	n/a
18	See Tholos VIII	n/a	n/a	n/a	n/a	n/a	n/a
19	1	Adult	20–40?	Unknown	n/a	n/a	n/a
	2	Adult		Female	n/a	n/a	n/a
	3	Fetus	22–36 weeks	Unknown	n/a	n/a	n/a
	4	Adult	60+	Male	n/a	Missing posterior dentition antemortem, extensive peridontal disease, dental abscess	n/a
20	1	Adult	60+	Male	Porotic hyperostosis, temporo-mandibular joint arthritis	Missing anterior maxillary teeth antemortem	n/a
	2	Adult	n/a	Male?	Porotic hyperostosis	n/a	n/a
	3	Adult	n/a	Female	n/a	n/a	n/a
	4	Fetus	18–22 weeks	Unknown	n/a	n/a	n/a
	5	Adult	60+	Male	Porotic hyperostosis	Periodontal disease, missing teeth antemortem	n/a
	6	Adult	n/a	Male	n/a	n/a	n/a
	7	Adult	45–50	Male	Periosteal bone on tibiae, vertebral osteoarthritis	n/a	n/a

Table 12, cont. Pathologies and anomalies on skeletons from the Vronda enclosure graves.

TABLE 12

Grave	Burial	Age Category	Age (Years)	Sex	Bone Pathology	Dental Pathology	Anomalies
21	1	Juvenile	3–4	Unknown	n/a	Shovel-shaped incisors	n/a
	2	Adult	45–55	Female	Vertebral lipping and osteoarthritis on facets (pitting and eburnation), cribra orbitalia, osteochondritis dessicans	Dental abscess	n/a
	3	Adult	50+	Male	Vertebral lipping and osteoarthritis on facets (pitting and eburnation), cribra orbitalia	Caries	n/a
	4	Adult	n/a	Female	Cribra orbitalia	n/a	Metopic suture
	5	Adult	40–60	Male	TMJ inflammation, arthritic vertebrae	n/a	n/a
	6	Adult	n/a	Male?	Cribra orbitalia	n/a	n/a
	7	Fetus	20–24 weeks	Unknown	n/a	n/a	n/a
22	See Grave 21	n/a	n/a	n/a	n/a	n/a	n/a
23	1	Infant	40 weeks	Unknown	Periosteal bone on tibia	Linear enamel hypoplasia on deciduous tooth	n/a
	2	Adult	n/a	Unknown	n/a	n/a	n/a
	3	Adult	n/a	Unknown	Endocranial lytic lesions	n/a	n/a
	4	Adult	40–60	Unknown	Tibia periostitis	Linear enamel hypoplasia on canine, heavy wear on teeth from tool use	n/a
24	1	Juvenile	6–7	Unknown	Probable histiocytosis, porotic hyperostosis	n/a	n/a
25	See Grave 32	n/a	n/a	n/a	n/a	n/a	n/a
26	1	Adult	n/a	Unknown	n/a	Caries	n/a
	2	Juvenile	16–18	Unknown	n/a	n/a	n/a
	3	Adult	n/a	Unknown	n/a	n/a	n/a
27	1	Adult?	n/a	Unknown	n/a	n/a	n/a
28	1	Adult	40–60	Male	n/a	Dental caries in premolar	n/a
	2	Juvenile	7–14	Unknown	Porotic hyperostosis	Linear enamel hypoplasia on deciduous tooth	n/a
	3	Adult	20–40	Female?	Widespread endocranial porosity (infection?)	n/a	n/a
	4	Adult	60+	Male?	Slight periosteal bone above left orbit, osteopenia	Dental abscess	n/a
	5	Adult	20–40	Unknown	n/a	n/a	n/a

Table 12, cont. Pathologies and anomalies on skeletons from the Vronda enclosure graves.

TABLE 12

Grave	Burial	Age Category	Age (Years)	Sex	Bone Pathology	Dental Pathology	Anomalies
28, cont.	6	Adult	n/a	Unknown	Endocranial lytic lesions, osteoporosis	Peridontal disease, dental abscess	n/a
	7	Adult	n/a	Unknown	n/a	n/a	n/a
	8	Adult	60+	Male	Porotic hyperostosis	Edentulous	n/a
29	1	Adult?	n/a	Unknown	n/a	n/a	n/a
30	1	Adult	20–40	Male?	(From Grave 7 deposit: osteoarthritis on distal metacarpal, tibia periostitis, endocranial lytic lesions)	n/a	n/a
	2	Adult	40–60	Male	Vertebral osteoarthritis and gluteus maximus enthesopathy, right and left femora	n/a	n/a
	3	Adult	20–40	Unknown	Disrupted linea aspera indicating injury	n/a	n/a
	4	Infant	0–12 months	Unknown	n/a	n/a	n/a
	5	Adult	35–39	Female	Ulna fracture at elbow (olecranon process)	Periodontal inflammation, neck (gumline) caries on premolar	n/a
31	1	Adult	n/a	Female	n/a	n/a	n/a
32	1	Adult	40–60	Female	Tibia periostitis	Antemortem tooth loss	n/a
	2	Adult	20–40	Female	n/a	n/a	n/a
	3	Infant	36–40 weeks	Unknown	n/a	n/a	n/a
33	See Grave 30	n/a	n/a	n/a	n/a	n/a	n/a
34	1	Adult	35–40	Female	Remodeled porotic hyperostosis	n/a	n/a
	2	Juvenile	2–8	Unknown	n/a	n/a	n/a
35	1	Adult	20–40	Unknown	Endocranial lytic lesions on parietals	n/a	n/a
36	1	Infant	0.5–1.0	Unknown	n/a	n/a	n/a
	2	Infant	0.5–1.0	Unknown	n/a	n/a	n/a
	3	Adult	20–40	Unknown	Remodeled porotic hyperostosis	n/a	Metopic suture
	4	Juvenile	18–20	Unknown	n/a	n/a	n/a
	5	Juvenile	3–6	Unknown	Cribra orbitalia (anemia)	n/a	Metopic suture
	6	Adult	20–40	Unknown	n/a	n/a	Metopic suture
	7	Adult	40–60	Male	n/a	n/a	n/a
37	1	Adult	n/a	Unknown	Porotic hyperostosis	n/a	n/a

Table 12, cont. Pathologies and anomalies on skeletons from the Vronda enclosure graves.

TABLE 13

Species	Number of Specimens	Locus	Context
Olea europaea	1 fragment	V 4701.2	Grave 20
	2 fragments	V 4705.2	Grave 20
	9 fragment = 1 whole? (fresh breaks)	V 4708.3	Grave 20
	5 fragments	V 5315.1	Grave 9
	1 fragment	V 5348.1	Grave 21
	1 fragment	V 5349.1	Grave 21
	1 nearly whole	VW 8104.3	Grave 23
Vitis vinifera	1 whole pip	V 4701.2	Grave 20
	1 fruit fragment	V 4701.3	Grave 20
	1 whole pip	V 4704.1	Grave 20
	1 stem	V 4705.2	Grave 20
	1 pip fragment	V 4706.1	Grave 20
	1 pip fragment	V 5312.2	Grave 9
	3 pip fragments	V 5312.4, 5	Grave 9
	1 pip fragment	V 5314.1–5	Grave 9
	1 whole pip	V 5319.2	Grave 9
	2 whole pips, 1 pip fragment	V 5319.5, 6	Grave 9
	2 fruit fragments	V 5348.1	Grave 21
	1 nearly whole pip	V 5350.1	Grave 21
	2 pip fragments, 10 fruit fragments	V 5350.2	Grave 21
	6 fruit fragments	V 8732.2, 3	Grave 26
	15 whole pips, 47 fruit fragments	V 8732.4	Grave 26
	4 fruit fragments	V 12802.2	Grave 36
	1 whole pip, 1 pip fragment, 1 fruit fragment	V 12806.1	Grave 36
	1 whole pip	V 12807.2	Grave 36
	2 fruit fragments	VW 8000	Removal of modern terrace wall, possibly associated with Grave 30
	9 fruit fragments	VW 8104.2	Grave 23
	1 whole pip	VW 10012.1	Grave 15
	1 pip fragment	VW 11110.6	Grave 28
	1 whole pip	VW 11110.9	Grave 28
	1 pip fragment	VW 11118.1	Grave 28
Pistacia vera	1 whole	V 4709.2	Grave 20

Table 13. Palaeobotanical remains from the Vronda enclosure graves.

TABLE 13

Species	Number of Specimens	Locus	Context
Pistacia vera, cont.	1 whole	V 5350.2	Grave 21
Lens culinaris s.l.	1 whole	V 4805.5	Grave 12
	1 whole	V 4809.1	Grave 17
	1 whole, 1 fragment	V 5312.2	Grave 9
Vicia ervilia	1 whole	V 5348.3	Grave 21
Lathyrus cicera s.l.	1 whole	VW 9118.1	Grave 23
Vicia/Lathyrus	1 whole	V 4709.3	Grave 20
Pisum sp.	3 fragments	V 8732.2+3	Grave 26
Pisum sp., *granular testa* (*P. elatius? P. humilis?*)	1 whole	V 4804.3	Grave 10
	2 fragments, same seed	V 8732.2+3	Grave 26
Legume	1 fragment	V 4701.1	Grave 20
	1 fragment	V 4805.2	Grave 12
	1 fragment	V 5348.3	Grave 21
	1 fragment	V 5349.1	Grave 21
	1 fragment	V 8732.2	Grave 26
	1 fragment	VW 11114.2	Grave 28
	3 fragments	VW 11118.1	Grave 28
Hordeum vulgare s.l.	1 whole (very tiny)	V 5348.3	Grave 21
Gramineae s.l.	1 fragment (spikelet fragment?)	V 9406.1+2	Grave 19
Aethusa cynapium	2 whole, 1 half, 6 fragments	V 4701.1, 2	Grave 20
	2 whole, 4 halves, 1 small fragment	V 4705.2	Grave 20
	1 whole	V 4709.2	Grave 20
	1 whole, 1 half	V 4809.2	Grave 17
	1 whole	V 5314.1–5	Grave 9
	2 fragments	V 8732.4	Grave 26
	1 whole	V 12806.1	Grave 36
	1 whole	VW 8104.2	Grave 23
	4 whole	VW 8104.3	Grave 23
	1 half	VW 8104.7	Grave 23
	5 whole	VW 9118.1	Grave 23
	1 whole, 1 half	VW 9208.2	Grave 24
	1 whole	VW 10012.1	Grave 15
	1 whole	VW 11110.2	Grave 28

Table 13, cont. Palaeobotanical remains from the Vronda enclosure graves.

Species	Number of Specimens	Locus	Context
Aethusa cynapium, cont.	1 whole, 1 nearly whole	VW 11110.6	Grave 28
	2 whole	VW 11114.2	Grave 28
	3 whole, 3 fragments	VW 12012.1	Grave 34
Polygonum convolvulus s.l.	1 whole	V 9406.1+2	Grave 19
Lithospermum arvense s.l.	1 whole	VW 9118.1	Grave 23
Medicago sp.	1 fragment	V 4705.2	Grave 20
	1 whole	V 5349.3	Grave 21
	1 whole	VW 8104.2	Grave 23
	1 whole	VW 9118.1	Grave 23
	1 fragment	VW 10012.1	Grave 15

Table 13, cont. Palaeobotanical remains from the Vronda enclosure graves.

Tomb	I	II	III	IV	V	VI	VII	VIII	IX	X	XI
Pres. h.	0.86	1.30	2.00	1.60	1.74	1.70	?	0.50	1.30	1.34	1.70?
Length	1.68	1.30	2.00	1.80	1.84	1.90	?	2.00	?	1.60	1.65–1.85
Width	1.64	1.70	2.00	1.70	1.80	1.70	?	2.00	1.60	1.30	1.50–1.60
Stomion height	0.50	0.60	0.80	0.60	0.50	0.50	0.56	?	?	?	0.59
Stomion width	0.72	0.58	?	0.86	0.68	0.56	0.49	0.72	?	0.70	0.57
Stomion length	0.64	1.14	0.85	0.82	0.82	0.73	?	0.75	?	0.90–1.06	0.70–0.80
Pseudo-dromos L.	1.50	1.60	?	1.04	1.06	0.90	?	0.83	?	?	1.30
Pseudo-dromos w.	0.67–0.83	1.22	?	0.90	0.86	1.10	?	0.63–0.80	?	?	0.72–0.88
Cairn over pit	Yes	Yes	?	Rocks	Yes	Yes		?	?	?	?
Pit stones	2 big flat rocks	2 big flat rocks	?	Rocks	4 flat rocks	2 big flat rocks	?	1 sloping flat rock	?	?	Many flat rocks
Lintel w.	1.04	1.00	0.75	0.96	0.83	0.80	1.02	?	?	?	?
Lintel material	Brec	Lime	?	Lime	Lime	Brec, lime	Lime	?	?	?	Brec
Shape	Round	Oval	Square	Oval	Square	Oval	?	Round or square	Square	Horse-shoe	Square

Table 14. Location, orientation, measurements, and architectural details of tholos tombs. All measurements are in meters. Abbreviations of stone types: brec = breccia, lime = limestone; abbreviations of relations to slope: para = parallel, perp = perpendicular.

Tomb	I	II	III	IV	V	VI	VII	VIII	IX	X	XI
Orientation	West	North-west	?	North-west	South-west	West		North	?	North	Southwest
Jambs	Lime	Lime	?	Brec	Lime	Lime	Brec	Lime	?	Brec	Lime
Floor of tomb	Soil over *tsakali*	Soil over *tsakali*	?	Soil	Soil	Soil	?	Soil over *tsakali*	Soil	?	Soil over bedrock
Floor of stomion	Stone slab level with tomb	3 stones, slopes down to tomb	?	Slopes down to tomb	Slopes down to tomb, possible paver	Slopes down to tomb	?	Level with tomb	?	Level with tomb	Slopes down to tomb
Blocking of stomion	2 big flat rocks	2 big flat rocks	?		2 big flat rocks	3 big flat rocks	?	2 big flat rocks	?		?
Relation to slope	Para	Para	?	Perp	Para	Para	Perp	Perp	?	Perp	Para

Table 14, cont. Location, orientation, measurements, and architectural details of tholos tombs. All measurements are in meters. Abbreviations of stone types: brec = breccia, lime = limestone; abbreviations of relations to slope: para = parallel, perp = perpendicular.

Grave(s)	Length (m)	Width (m)	Maximum Preserved Height (m)	Building and Room	Use of LM IIIC Walls	Floor	Orientation	Number of Burials
1	2.00 east–west	Ca. 1.75 north–south	0.69	E3	North and west	Roofing clay	Northwest–southeast	2
3	1.75–1.87 east–west	1.00–1.07 north–south	0.80	n/a	Terrace wall east	Bedrock	Northeast–southwest	2
4	Ca. 1.70 north–south	Ca. 1.00 east–west	0.85	D3	North, east, south	Roofing clay	Northwest–southeast	2
5, 11	2.00–2.05 north–south	1.08 east–west	0.50	C4	None	Bedrock, LM IIIC hearth	Northwest–southeast	7
6	1.90 north–south	1.17–1.46 east–west	0.66	n/a	East?	Bedrock	Northwest–southeast	5
9, 14	1.81–1.83 east–west	1.10–1.15 north–south	0.53	J1	South	Roofing clay	East–west	7
10	1.80–2.20 north–south	0.70–0.84 east–west	0.43	J4	South? east?	Bedrock	North–south	1 (in pithos)
12	1.88–1.93 east–west	0.93–1.00 north–south	0.51	J4	South	Bedrock	East–west	8
15	1.22 north–south	1.15–1.20 east–west	0.25	IC1	East	Upper courtyard floor	?	4

Table 15. Location, orientation, measurements, and architectural details of enclosure graves.

Grave(s)	Length (m)	Width (m)	Maximum Preserved Height (m)	Building and Room	Use of LM IIIC Walls	Floor	Orientation	Number of Burials
16	2.10 east–west	0.78–0.95 north–south	0.41	K1	None	Bedrock	East–west	2
17	1.88–2.15 east–west	Ca. 0.85–1.00 north–south	0.38	South of J4	North	Bedrock	East–west	3
19	1.40 north–south	1.20 east–west	0.59	G1	East	Roofing clay	North–south	4
20	1.75–1.90 north–south	0.93–1.10 east–west	0.40	West of J4	East	Bedrock	North–south	7
21, 22	1.88–2.25 east–west	Ca. 1.13–1.25 north–south	0.64	J1	None	Bedrock	East–west	7 (3 in pithos)
23	1.55 north–south	0.95–1.05 east–west	0.46	South of O1	None	Bedrock	Northwest–southeast	4
26	1.98 north–south	1.14 east–west	0.77	West of G1	None	Red soil	North–south	3 (1 in pot)
27	2.08 north–south	1.23–1.32 east–west	0.74	West of G1	East?	Bedrock	North–south	1
28	1.76 north–south	1.60 east–west	0.64	O3	East	House floor north; roofing clay south	Northeast–southwest	8 (2 in pots)
30, 7, 33	1.91 east–west	1.09 north–south	0.40	South of I5	None	Brecciating surface	Northeast–southwest	5
32, 25	2.29 north–south	Ca. 0.80 east–west	0.29	Southwest of G1	None	Ancient surface	North–south	3
34	1.50–1.60 north–south	Ca. 1.13 east–west	0.73	O4	East, south	Roofing clay and slope wash	North–south	2
36	1.80–1.95 north–south	1.08–1.15 east–west	0.54	West of D2	North, east, west	Bedrock	Northeast–southwest	7

Table 15, cont. Location, orientation, measurements, and architectural details of enclosure graves.

Grave	Location	Dimensions North–South	Dimensions East–West	Total Area
Certain Platforms				
Grave 3	South of enclosure	2.50 m	1.50 m	3.75 m²
Grave 26	North of enclosure	1.25 m	1.75 m	2.19 m²
Grave 27	South of enclosure	1.35–1.50 m	2.25 m	3.04–3.38 m²
Possible Platforms				
Grave 6	South of enclosure	2.30 m	1.60–1.85 m	3.68–4.26 m²
Grave 12	West of enclosure	1.60 m	1.60 m	3.20 m²
Grave 32	North of enclosure	1.00 m	1.50 m	1.50 m²

Table 16. Paved platforms associated with enclosure graves.

Tholos	Total Count	Fine	Medium Coarse	Coarse	Fine %	Medium Coarse %	Coarse %
Tomb IV	18	12	5	1	67%	28%	5%
Tomb IX	57	48	6	3	84%	11%	5%
All tombs	110	87	18	5	79%	16%	5%

Table 17. Counts of pottery sherds by fabric and percentages of pottery fabrics in the tholos tombs.

Grave(s)	Total Count	Fine	Medium Coarse	Coarse	Fine %	Medium Coarse %	Coarse %
1	33	32	1	0	97%	3%	0%
2	2	1	1	0	50%	50%	0%
3	20	15	5	0	75%	25%	0%
4	25	19	4	2	76%	16%	8%
5 and 11	17	12	4	1	71%	24%	5%
6	30	21	5	4	70%	17%	13%
8	3	2	0	1	67%	0%	33%
9 and 14	58	32	15	10	55%	27%	18%
10	1	0	0	1	0%	0%	100%
12	44	31	9	4	70%	21%	9%
13	14	13	1	0	93%	7%	0%
15	4	4	0	0	100%	0%	0%
16	22	13	6	3	59%	27%	14%
17	11	8	1	2	73%	9%	18%
19	19	15	4	0	79%	21%	0%
19 dump	4	1	3	0	25%	75%	0%
20	21	16	5	0	76%	24%	0%
21 and 22	13	7	5	1	54%	38%	8%
23	8	7	1	0	88%	12%	0%
26	23	19	4	0	83%	17%	0%
27	13	10	2	1	77%	15%	8%
28	28	18	5	5	64%	18%	18%
29	1	0	0	1	0%	0%	100%
30, 33, and 7	33	23	9	1	70%	27%	3%
32	11	8	2	1	73%	18%	9%
34	5	3	2	0	60%	40%	0%
36	18	14	3	1	78%	17%	5%
37	2	2	0	0	100%	0%	0%

Table 18. Counts of pottery sherds by fabric and percentages of pottery fabrics in the enclosure graves.

TABLE 19

Petrographic Fabric	Sample Number	Description	Pot Number
1a brown metamorphic semi-coarse	KAV 15/7	Cup	GR9 P55
1a brown metamorphic semi-coarse	KAV 15/9	Cup	GR9 P33
1a brown metamorphic semi-coarse	KAV 15/11	Cup	GR9 P41
1a brown metamorphic semi-coarse	KAV 15/17	Skyphos	GR9 P45
1a brown metamorphic semi-coarse	KAV 15/35	Skyphos	GR3 P17
1a brown metamorphic semi-coarse	KAV 15/76	Krater	GR28 P24
1a brown metamorphic semi-coarse	KAV 15/78	Krater	GR28 P25
1a brown metamorphic semi-coarse	KAV 15/85	Skyphos	GR30 P29
1a brown metamorphic semi-coarse	KAV 15/87	Skyphos/cup	GR30 P25
1a brown metamorphic semi-coarse	KAV 15/91	Bowl	GR17 P10
1b brown metamorphic semi-fine	KAV 15/8	Cup	GR9 P43
1b brown metamorphic semi-fine	KAV 15/10	Cup	GR9 P34
1b brown metamorphic semi-fine	KAV 15/25	Stemmed skyphos	GR6 P3
1b brown metamorphic semi-fine	KAV 15/33	Amphora	GR5 P13
1b brown metamorphic semi-fine	KAV 15/37	Cup	GR3 P3
1b brown metamorphic semi-fine	KAV 15/40	Krater	GR4 P16
1b brown metamorphic semi-fine	KAV 15/41	Cup	GR4 P22
1b brown metamorphic semi-fine	KAV 15/42	Skyphos	GR4 P15
1b brown metamorphic semi-fine	KAV 15/43	Lid	GR4 P24
1b brown metamorphic semi-fine	KAV 15/60	Amphora V98.103	GR16 P17
1b brown metamorphic semi-fine	KAV 15/65	Amphora V98.115	GR20 P7
1b brown metamorphic semi-fine	KAV 15/67	Amphora or necked jar	GR20 P20
1b brown metamorphic semi-fine	KAV 15/70	Oinochoe V98.123	GR26 P23
1b brown metamorphic semi-fine	KAV 15/71	Amphora/hydria	GR27 P11
1b brown metamorphic semi-fine	KAV 15/72	Krater	GR27 P4
1b brown metamorphic semi-fine	KAV 15/73	Cup	GR27 P2
1b brown metamorphic semi-fine	KAV 15/74	Amphora/hydria	GR27 P12
1b brown metamorphic semi-fine	KAV 15/75	Closed vessel	GR27 P13
1b brown metamorphic semi-fine	KAV 15/79	Jar	GR28 P28
1b brown metamorphic semi-fine	KAV 15/84	Pyxis V98.120	GR30 P5
1b brown metamorphic semi-fine	KAV 15/86	Open vessel	GR30 P24
1c brown metamorphic fine	KAV 15/5	Skyphos	GR9 P3
1c brown metamorphic fine	KAV 15/12	Cup/skyphos	GR9 P23
1c brown metamorphic fine	KAV 15/18	Cup	GR9 P16

Table 19. Concordance of vessel shapes and petrographic fabrics.

TABLE 19

Petrographic Fabric	Sample Number	Description	Pot Number
1c brown metamorphic fine	KAV 15/38	Pyxis	GR4 P8
1c brown metamorphic fine	KAV 15/81	Cup V89.85	GR28 P6
1c brown metamorphic fine	KAV 15/82	Cup V89.82	GR28 P11
1c brown metamorphic fine	KAV 15/90	Necked jar	GR36 P10
1c brown metamorphic fine	KAV 15/96	Oinochoe	IX P46
1c brown metamorphic fine	KAV 15/102	Krater	IX P36
1c brown metamorphic fine	KAV 15/104	Amphora	IX P47
2 red metamorphic	KAV 15/3	Cup	GR9 P53
2 red metamorphic	KAV 15/6	Cup	GR9 P40
2 red metamorphic	KAV 15/13	Cup	GR9 P54
2 red metamorphic	KAV 15/14	Necked jar	GR9 P36
2 red metamorphic	KAV 15/16	Skyphos or basin	GR9 P46
2 red metamorphic	KAV 15/19	Cup	GR9 P52
2 red metamorphic	KAV 15/49	Cup/skyphos	GR12 P39
2 red metamorphic	KAV 15/55	Amphora	GR12 P43
2 red metamorphic	KAV 15/63	Cup	GR17 P9
2 red metamorphic	KAV 15/77	Jug	GR28 P20
2 red metamorphic	KAV 15/80	Cup V89.84	GR28 P5
2 red metamorphic	KAV 15/88	Cup	GR36 P15
2 red metamorphic	KAV 15/94	Cup	IX P30
2 red metamorphic	KAV 15/98	Cup	IX P51
3 metamorphic with greenstone	KAV 15/24	Amphora	GR9 P38
3 metamorphic with greenstone	KAV 15/51	Oinochoe	GR12 P35
3 metamorphic with greenstone	KAV 15/52	Jug/olpe	GR12 P34
3 metamorphic with greenstone	KAV 15/54	Amphora	GR12 P42
3 metamorphic with greenstone	KAV 15/59	Cup	GR16 P21
3 metamorphic with greenstone	KAV 15/92	Burial pithos V98.89	GR 10 P1
3 metamorphic with greenstone	KAV 15/95	Cup	IX P60
3 metamorphic with greenstone	KAV 15/97	Cup	IX P52
Small group metamorphic with mica	KAV 15/4	Cup	GR9 P51
Small group metamorphic with mica	KAV 15/58	Bowl	GR16 P22
Small group metamorphic with mica	KAV 15/68	Jug/oinochoe	GR23 P8
Small group metamorphic low fired	KAV 15/27	Cup/skyphos	GR6 P26
Small group metamorphic low fired	KAV 15/46	Cup	GR1 P33

Table 19, cont. Concordance of vessel shapes and petrographic fabrics.

TABLE 19

Petrographic Fabric	Sample Number	Description	Pot Number
Small group metamorphic low fired	KAV 15/56	Ovoid krater	GR12 P41
Small group metamorphic low fired	KAV 15/62	Basin	GR17 P11
Small group metamorphic low fired	KAV 15/93	Burial pithos	GR21 P13
4 granitic dioritic	KAV 15/20	Jug	GR9 P49
4 granitic dioritic	KAV 15/44	Lekythos V87.89	GR4 P20
4 granitic dioritic	KAV 15/48	Necked jar	GR12 P19
4 granitic dioritic	KAV 15/50	Oinochoe	GR12 P14
4 granitic dioritic	KAV 15/57	Bell krater	GR12 P11
5 gray siltstone	KAV 15/15	Krater	GR9 P35
5 gray siltstone	KAV 15/21	Jug/oinochoe	GR9 P37
5 gray siltstone	KAV 15/22	Amphora	GR9 P50
5 gray siltstone	KAV 15/26	Skyphos	GR6 P2
5 gray siltstone	KAV 15/29	Krater	GR6 P27
5 gray siltstone	KAV 15/31	Oinochoe V98.85	GR6 P29
5 gray siltstone	KAV 15/69	Hydria V98.122	GR26 P20
6 ophiolitic	KAV 15/23	Amphora	GR9 P39
6 ophiolitic	KAV 15/61	Amphora	GR16 P20
6 ophiolitic	KAV 15/66	Cup V98.116	GR20 P1
6 ophiolitic	KAV 15/83	Pyxis V98.119	GR30 P28
6 ophiolitic	KAV 15/89	Lekythos	GR36 P11
6 ophiolitic	KAV 15/100	Jug	IX P15
7 fine with clay pellets	KAV 15/1	Cup	GR9 P20
7 fine with clay pellets	KAV 15/32	Necked jar	GR5 P3
7 fine with clay pellets	KAV 15/36	Skyphos	GR3 P10
7 fine with clay pellets	KAV 15/39	Cup V87.90	GR4 P1
7 fine with clay pellets	KAV 15/45	Amphora	GR1 P11
7 fine with clay pellets	KAV 15/47	Skyphos	GR1 P16
7 fine with clay pellets	KAV 15/53	Kalathos	GR12 P10
7 fine with clay pellets	KAV 15/99	Cup	IX P31
7 fine with clay pellets	KAV 15/103	Stirrup jar V98.43	IX P10
Loner	KAV 15/2	Cup	GR9 P18
Loner	KAV 15/30	Jug	GR6 P28
Loner	KAV 15/101	Necked jar	IX P9
Off-island import?	KAV 15/28	Cup	GR6 P22

Table 19, cont. Concordance of vessel shapes and petrographic fabrics.

Petrographic Fabric	Sample Number	Description	Pot Number
Off-island import	KAV 15/34	Jug	**GR5 P15**
Off-island import?	KAV 15/64	Cup	**GR19 P17**

Table 19, cont. Concordance of vessel shapes and petrographic fabrics.

Shape	Matrix	Coarse Fraction	Fine Fraction	Geological Association
Fabric Group 1	Fine dark reddish brown to dark brown; optically inactive	Frequent to common small quartz fragments; fine-grained dark phyllite, rare schist, quartzite, and sandstone	Small quartz fragments, biotite mica laths	Phyllite-Quartzite series
Fabric Group 2	Fine, reddish brown; optically inactive	Fine-grained brown phyllite occasionally containing biotite; small quartz fragments, very little quartzite and sandstone	Biotite mica laths, rare small quartz fragments	Phyllite-Quartzite series
Fabric Group 3	Fine, reddish brown; optically inactive	Frequent greenstone, rounded to subrounded; rare phyllite (brown, fine grained), quartzite/ polycrystalline quartz; very rare to absent pyroxene; sample KAV 15/54 also contains micritic limestone and microfossils	Biotite mica laths, rare small quartz fragments	Phyllite-Quartzite series
Fabric Group 4	Very fine dark reddish brown to dark brown with mottled areas due to high firing; optically inactive	Rare to very rare fragments of granite and diorite, very rare to absent sandstone, very little quartz; dark brown/black clay pellets	Very rare biotite mica laths	Granitic-dioritic outcrops
Fabric Group 5	Very fine dark reddish brown with mottled areas due to high firing; optically inactive	Siltstone, gray to black, subrounded to rounded; rare: quartz-biotite mica schist, fine-grained phyllite, small quartz fragments	Rare quartz fragments and small biotite mica laths	Ophiolite series/ flysch mélange
Fabric Group 6	Very fine dark reddish brown; optically inactive	Very few: phyllite, quartzite, basalt, sandstone, polycrystalline quartz; very rare quartz	Rare small quartz fragments and biotite mica laths	Ophiolite series/ flysch mélange
Fabric Group 7	Very fine, dark reddish brown; optically inactive	Rare to absent: small quartz fragments, sandstone, clay pellets	Very few to rare small quartz fragments and biotite mica laths	Ophiolite series/ flysch mélange

Table 20. Summary of the characteristics of the main petrographic fabric groups.

TABLE 21

Catalog Number	Length	Max. Pres. Length	Maximum Width	Socket Diameter	Socket Length	Shoulder	Midrib	Javelin or Spear
GR5 M2	25.2	—	2.7	1.8	6.5	Sloping	No	Javelin
GR5 M3	22.5	—	2.2	1.8	9.0	Sloping	No	Javelin
GR5 M4	—	15.9	2.3	2.3	10.5	Sloping	No	Javelin
GR5 M5	—	7.6	—	1.6	—	Sloping	No	?
GR5 M6	—	14.0	—	2.0	—	n/a	n/a	?
GR6 M5	32.5+	—	2.4	1.6	9.0	Sloping	No	Javelin
GR6 M6	25.3+	—	2.2	1.6	9.0	Sloping	No	Javelin
GR6 M7	—	16.3	2.7	1.7	9.0	Sloping	No	Javelin?
GR9 M14	—	33.5	2.3	1.6	5.6	Rectangular	Yes	Spear?
GR9 M15	36.5	—	2.5	1.8	7.0	Rectangular	Yes	Spear
GR9 M16	—	23.6	2.9	1.6–1.8	?	n/a	No	Javelin?
GR9 M17	30.0	—	2.2	1.9	7.8	Rectangular	Yes	Javelin
GR9 M18	22.3	—	2.8	1.9	7.5	Rectangular	Yes	Javelin
GR9 M19	41.2	—	2.6	1.6	7.8	Rectangular	Yes	Spear
GR9 M20	36.0	29.5	2.3	1.8	11.6	Rectangular	Yes	Spear?
GR9 M21	26.0	—	1.9	1.7	8.5	Sloping	No	Javelin
GR9 M22	24.0	—	2.5	1.8–1.9	8.0	Rectangular	Yes	Javelin
GR9 M23	—	18.1	2.3	1.6–2.0	8.3	Angular	No	Javelin
GR9 M24	21.0	—	2.6	1.9	7.5	Rectangular	Yes	Javelin
GR9 M25	ca. 28.2	—	2.2	1.8	7.0	Rectangular	Yes	Javelin?
GR9 M26	—	9.9	?	1.9	—	Sloping	No	Javelin?
GR9 M27	—	23.0	1.7	1.5–1.7	10.0	Sloping	No	Javelin?
GR9 M28	—	26.3	2.1	—	?	n/a	No	Javelin?
GR12 M24	ca. 23.0	—	2.1	1.5–2.0	10.0	Rectangular	Yes	Javelin
GR12 M25	26.0	—	2.5	1.8	8.5	Sloping	No	Javelin
GR12 M26	24.0	—	2.7	2.4	9.5	Sloping	No	Javelin
GR12 M27	—	9.5	2.1	1.6	—	Angular	No	Spear?
GR12 M28	—	23.0	2.1	—	—	n/a	Yes	Spear?
GR16 M4	23.6	—	1.9	2.0	8.0	Sloping	No	Javelin
GR16 M5	23.5	—	1.8	2.0	8.0	Sloping	No	Javelin
GR17 M6	—	6.2+9.7	2.6	1.9	6.2	Sloping	No	Javelin
GR20 M7	—	21.0	2.1	1.7	8.2	Sloping	Yes	Javelin
GR20 M8	23.6	—	2.0	2.0	8.2	Sloping	Yes	Javelin

Table 21. Iron spears or javelins from the Vronda enclosure graves.

Catalog Number	Length	Max. Pres. Length	Maximum Width	Socket Diameter	Socket Length	Shoulder	Midrib	Javelin or Spear
GR21 M1	—	14.8	2.1	2.3	8.6	Sloping?	No	Javelin?
GR26 M2	28.3	—	1.9	1.4	9.3	Angular	No	Javelin
GR26 M3	34.0	—	2.3	1.8	11.5	Angular	No	Spear
GR28 M2	15.4	—	2.1	2.5	8.4	Sloping	Yes	Javelin
GR28 M3	16.1	—	1.8	2.0	8.0	Sloping	No	Javelin
GR30 M8	—	18.4	2.2	1.8	9.5	Sloping	Yes	Javelin?
GR30 M9	—	11.0+10.0	?	1.6	11.8+	n/a	No	Spear/ javelin

Table 21, cont. Iron spears or javelins from the Vronda enclosure graves.

Catalog Number	Max. Pres. Length	Length (Est.)	Blade Length	Maximum Width	Rivets	Type
GR6 M8	36.5+	37.7	28.5	3.4	3: 2 bronze,1 not pres.	Dirk
GR9 M30	21.8	—	15.5	3.3	3: 1 bronze, 1 hole, 1 not pres.	Dagger
GR9 M31	41.3	—	34.3	3.3	3: holes	Dirk
GR9 M32	31.6	31.6+	33.8	3.5	3: 2 holes, 1 not pres.	Dagger?
GR9 M33	38.6	—	29.0	3.6	3 bronze	Dirk
GR9 M34	17.7+	—	—	3.9	3 bronze	Dirk?
GR12 M31	35.3	—	26.0	3.5	3: 1 bronze, 1 hole, 1 not pres.	Dirk
GR16 M6	37.0	—	27.0	4.0	3 iron	Dirk?
GR21 M2	41.5	—	34.2	3.0	3: 2 bronze, 1 hole	Dirk
GR26 M4	36.2	39.0	25.0	3.6	3: holes	Dirk
GR30 M10	26.9	30.5	21.0	3.7	3: 2 iron, 1 hole	Dirk?

Table 22. Iron short swords (dirks) and daggers from the Vronda enclosure graves.

Catalog Number	Inventory Number	Material	Shape	Height	Maximum Diameter	Hole Diameter	Weight (g)	Burning?
GR1 S1	V84.67	Carnelian?	Biconical	1.10	1.10	0.20	1	No
GR9 S1	V88.77	Serpentinite	Conical	1.30	1.20	0.40	4	No
GR20 S1	V88.241	Serpentinite	Disk	0.20	0.50	0.30	Not measurable	No
GR23 S1	V89.26	Serpentinite	Disk	1.10	2.25	0.65	8	Yes
GR23 S2	V89.27	Limestone	Disk	0.90	1.65	0.60	4	No
GR36 S1	V90.55	Rock crystal	Depressed globular	1.45	2.00	0.50	8	No

Table 23. Stone beads from the Vronda enclosure graves.

Catalog Number	Inventory Number	Shape	Height	Maximum Width	Hole Diameter	Weight (g)	Surface Treatment
GR3 TC1	V87.21	Tall biconical	2.0	2.2	0.50	6	Melon incision; burned
GR4 TC1	V87.14	Biconical	1.9	2.5	0.40	8	Burned
GR6 TC1	V87.64	Depressed globular	1.2	1.8	0.30	2	Monochrome; no burning
GR12 TC1	V88.74	Depressed globular	1.2–1.5	2.1	0.55	0.5	Three parts, incised with circles/bands; some burning
GR19 TC1	V88.76	Biconical	1.9	2.2	0.65	11	Buff slip; burning only on one side
GR26 TC1	V90.50	Disk	1.0	2.1	0.40	6	Burnished; incised decoration; burned?
GR30 TC1	V90.37	Globular	1.95	2.3	0.40	10	Melon incisions; no burning
GR30 TC2	V90.39	Biconical	n/a	2.5	0.50	8	Monochrome; burned
GR34 TC1	VW 12014.1	Cylindrical, cut from kylix stem	1.3–1.7	1.4–1.6	0.50	12	Painted bands
GR36 TC1	V90.116	Biconical	1.8	1.8	0.50	10	Burned
GR36 TC2	V90.117	Globular	1.5	1.8	0.40	4	Monochrome; burned
GR36 TC3	V90.118	Depressed globular	1.9	1.9	0.60	10	Incised circles; burned
GR36 TC4	V90.119	Globular	1.8	2.1	0.40	6	Monochrome; no burning
GR36 TC5	V90.120	Biconical	2.2	2.5	0.50	4	Incised melon; burned and melted

Table 24. Terracotta beads or whorls from the Vronda enclosure graves.

Grave	Identifiable Male Burials	Kraters	Weapons
1	1	1	17
4	—	1	—
5	3	—	5
6	1	1	4
9	2	1	19
12	1	3	28
16	—	—	3
17	1	1? (basin)	1
19	1	—	—
20	5	1? (small)	2

Table 25. Co-occurrence of male burials with kraters and weapons in the enclosure graves.

Grave	Identifiable Male Burials	Kraters	Weapons
21	2	1	1
21 pithos	1	—	1
23	—	1	—
26	—	—	3
27	—	1	?
28	3	4 (1 small)	2
30	2	1? (small)	3
36	1	—	—

Table 25, cont. Co-occurrence of male burials with kraters and weapons in the enclosure graves.

Grave/ Tomb	Subminoan 1050–970	Protogeometric 970–810	Geometric 810–745	Late Geometric 745–700	Early Orientalizing 700–650	Late Orientalizing 650–600
I	▓	▓				
II	▓	▓		▓		
IV	▓	▓		▓		
V				▓		
VI						
VII	▓	▓		▓		
VIII	▓	▓				
IX	▓	▓	▓	▓		
X	▓	▓	▓			
XI	▓	▓	▓			
1				▓		
2				▓	▓	
3				▓	▓	
4					▓	▓
5				▓		
6				▓		
8				▓		
9				▓		
10				▓		
12				▓	▓	

Table 26. Chronology of use of the tholos tombs and enclosure graves (years B.C.).

Grave/ Tomb	Subminoan 1050–970	Protogeometric 970–810	Geometric 810–745	Late Geometric 745–700	Early Orientalizing 700–650	Late Orientalizing 650–600
13				▓		
15				▓	▓	▓
16				▓	▓	
17					▓	▓
19			▓	▓		
20				▓	▓	
21				▓	▓	
23				▓	▓	▓
26				▓	▓	
27				▓	▓	
28				▓	▓	
29				▓	▓	
30					▓	▓
32					▓	▓
34				▓		
36				▓		
37				▓		

Table 26, cont. Chronology of use of the tholos tombs and enclosure graves (years B.C.).

Cemetery	Knossos, North Cemetery (Coldstream and Catling, eds., 1996)	Fortetsa (Brock 1957)	Eltyna (Rethemiotakis and Englezou 2010)	Vronda, Enclosure Burials
Number of graves	120	22	16	36
Number of graves with objects	82	18	12	20
Number of graves with weapons*	32	7	8	12
Percentage of all graves that had weapons	27%	32%	50%	33%
Percentage of graves with objects that have weapons	39%	39%	67%	60%

Table 27. Comparison of numbers and percentages of burials with weapons in fully published EIA Cretan cemeteries.
    *Weapons include only swords, daggers, spearheads, javelin heads, and arrowheads.

TABLE 28

Catalog Number	Capacity (L)	Catalog Number	Capacity (L)
Cups		Cups, cont.	
GR4 P17	0.049	GR27 P2	0.580
GR1 P1	0.162	GR36 P12	0.609
GR4 P12	0.178	GR6 P13	0.636
GR12 P20	0.178	GR16 P7	0.641
IV P1	0.263	GR3 P2	0.655
GR12 P32	0.267	GR3 P7	0.665
GR4 P22	0.295	GR9 P42	0.666
IX P60	0.301	GR9 P51	0.666
GR9 P23	0.314	GR9 P52	0.670
IX P50	0.318	GR19 P1	0.676
GR9 P1	0.330	GR5 P6	0.676
GR9 P34	0.336	GR21 P3	0.696
GR17 P1	0.343	GR19 P7	0.697
IX P33	0.364	GR12 P23	0.718
IX P29	0.372	GR6 P18	0.719
GR9 P43	0.374	GR27 P7	0.733
IX P28	0.380	GR28 P6	0.737
GR9 P18	0.380	GR12 P38	0.746
IX P30	0.396	GR30 P6	0.765
GR6 P9	0.412	GR3 P19	0.770
IX P51	0.415	GR28 P4	0.782
GR27 P1	0.416	GR36 P13	0.782
GR16 P14	0.422	GR9 P15	0.810
IX P59	0.423	GR16 P10	0.813
GR21 P12	0.462	GR30 P7	0.822
GR9 P55	0.466	GR5 P4	0.823
GR9 P41	0.469	GR5 P5	0.824
GR9 P19	0.474	GR26 P7	0.828
IX P31	0.474	GR9 P16	0.848
GR3 P3	0.480	GR9 P17	0.854
GR20 P9	0.494	GR30 P10	0.860
GR1 P13	0.497	GR19 P8	0.861
GR9 P33	0.503	GR28 P9	0.864
GR9 P20	0.510	GR16 P8	0.865
GR19 P16	0.515	GR30 P8	0.868
GR12 P1	0.549	GR30 P16	0.915
GR9 P24	0.552	GR21 P11	0.919

Table 28. Estimates of maximum vessel capacities for the cups, kantharos, mug-like cups, wide-mouthed jugs, skyphoi, and kraters from graves and tholos tombs at Vronda, sorted by shape and volume. AutoCAD calculations by S. Zarrinmehr.

TABLE 28

Catalog Number	Capacity (L)	Catalog Number	Capacity (L)
Cups, cont.		*Jugs, cont.*	
GR9 P13	0.976	GR9 P22	0.531
GR27 P6	0.977	Average (n=5)	0.420
GR9 P14	0.983	*Skyphoi*	
GR28 P7	0.985	GR26 P13	0.242
GR16 P6	0.994	GR20 P2	0.275
GR28 P5	1.024	GR26 P10	0.276
GR28 P10	1.038	GR26 P9	0.330
GR4 P13	1.045	GR26 P8	0.343
GR28 P8	1.053	GR12 P6	0.383
GR12 P21	1.072	GR3 P9	0.417
GR5 P8	1.153	GR36 P2	0.441
GR9 P40	1.154	GR12 P5	0.445
GR21 P5	1.176	GR19 P3	0.486
GR6 P12	1.220	GR12 P7	0.571
Average (n=88)	0.648	GR16 P15	0.710
Kantharos		GR36 P3	0.714
GR5 P11	0.981	GR9 P3	0.744
Footed Cups		GR19 P2	0.791
IX P34	0.168	GR6 P23	0.805
IX P2	0.546	GR36 P1	0.950
IX P4	1.037	GR3 P10	1.024
Average (n=3)	0.584	GR1 P17	1.044
Mug-like Cups		GR16 P2	1.055
GR12 P2	0.380	GR36 P16	1.183
GR28 P11	0.420	GR30 P29	1.244
GR3 P1	0.550	GR4 P15	1.247
GR16 P4	0.586	Average (n=23)	0.683
GR16 P3	0.608	*Stemmed Skyphoi*	
GR21 P4	0.758	GR1 P2	0.464
GR12 P3	0.879	GR28 P1	0.480
GR4 P1	1.758	GR19 P4	0.617
Average (n=8)	0.742	GR6 P3	0.675
Jugs		Average (n=4)	0.559
GR12 P22	0.294	*Kraters*	
GR3 P4	0.313	GR4 P16	5.375
GR12 P4	0.448	GR6 P27 (restored)	34.643
GR19 P5	0.514	Average (n=2)	20.009

Table 28, cont. Estimates of maximum vessel capacities for the cups, kantharos, mug-like cups, wide-mouthed jugs, skyphoi, and kraters from graves and tholos tombs at Vronda, sorted by shape and volume. AutoCAD calculations by S. Zarrinmehr.

TABLE 29

Sample No.	Catalog No.	Inventory No.	Context	Type	Metallic?
KAV1	n/a	K 88.93	Kastro, Room 56	Iron bloom	Yes
KAV2	**GR6 M16**	V87.144	Grave 6	File	No
KAV3	**GR9 M41**	V88.202	Grave 9	Axe-head, near handle	No
KAV4	n/a	K 20014 (1)	Kastro, Room 33	Iron billet	Yes
KAV5	**GR9 M14**	V88.179 (2)	Grave 9	Spearhead, end	No
KAV6	**GR9 M29**	V88.198	Grave 9	Socketed weapon or tool	No
KAV7	**GR9 M33**	V88.186	Grave 9	Dirk	No?
KAV8	**GR28 M5**	V89.66 (2)	Grave 28	Axe-head	
KAV9	**GR28 M5**	V89.66 (1)	Grave 28	Axe-head	Yes
KAV10	n/a	K 20014 (2)	Kastro, Room 33	Iron billet	Yes
KAV11	**GR9 M40**	V88.196 (1)	Grave 9	Axe-head, edge	Yes
KAV12	**GR9 M19**	V88.155	Grave 9	Spearhead	No
KAV13	**GR9 M39**	V88.175	Grave 9	Sickle	No
KAV14	n/a	K 15903	Kastro, Rooms 32, 33	Smithing hearth bottom?	Yes
KAV15	**GR9 M2**	V88.130 (1)	Grave 9	Copper-iron fibula	Yes
KAV16	n/a	K 11705 (1)	Kastro, Room 47	Iron bloom, ca. 5 cm wide	Yes
KAV17	n/a	K 15502 (2)	Kastro, Room 44	Iron billet or bloom, ca. 3 cm thick	Yes
KAV18	**GR12 M9**	V88.109 (1)	Grave 12	Arrowhead	No
KAV19	**GR12 M9**	V88.109 (2)	Grave 12	Arrowhead	No
KAV20	**GR12 M19**	V88.131b	Grave 12	Arrowhead	No
KAV21	**GR9 M2**	V88.130 (2)	Grave 9	Copper-iron fibula	Yes
KAV22	**GR12 M9**	V88.109 (3)	Grave 12	Arrowhead	No
KAV23	**GR1 M6**	V84.65a	Grave 1	Arrowhead	No
KAV24	**GR26 M4**	V90.138a (2)	Grave 26	Dirk, edge	No
KAV25	**GR16 M6**	V88.85 (1)	Grave 1	Dirk, edge	No
KAV26	**GR9 M40**	V88.196 (2)	Grave 9	Axe-head	Yes
KAV27	**GR9 M44**	V88.181 (1)	Grave 9	Iron scraper	Yes?
KAV28	**GR9 M44**	V88.181 (2)	Grave 9	Iron scraper	No
KAV29	**GR26 M4**	V90.138a (1)	Grave 26	Dirk, edge	Yes
KAV30	**GR5 M7**	V87.96/102	Grave 5	Knife, edge	No

Table 29. List of ferrous and nonferrous Kavousi artifacts deriving from both Vronda and the Kastro. The KAV numbers (KAV1–KAV40) refer to polished blocks prepared for this study. Numbers in parentheses correspond to subsamples taken from the same object.

Sample No.	Catalog No.	Inventory No.	Context	Type	Metallic?
KAV31	**GR16 M6**	V88.85 (2)	Grave 16	Dirk, edge	No
KAV32	**GR9 M34**	V88.206	Grave 9	Dirk, edge near hilt	No
KAV33	**GR26 M3**	V90.135 (1)	Grave 26	Spearhead	Yes
KAV34	**GR26 M3**	V90.135 (2)	Grave 26	Spearhead	No
KAV35	**GR26 M2**	V90.137 (1)	Grave 26	Spearhead	Yes
KAV36	**GR26 M2**	V90.137 (2)	Grave 26	Spearhead	No
KAV37	GR30 M12	V90.139	Grave 30	Sickle	No
KAV38	**GR9 M14**	V88.179 (1)	Grave 9	Spearhead	Yes
KAV39	**GR30 M10**	V90.138b	Grave 30	Dagger, edge	No
KAV40	**GR9 M15**	V88.183	Grave 9	Spearhead	No

Table 29, cont. List of ferrous and nonferrous Kavousi artifacts deriving from both Vronda and the Kastro. The KAV numbers (KAV1–KAV40) refer to polished blocks prepared for this study. Numbers in parentheses correspond to subsamples taken from the same object.

Sample Identification	Context	Optical Examination/ SEM Image	Hardness Testing (H_v)	Slag Inclusions	Comments
Group I					
KAV1 Iron bloom/billet (Pl. 76A)	Iron bloom found in K 4120.8, a level of rock tumble above roofing on the floor of Kastro Room 56, with material dated to seventh century and earlier.	Uneven distribution of carbon content throughout matrix; low carbon areas: ferrite (light) with few slag inclusions (dark spots; Pl. 76A:a), ferrite with many slag inclusions (Pl. 76A:b); high carbon area: ferrite with pearlite (dark area; Pl. 76A:c).	Confirmation of ferrite areas (H_v = 130 and 135) and pearlite (H_v = 170 and 225)	Numerous (small and round) inclusions associated primarily with ferrite; also some Cu-Sn-Fe inclusions within metallic matrix.	Uneven carbon distribution shown in section is inherent in bloomery iron making and therefore is representative of iron blooms/billets of that period (but also later). Uniform carbon distribution only would have been possible had the iron metal been molten, which it never is in the bloomery; or it can be so in very small areas. It follows that the harder the section of the bloom the more difficult it would have been to work, and therefore it may have been discarded easily. For the presence of copper-tin inclusions within this artifact, see this vol., pp. 382–383, Table 31.

Table 30. Summary of observations gathered from optical examination with the metallographic microscope and SEM of polished blocks of Kavousi samples, and the hardness testing measurements of each block.

TABLE 30

Sample Identification	Context	Optical Examination/ SEM Image	Hardness Testing (H_v)	Slag Inclusions	Comments
		Group I, cont.			
KAV4 (1/2) Iron bloom/billet (first section) (Pls. 76B, 76C)	Iron bloom found in stone tumble and habitation debris of PG date in Kastro Room 33.	Compared to KAV1, higher distribution of carbon across section due to extensive presence of pearlite (Pl. 76B); large ferrite grains (Pl. 76C) with lamelar pearlite (Pl. 76B) at the grain boundaries; elongated slag inclusions (Pl. 76C).	Hardness varies across section; for areas with low to medium carbon $H_v = 141$ and 137	Two types of slag inclusions: fayalitic (globular) and silica rich (elongated); small amount of phosphorus (ca. 0.3%).	See KAV 10, below
KAV10 (2/2) Iron bloom/billet (second section) (Pls. 77A, 77B)	See KAV4, above	Uneven carburization with areas of high and low carbon (Pl. 77A), ranging from ferrite and pearlite (0.1% carbon, bottom of Pl. 77A) to areas of ca. 0.7% carbon (top of Pl. 77A), with pearlite being the major phase and ferrite at the grain boundaries; pearlite is primarily lamellar, as seen in Pl. 77B; volume expansion as a result of weathering (converting metallic iron back to iron oxide) is evident at the bottom of Pl. 77A.	—	Only a few globular slag inclusions, their composition primarily calcium aluminosilicate; no distinguishing elements that would point to a particular ore type (see Table 31).	Samples KAV4 and KAV10 are fragments of the same artifact, an iron bloom/billet (object K 20014.2). Both sections show increased levels of carburization compared to KAV1; this carburization is mostly distributed evenly throughout, making it a medium carbon steel rather than wrought iron. It may have been the raw material for objects like KAV29, a dagger/dirk (see below).
KAV14 Smithy hearth bottom? Pls. 78A, 78B)	Fragment of smithing or smelting slag found in dense stone tumble above clay fill dated to seventh century or earlier in Kastro Room 32/31.	Smithing/smelting slag (or fragment of smithing hearth bottom?) consisting of globular iron oxides amid a silicate matrix of fayalite (Fe_2SiO_4) and interstitial glass (Pl. 78A); remnants of metallic iron (Pl. 78A), most of which have weathered to iron oxides (oxyhydroxides rather than wustite) amid an equally weathered silicate matrix; remnants of charcoal, used as fuel, can be seen in Pl. 78B, trapped within a matrix of partially reduced iron ore.	—	—	This fragment, which cannot be securely identified as smithing or smelting, testifies to both activities taking place on site, as indeed would have been expected from a "smithy" of eighth–seventh centuries B.C. Crete.

Table 30, cont. Summary of observations gathered from optical examination with the metallographic microscope and SEM of polished blocks of Kavousi samples, and the hardness testing measurements of each block.

TABLE 30

Sample Identification	Context	Optical Examination/ SEM Image	Hardness Testing (H$_v$)	Slag Inclusions	Comments
Group I, cont.					
KAV16 Iron bloom (Pl. 79A)	Iron bloom found in destruction debris above floor of Kastro Room 47 and dating to seventh century.	Fragment of unconsolidated bloom consisting of a silicate phase, metal, and iron oxides as well as unreacted or partially reacted ore; latter (Pl. 79A) consisted of iron oxides and calcium with chlorine (soil contaminant); no phosphorus in ore; silicate matrix is calcium rich, wustite is "fine" iron oxide with no diagnostic elements. Of interest is the metal composition, consisting of minor quantities of copper (1.80%) dissolved in the iron.	—	Composition of slag in matrix is calcium aluminosilicate; wustite contains no disgnostic elements (Table 31).	The presence of copper within the iron is an interesting observation that points to the choice of iron ores found in the proximity of and in association with copper (see this vol., pp. 382–383).
KAV17 Iron slag or within bloom? (Pl. 79B)	Iron slag or slag-rich fragment of a bloom found in stone tumble below the modern surface in Kastro Room 44, probably belonging to the seventh century or earlier.	Slag of the smithing type consisting of globular dendrites of wustite and fine fayalite needles in an interstitial glass (Pl. 79B).	—	—	Section of a smithing slag
Group II					
KAV11 (1/2) Axe-head (second section) (Pl. 80A)	See KAV26, below	Second section of **GR9 M40**: SEM shows large equiaxial ferrite grains with nitride needles and cementite inclusions; unresolved cementite lies within grain boundaries (Pl. 80A); diamond indentation on right testifies to softness of ferritic nature.	Two measurements reflect ferritic nature of matrix: H$_v$ = 105 and 119.	Very few in Pl. 80A	—

Table 30, cont. Summary of observations gathered from optical examination with the metallographic microscope and SEM of polished blocks of Kavousi samples, and the hardness testing measurements of each block.

TABLE 30

Sample Identification	Context	Optical Examination/ SEM Image	Hardness Testing (H_v)	Slag Inclusions	Comments
			Group II, cont.		
KAV26 (2/2) Axe-head (first section) (Pl. 80B)	Iron axe-head mended from numerous fragments; nearly complete, except for chips; L. 10.1, max. w. 4.1 cm; corroded, but with some well-preserved surfaces; long tang (3.9 cm); Grave 9 (Geometric).	First section of **GR9 M40**: optical examination reveals largely ferrite with cementite/nitride needles throughout; nitride needles concentrate at end of section; minimal pearlite and numerous slag inclusions (Pl. 80B).	—	—	The metallographic structure of the axe-head (KAV26 and KAV11; see above) is primarily ferrite that was hardened by exposure to the oxygen-starved atmosphere, with the formation of nitride needles. Nitrides also could have originated from exposure to the cremation pyre, and they may not necessarily reflect conditions within the hearth. Axe-heads were expected to be tough and to withstand impact rather than to have a sharp cutting edge, hence the largely ferritic structure of the object.
			Group III		
KAV33 Spearhead (Pls. 81A, 81B)	Iron spearhead, complete in two fragments but bent; L. est. (unbent) 34.0, max. w. 2.3, d. socket 1.8 cm; socket and blade corroded, but well-preserved surfaces on one side of blade; long socket (11.5 cm), folded tightly; no visible hole pierced in socket.	Metallographic section shows ferrite and many slag inclusions (Pl. 81A); SEM image reveals ferrite matrix with cementite growing within grains (Pl. 81B).	Two measurements reflect a ferritic composition: H_v = 90.7 and 91.8.	Numerous; fayalite type composition with much calcium; traces of copper	Ferritic spearhead with numerous slag inclusions; exposure in reducing atmosphere of hearth has resulted in nitriding of the surface, and, in the absence of carbon, imparted some hardness to the blade.

Table 30, cont. Summary of observations gathered from optical examination with the metallographic microscope and SEM of polished blocks of Kavousi samples, and the hardness testing measurements of each block.

TABLE 30

Sample Identification	Context	Optical Examination/ SEM Image	Hardness Testing (H$_v$)	Slag Inclusions	Comments
		Group III, cont.			
KAV35 Spearhead (Pl. 81C)	Iron spearhead, complete in four fragments; L. 28.3, max. w. 1.9, d. socket 1.4 cm; very corroded; long (9.3 cm) socket, wrapped very tightly without great diameter.	Metallographic section showing ferritic matrix with many slag inclusions elongated along line of working (Pl. 81C).	Measurements recorded on ferrite revealed H$_v$ = 128, 122, 96, and 101.	Numerous	Samples KAV33 and KAV35 are both spearheads whose metallographic composition is largely ferritic. Long exposure in the reducing atmosphere of the hearth has resulted in nitriding of the surface.
		Group IV			
KAV15 Fibula (first section) (Pls. 82B, 82D)	Bronze-iron fibula with iron coil; four fragments, including catch plate; missing only pin parts; Grave 9.	Photo of entire section in Pl. 82B; only two places with remnants of metal (white); metallic remains consist of copper-tin-bronze crystals (Pl. 82B) with SnCl$_2$ corrosion growing at grain boundaries (Pl. 82D); envelope of iron around copper alloy; difficult to ascertain how two sections (ferrous and nonferrous) were held/welded together.	—	Slag composition within area of iron is K, Ca aluminosilicate with titanium and manganese inclusions as well as barium; this type of slag differs (in Ti and Mn) from the iron in the other objects examined here.	A cross-section of a small fibula wherein the two copper tin "sections" are welded or held together by iron that is presently corroded (Pl. 82D). The alloy is actually leaded bronze, but the lead content is low and is dispersed in the matrix as small inclusions.
KAV21 Fibula (second section) (Pls. 82A, 82C)	—	Corrosion product is SnCl$_2$ (Table 31)	—	—	—
KAV29 Dirk (Pls. 83A, 83B)	Iron dirk, nearly complete in five fragments; missing tip of hilt and tip of blade; slightly bent; Grave 26.	Metallographic section (Pl. 83A) showing primarily lamellar pearlite, well formed and with small amounts of spheroidized pearlite; islands of ferrite (white) at grain boundaries; considerable orangish-yellow corrosion associated with the cementite/pearlite; areas with ferrite and pearlite have carbon contents of ca. 0.70%; SEM image (Pl. 83B) shows closeup of lamellar pearlite with single slag inclusion in between.	—	Very few inclusions; slag inclusion is K, Ca aluminosilicate glass with minor copper oxide (Table 31)	Dirk made of high carbon steel, perhaps from a highly carburized section of a bloom similar to KAV4/KAV10.

Table 30, cont. Summary of observations gathered from optical examination with the metallographic microscope and SEM of polished blocks of Kavousi samples, and the hardness testing measurements of each block.

TABLE 31

Sample	Na$_2$O	MgO	Al$_2$O$_3$	SiO$_2$	SO$_3$	P$_2$O$_5$	K$_2$O	CaO	TiO$_2$	MnO	FeO	BaO	CuO	SnO	Total
Group I															
KAV1 Iron bloom; Ca-Fe-Si phase (matrix) (average of three measurements)	0.3	1.6	6.2	40.6	0.1	0.2	5.0	17.7	0.2	0.4	27.3	0.0	0.1	0.0	99.7
KAV1 Cu-Sn-rich Fe oxide phase (average of three measurements)	0.0	0.2	0.0	0.2	0.2	0.0	0.0	0.0	0.0	0.0	90.4	0.0	4.6	4.1	100.0
KAV1 Sn-rich Fe oxide phase (average of two measurements)	0.0	0.1	0.0	0.1	0.2	0.0	0.0	0.0	0.0	0.0	96.9	0.0	0.1	2.4	99.7
KAV4 Iron bloom/billet; fayalite (Fe-Si) phase	0.4	0.3	2.9	22.5	0.2	0.3	0.8	3.0	0.1	0.2	69.3	0.1	nm	nm	100.0
KAV10 Iron bloom/billet; Ca-Fe-Si phase (matrix)	0.7	1.5	6.5	35.6	0.2	0.4	1.5	11.7	0.1	0.0	40.6	nm	0.0	0.0	98.9
KAV16 Iron bloom/billet; Ca-Fe-Si phase (matrix)	0.2	0.2	3.1	28.7	0.3	0.5	2.9	22.4	0.0	0.1	41.6	0.1	nm	nm	100.0
KAV16 Fe-O phase (wustite)	0.0	0.1	0.1	0.2	0.0	0.0	0.0	0.1	0.1	0.0	99.4	0.0	nm	nm	100.0
Group II															
KAV11 Axe-head; fayalite (Fe-Si) phase	0.0	0.8	2.2	26.0	0.1	0.1	1.1	2.2	0.0	0.2	67.0	0.1	0.0	0.2	100.0
KAV11 Fayalite (Fe-Si) phase	0.3	2.0	5.7	26.9	0.1	0.9	3.7	5.7	0.1	0.0	54.1	0.2	0.0	0.2	100.0
KAV26 Axe-head; fayalite (Fe-Si)-like phase	0.4	0.5	2.2	17.8	0.1	0.2	0.9	2.4	0.1	0.2	75.2	0.1	0.1	0.0	100.0
Group III															
KAV33 Spearhead; fayalite (Fe-Si) phase (average of two measurements)	0.0	0.5	0.4	22.3	0.1	0.1	0.3	6.3	0.0	6.0	63.9	0.1	0.1	0.0	100.0

Table 31. SEM-EDAX spot analyses on polished blocks of Kavousi samples, as shown in Table 29. Individual and average compositions expressed in oxide weight percent; nm = not measured. The analyses shown here are indicative of the composition of various phases illustrated. Of interest is the frequent presence of traces of both Cu and Sn in Fe (as in the case of the bloom KAV1, as well as in the sulfide-rich phase in the second copper-iron fibula KAV21).

TABLE 31

Sample	Na$_2$O	MgO	Al$_2$O$_3$	SiO$_2$	SO$_3$	P$_2$O$_5$	K$_2$O	CaO	TiO$_2$	MnO	FeO	BaO	CuO	SnO	Total
Group IV															
KAV15 Copper-iron fibula; Ca-Fe-Si phase (matrix)	0.0	1.9	5.0	24.9	0.3	0.1	5.0	16.6	0.6	1.1	43.4	1.0	0.0	0.2	100.0
KAV 21 Copper-iron fibula; unusual Sn-S phase	nm	nm	nm	nm	5.6	nm	nm	nm	nm	nm	0.2	nm	nm	88.5	94.3
KAV 21 Unusual Sn-O phase	nm	nm	nm	nm	0.2	nm	nm	nm	nm	nm	nm	nm	0.3	99.4	99.8
KAV21 Unusual Sn-S phase	nm	nm	nm	nm	80.6	nm	nm	nm	nm	nm	nm	nm	0.0	19.0	99.6
KAV29 Dirk edge; glassy Al-Si-Ca phase	0.4	3.8	8.7	40.0	0.1	0.0	8.0	33.0	0.3	0.8	3.0	1.0	0.1	0.9	100.0

Table 31, cont. SEM-EDAX spot analyses on polished blocks of Kavousi samples, as shown in Table 29. Individual and average compositions expressed in oxide weight percent; nm = not measured. The analyses shown here are indicative of the composition of various phases illustrated. Of interest is the frequent presence of traces of both Cu and Sn in Fe (as in the case of the bloom KAV1, as well as in the sulfide-rich phase in the second copper-iron fibula KAV21).

Charts

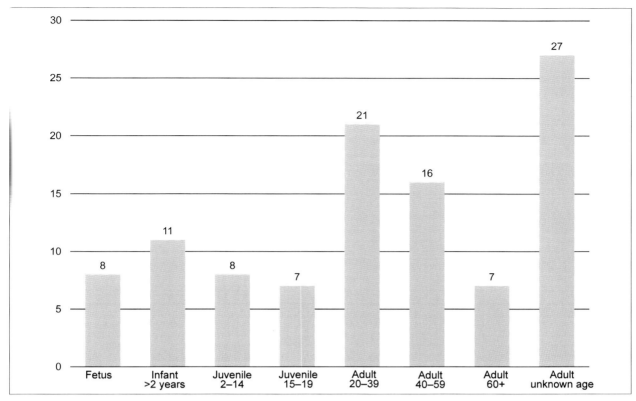

Chart 1. Total deaths by age group in Vronda enclosure graves.

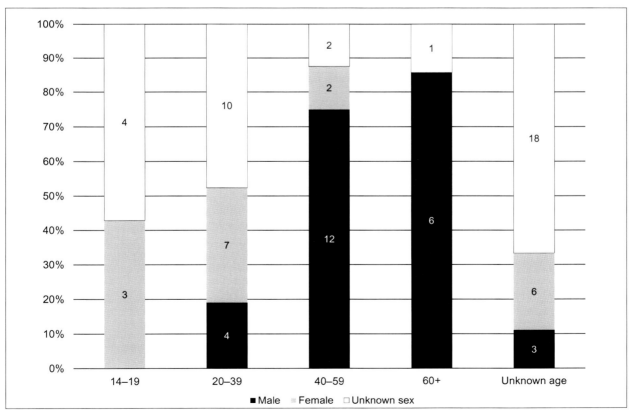

Chart 2. Number of individuals by age at death and sex in Vronda enclosure graves.

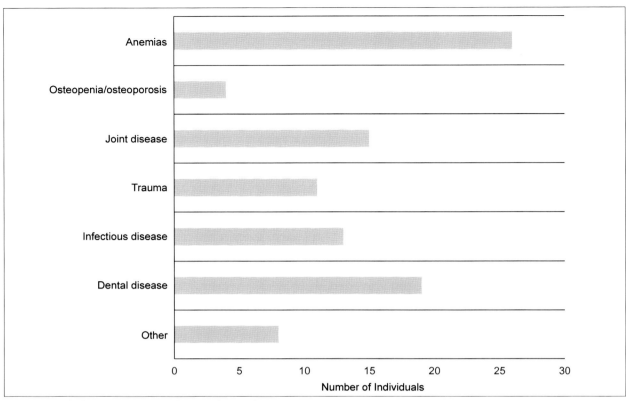

Chart 3. Pathologies in the population of Vronda enclosure graves.

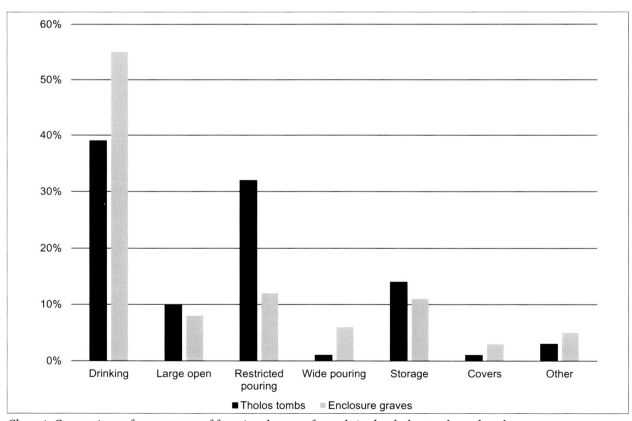

Chart 4. Comparison of percentages of functional types of vessels in the tholos tombs and enclosure graves.

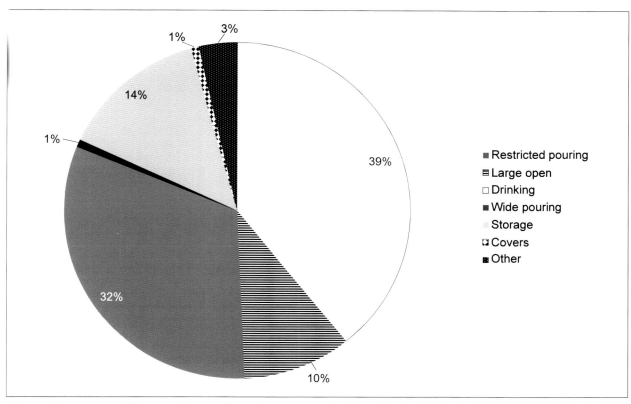

Chart 5. Percentages of functional types of vessels represented in the tholos tombs.

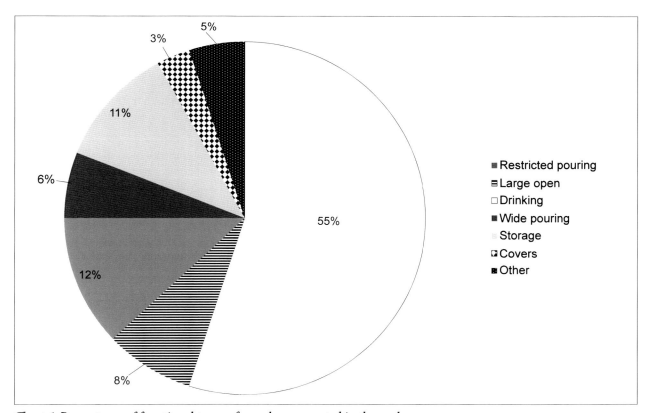

Chart 6. Percentages of functional types of vessels represented in the enclosure graves.

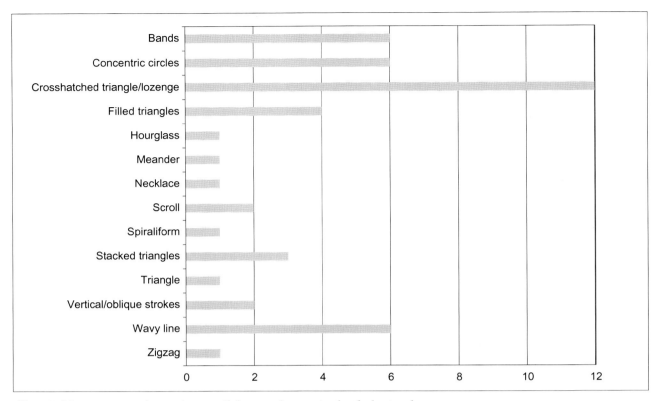

Chart 7. Most common decorative motifs by vessel count in the tholos tombs.

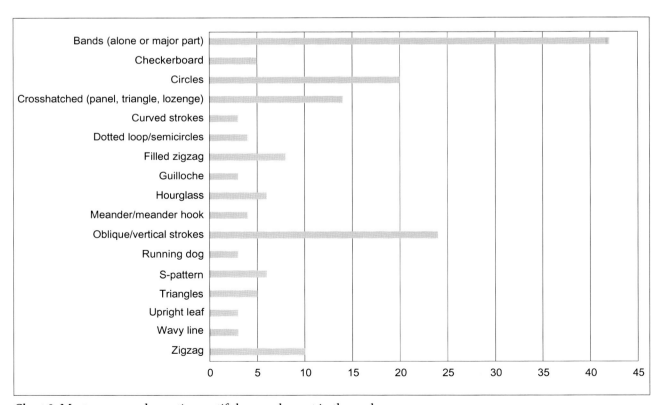

Chart 8. Most common decorative motifs by vessel count in the enclosure graves.

CHART 9 AND 10

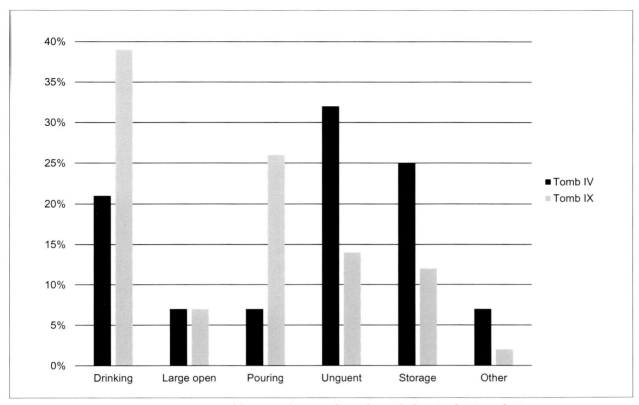

Chart 9. Comparison of the percentages of functional types of vessels in Tholos Tombs IV and IX.

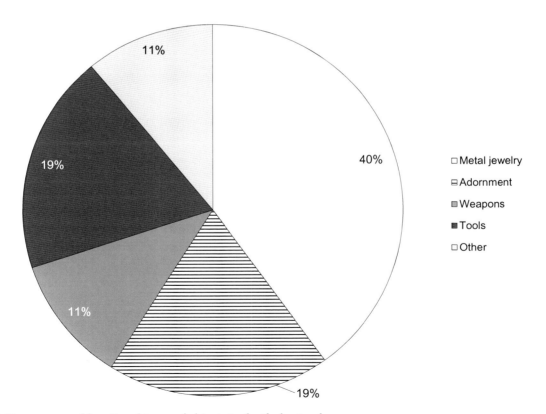

Chart 10. Percentages of functional types of objects in the tholos tombs.

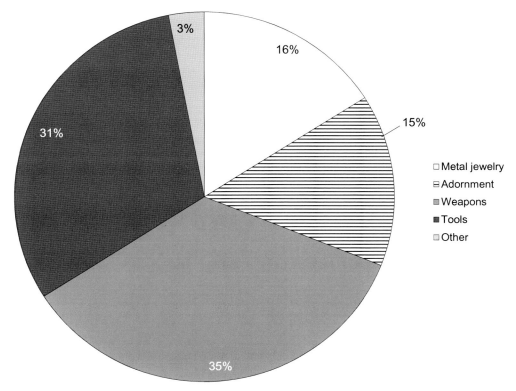

Chart 11. Percentages of functional types of objects in the enclosure graves.

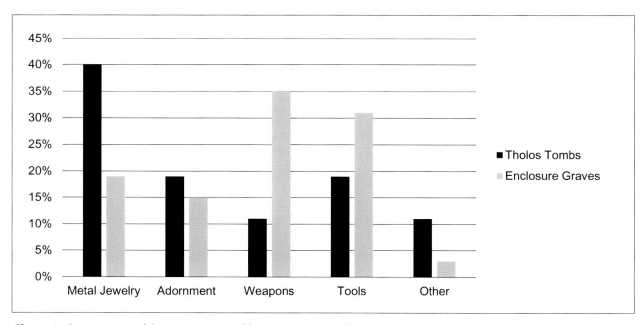

Chart 12. Comparison of the percentages of functional types of objects in the tholos tombs and enclosure graves.

CHART 13

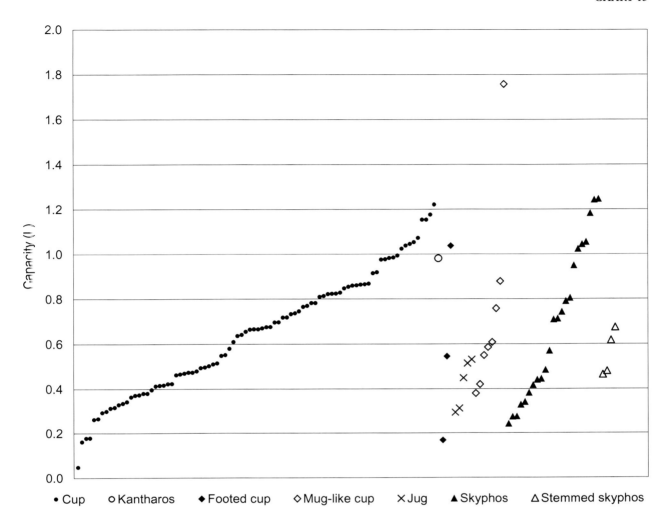

Chart 13. Scatter plot of estimated maximum capacities (L) of drinking vessels from grave contexts at Vronda, separated by shape.

CHART 14

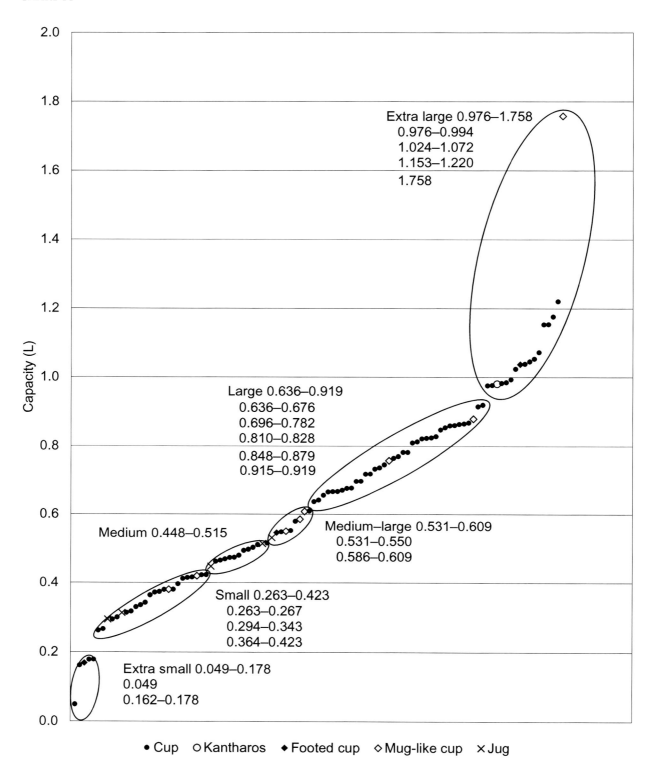

Chart 14. Scatter plot of estimated maximum capacities (L) of all the cups, kantharos, footed cups, mug-like cups, and wide-mouthed jugs, with suggested size categories. Possible subgroups within each size category are also indicated.

CHART 15

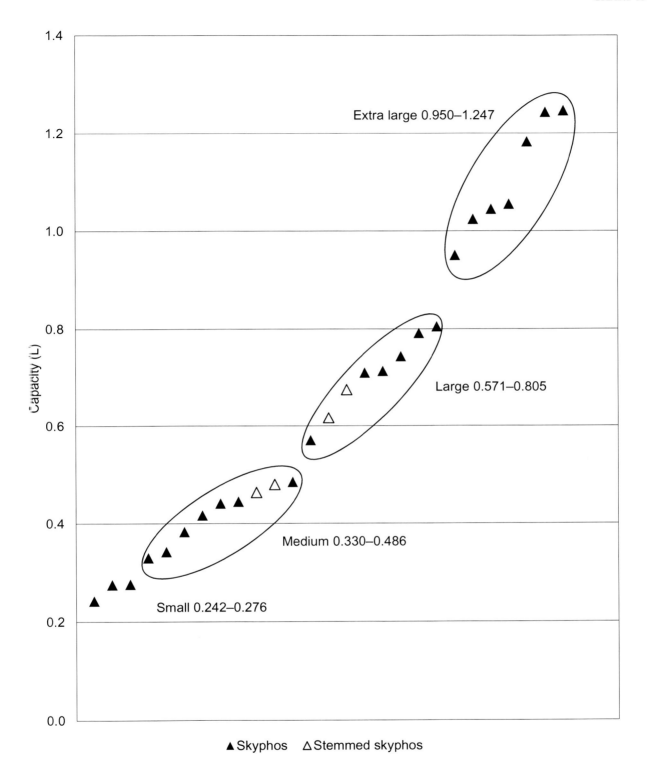

▲ Skyphos △ Stemmed skyphos

Chart 15. Scatter plot of estimated maximum capacities (L) of all skyphoi and stemmed skyphoi, with suggested size categories.

Figures

FIGURE 1

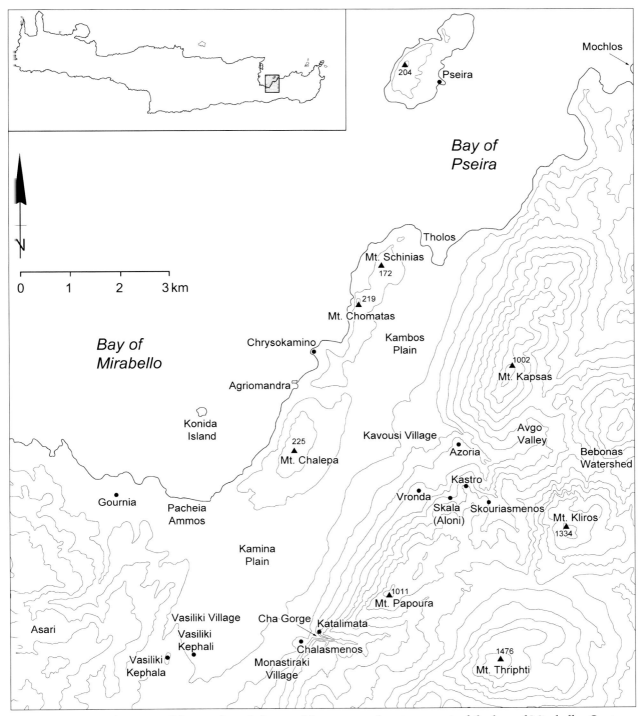

Figure 1. Topographic map of the northern isthmus of Ierapetra and eastern coast of the bay of Mirabello. Contour lines at 100 m intervals. Adapted from Haggis 2005, fig. 2.

FIGURE 2

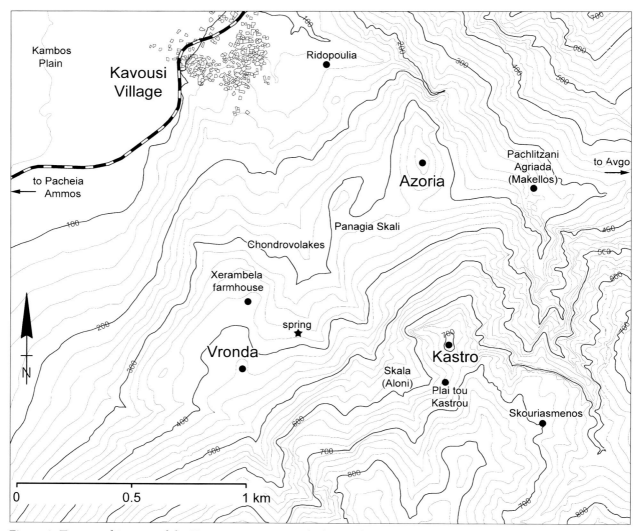

Figure 2. Topographic map of the Kavousi region, Vronda (Xerambela), and the north Papoura area. Contour lines at 20 m intervals. Adapted from Haggis 2005, fig. 22.

FIGURE 3

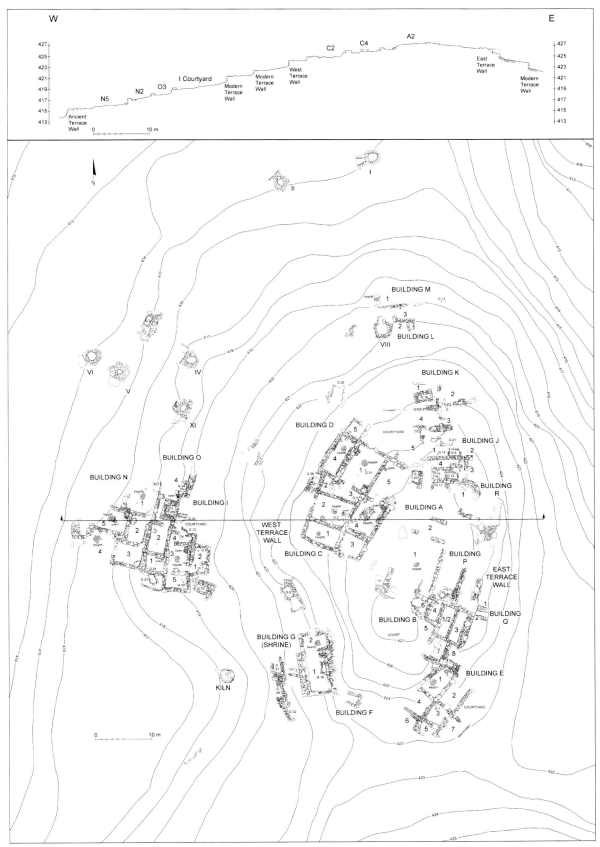

Figure 3. Vronda: state plan and site section. Topographic contours (1 m intervals) based on 1984 survey by
J. Rehard. Grid north reflects magnetic north (declination 2.1584°) in July, 1984. G. = Grave.

FIGURE 4

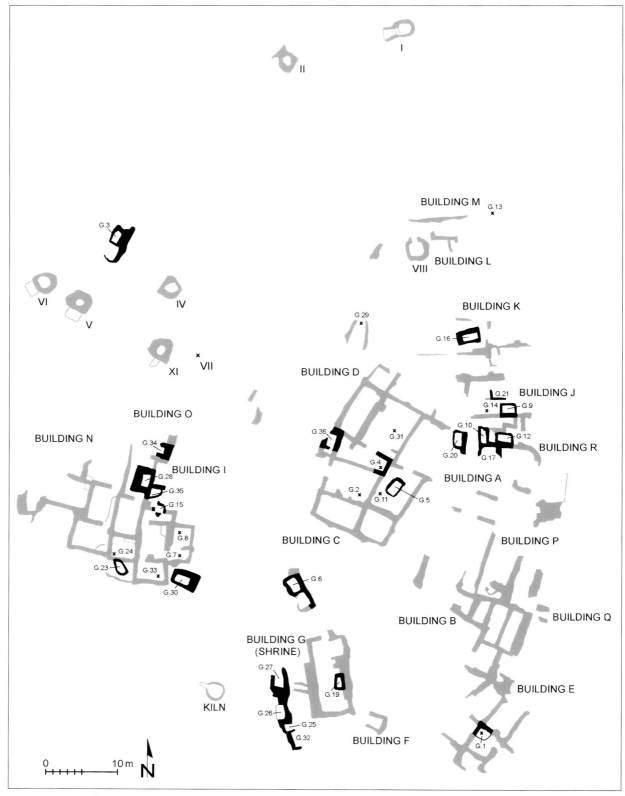

Figure 4. Plan of Vronda ridge showing position of the LM IIIC settlement, tholos tombs, and cremation enclosures.
G. = Grave. D. Faulmann.

FIGURE 5

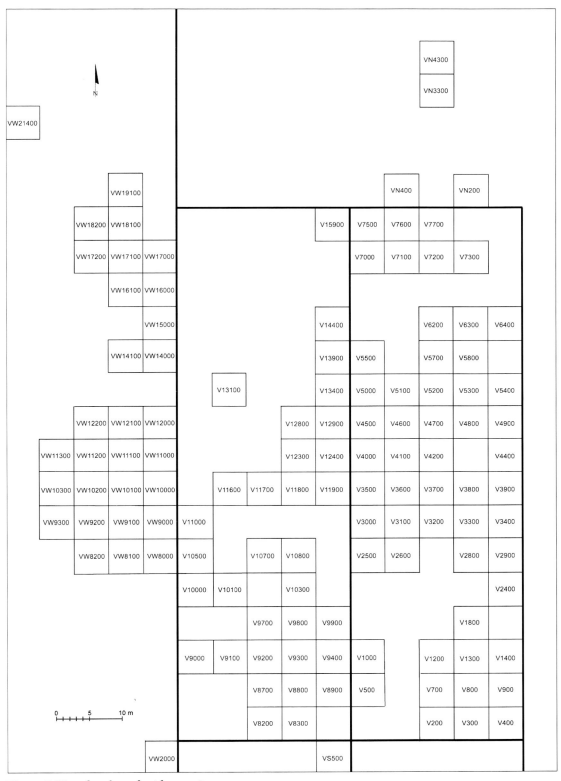

Figure 5. Vronda: plan of grid over site.

FIGURE 6

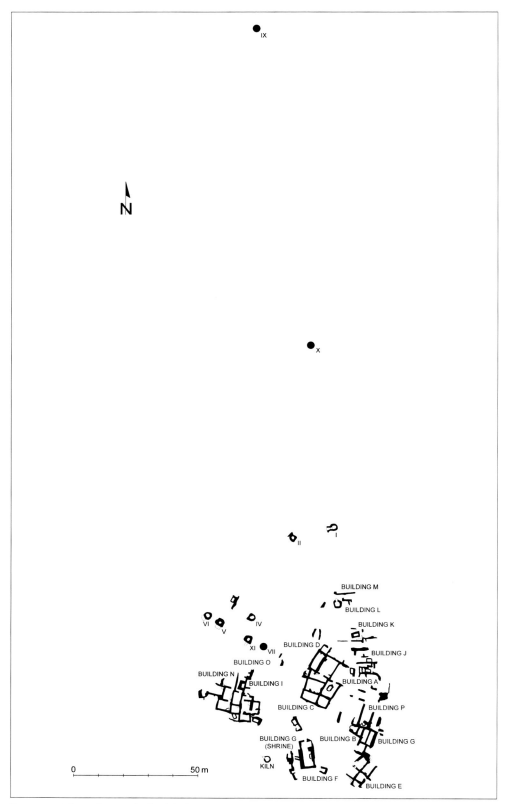

Figure 6. Plan of Vronda highlighting position of tholos tombs in relation to the LM IIIC settlement. D. Faulmann.

FIGURE 7

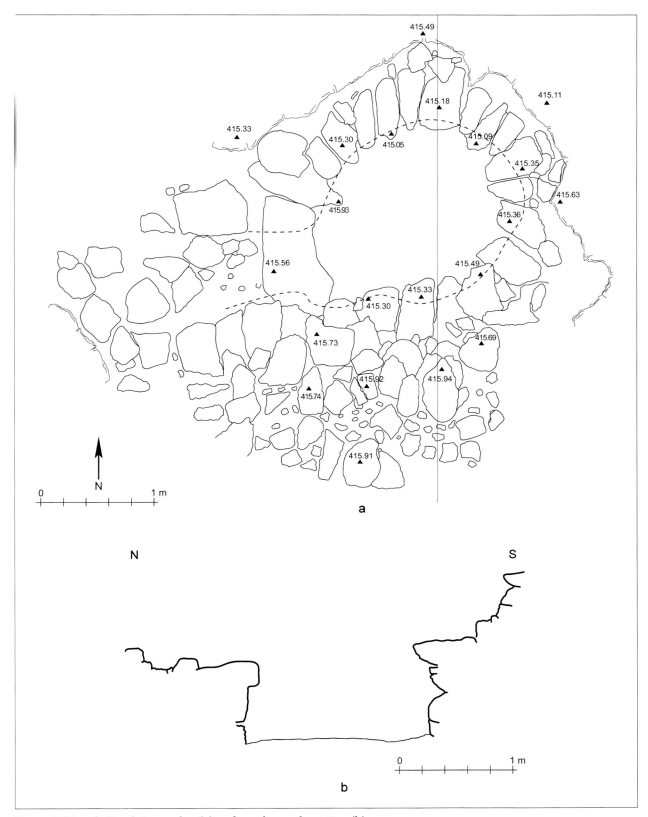

Figure 7. Vronda Tomb I: top plan (a) and north–south section (b).

FIGURE 8

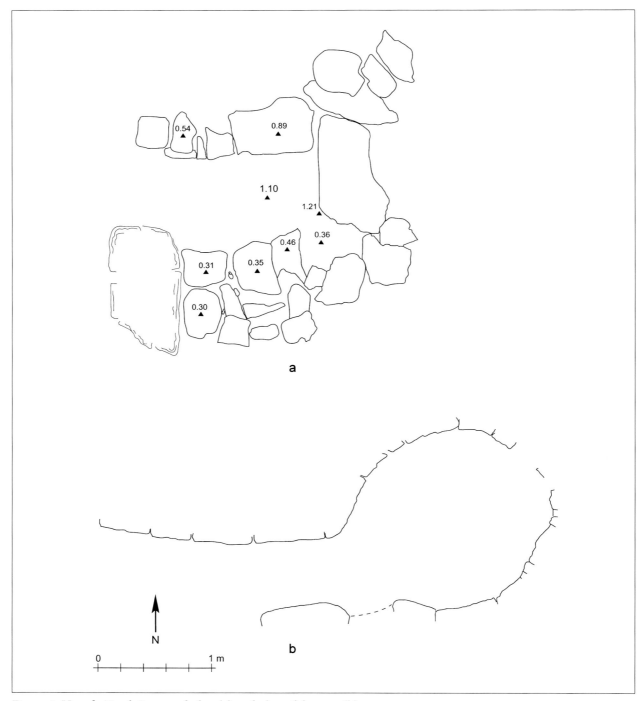

Figure 8. Vronda Tomb I: ground plan (a) and plan of dromos (b).

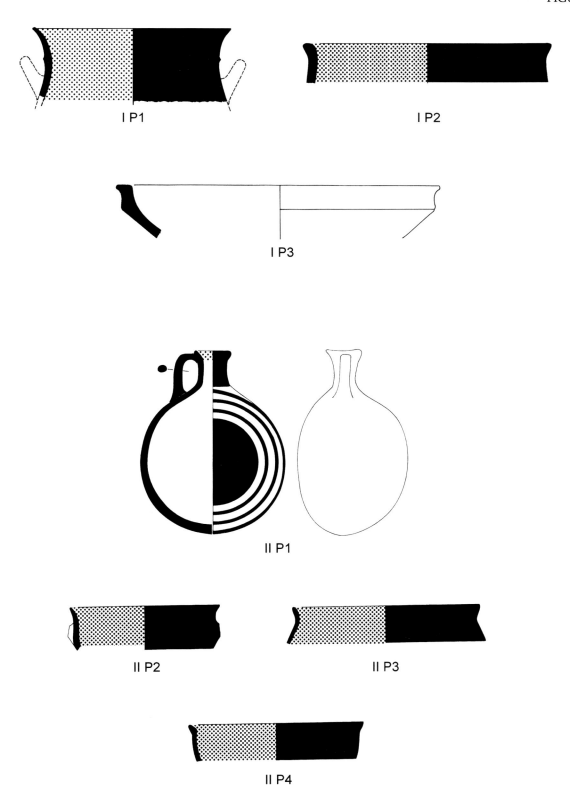

FIGURE 9

Figure 9. Tomb I, pottery (**I P1**–**I P3**); Tomb II, pottery (**II P1**–**II P4**). Scale 1:3.

FIGURE 10

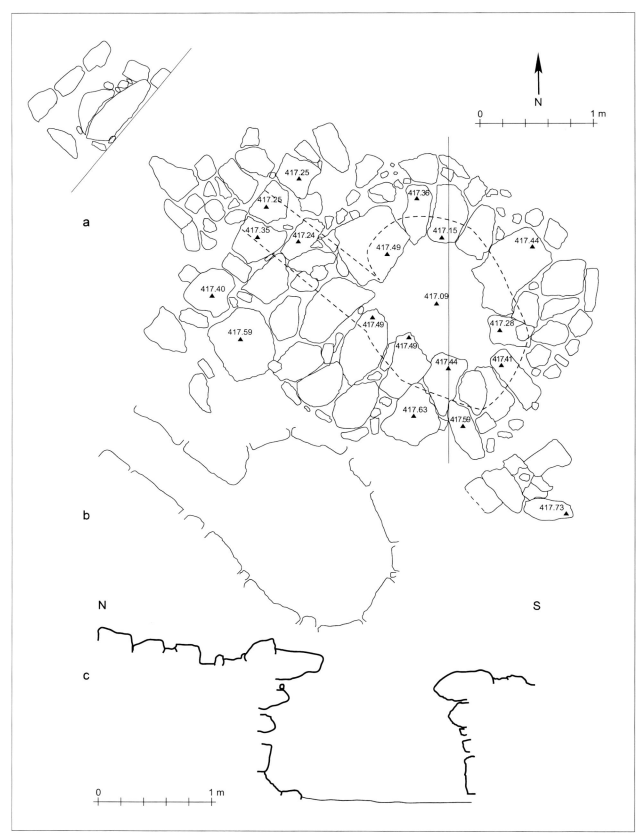

Figure 10. Vronda Tomb II: top plan (a), ground plan (b), and north–south section (c).

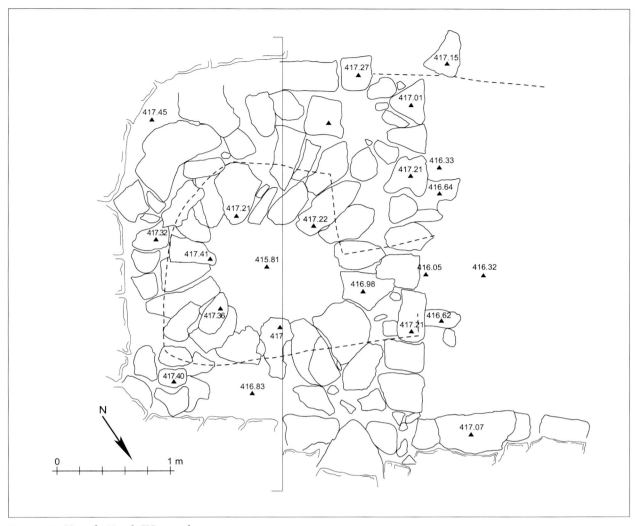

FIGURE 11

Figure 11. Vronda Tomb IV: top plan.

FIGURE 12

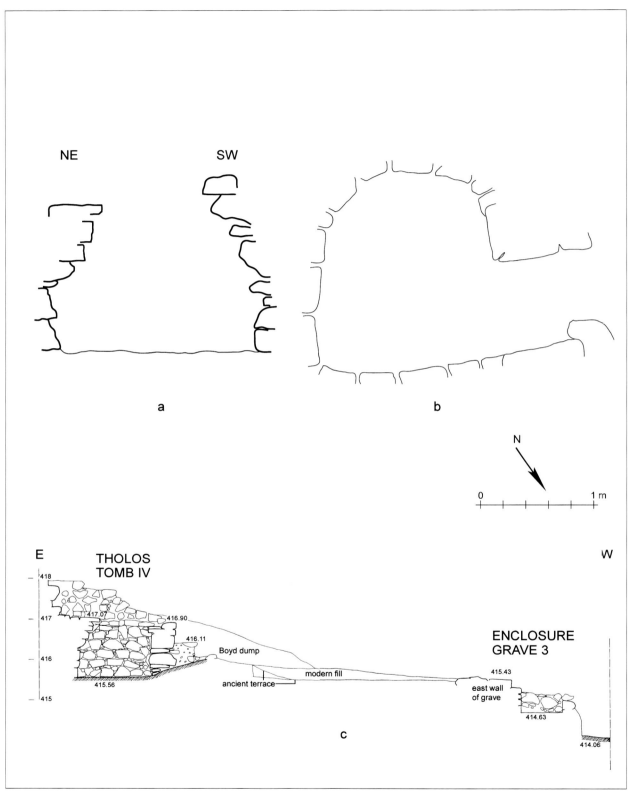

Figure 12. Vronda Tomb IV: ground plan (a) and section (b); east–west stratigraphic section through Tomb IV and Grave 3 (c). Drawing (c) J. Soles.

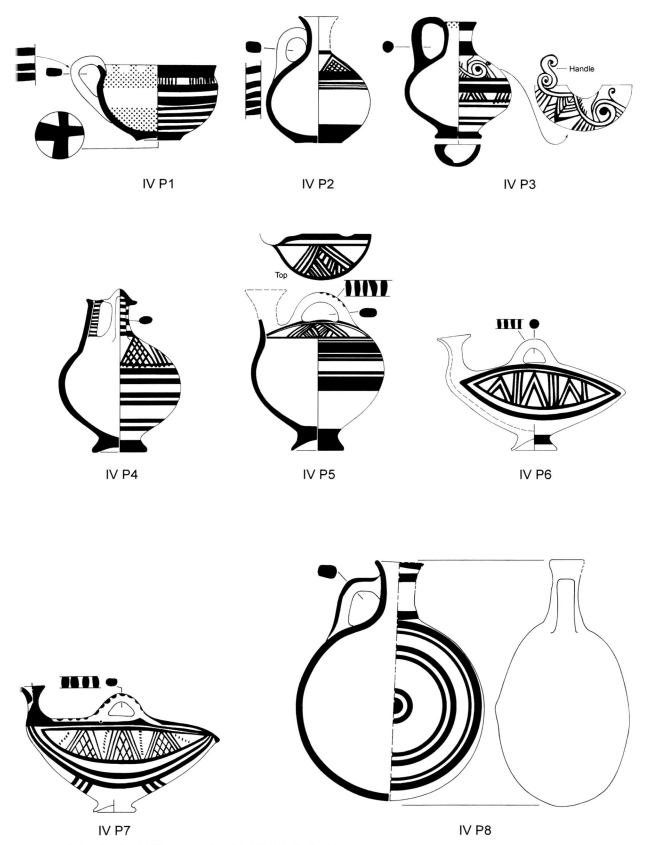

FIGURE 13

IV P1

IV P2

IV P3

Handle

Top

IV P4

IV P5

IV P6

IV P7

IV P8

Figure 13. Vronda Tomb IV: pottery (**IV P1–IV P8**). Scale 1:3.

FIGURE 14

Figure 14. Vronda Tomb IV: pottery (**IV P9**, **IV P10**); Tomb IV, cleaning: pottery (**IV P11–IV P17**), stone lid (**IV S1**). Scale 1:3 unless otherwise stated.

FIGURE 15

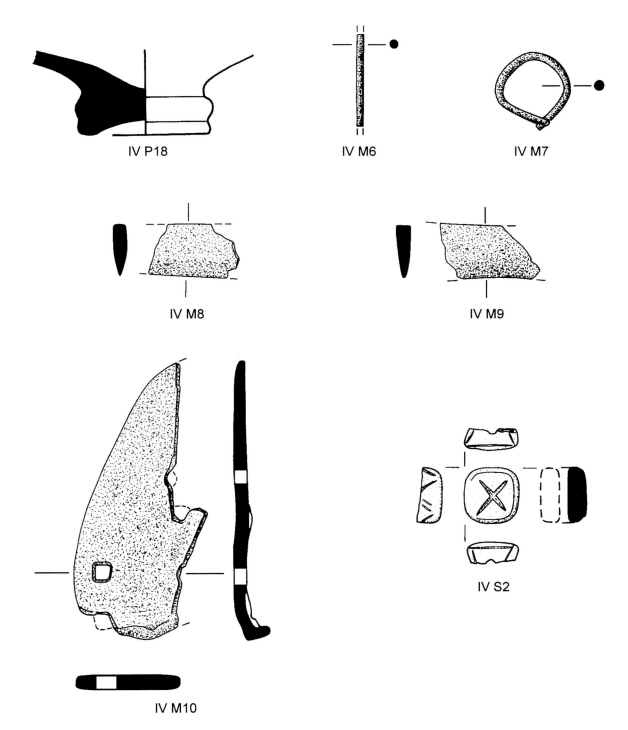

F gure 15. Vronda Tomb IV, dump: pottery (**IV P18**), bronze jewelry (**IV M6**, **IV M7**), iron weapons or tools (**IV M8**–**IV M10**), stone bead (**IV S2**). Scale 1:1.

FIGURE 16

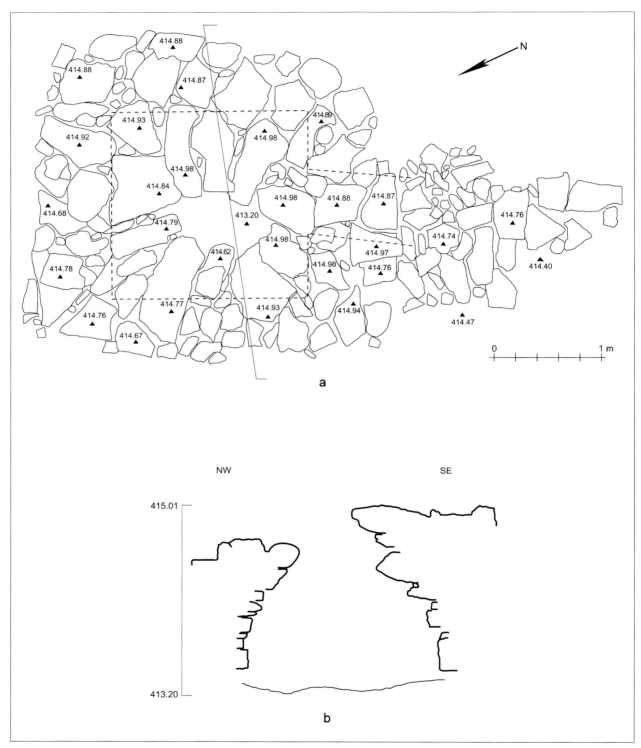

Figure 16. Vronda Tomb V: top plan (a) and northwest–southeast section (b).

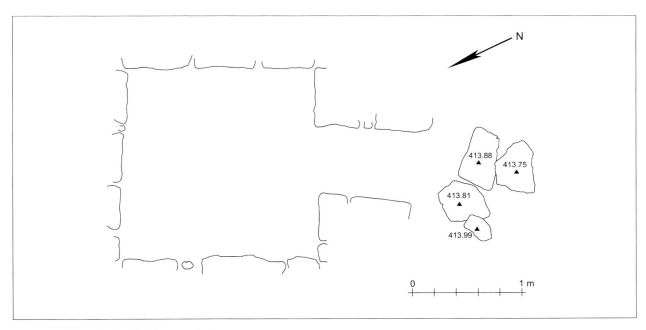

Figure 17. Vronda Tomb V: ground plan.

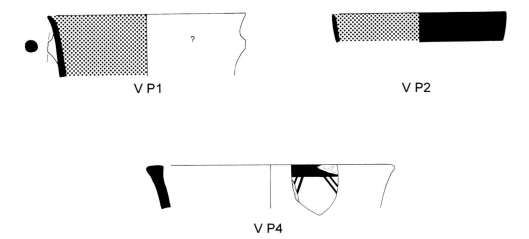

Figure 18. Vronda Tomb V: pottery (**V P1**, **V P2**, **V P4**). Scale 1:3.

FIGURE 19

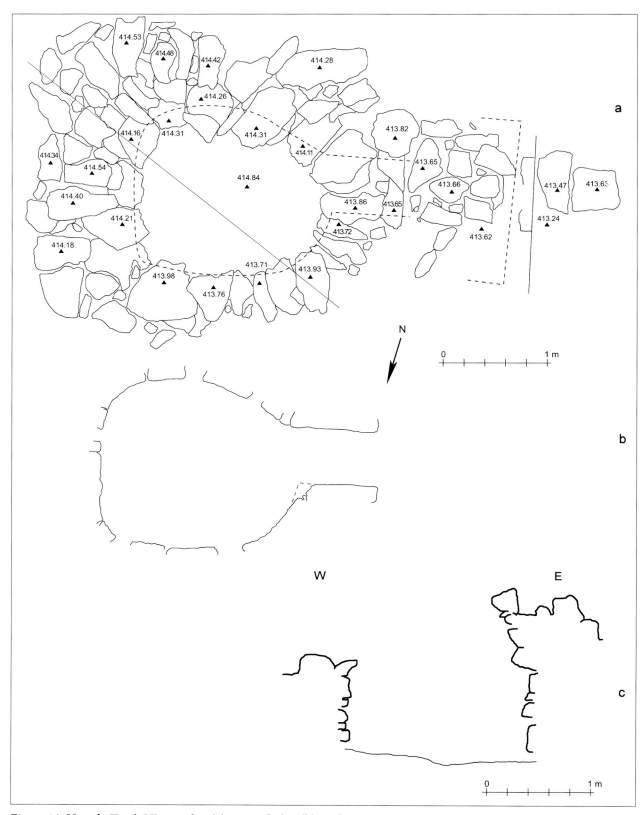

Figure 19. Vronda Tomb VI: top plan (a), ground plan (b), and west–east section (c).

FIGURE 20

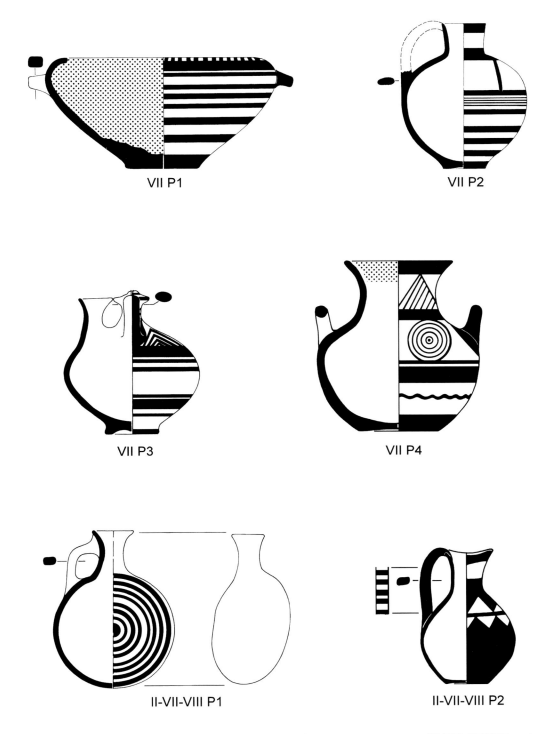

VII P1

VII P2

VII P3

VII P4

II-VII-VIII P1

II-VII-VIII P2

Figure 20. Tomb VII: pottery (**VII P1–VII P4**); Tombs II-VII-VIII: pottery (**II-VII-VIII P1** and **II-VII-VIII P2**). Scale 1:3.

FIGURE 21

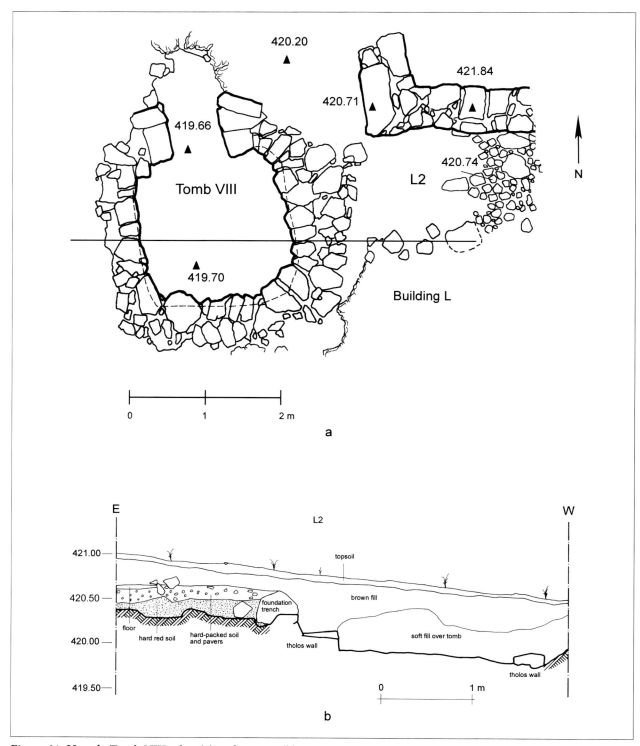

Figure 21. Vronda Tomb VIII: plan (a) and section (b).

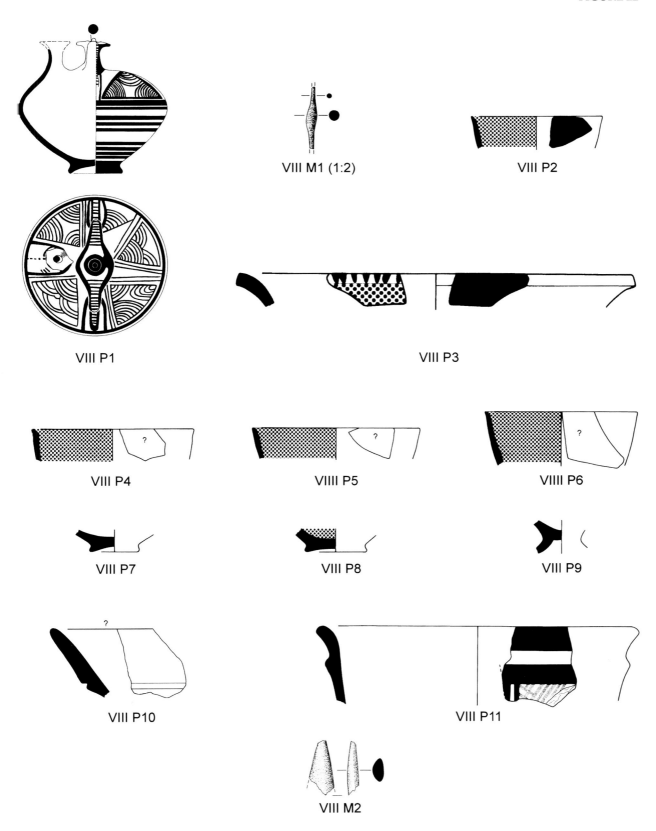

FIGURE 22

VIII M1 (1:2)

VIII P2

VIII P1

VIII P3

VIII P4

VIIII P5

VIIII P6

VIII P7

VIII P8

VIII P9

VIII P10

VIII P11

VIII M2

Figure 22. Vronda Tomb VIII, interior: pottery (**VIII P1**), bronze pin (**VIII M1**); Tomb VIII, fill: pottery (**VIII P2–VIII P11**), iron object (**VIII M2**). Scale 1:3 unless otherwise indicated.

FIGURE 23

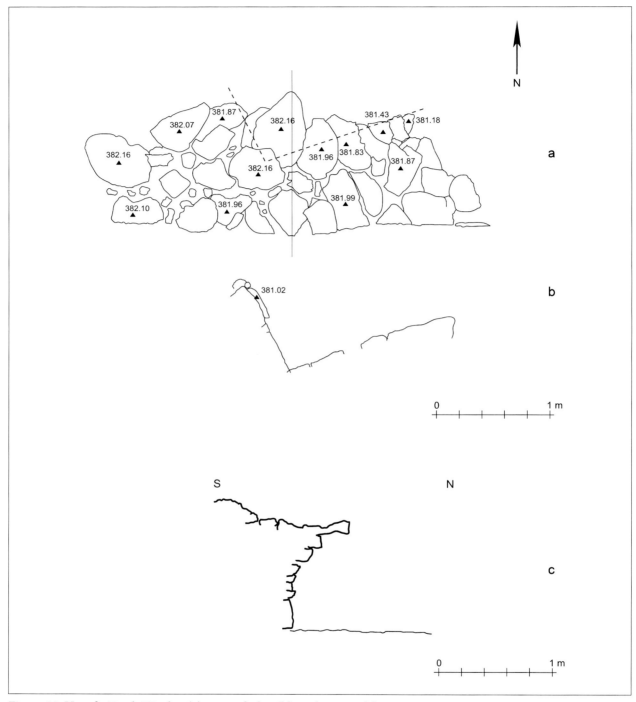

Figure 23. Vronda Tomb IX: plan (a), ground plan (b), and section (c).

FIGURE 24

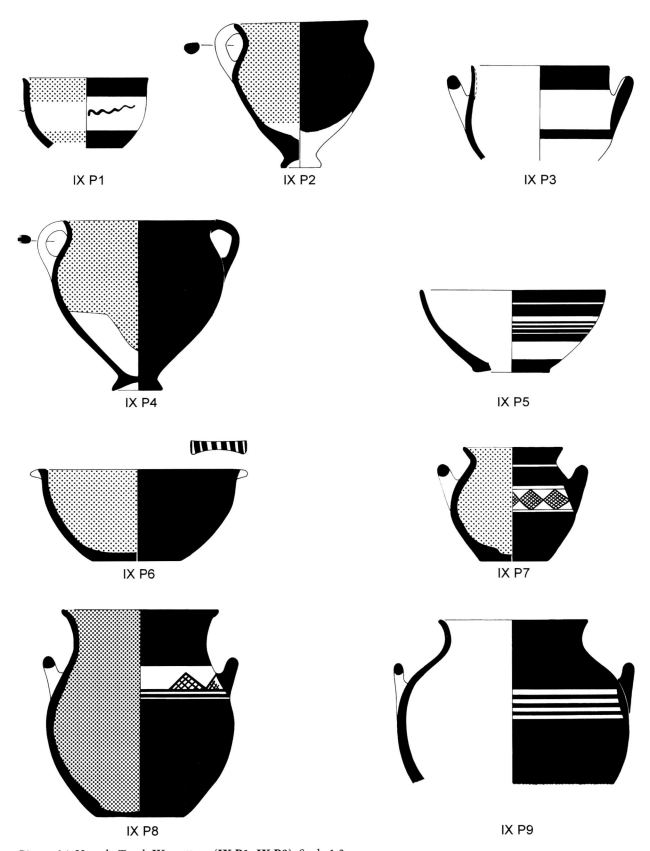

IX P1

IX P2

IX P3

IX P4

IX P5

IX P6

IX P7

IX P8

IX P9

Figure 24. Vronda Tomb IX: pottery (**IX P1–IX P9**). Scale 1:3.

FIGURE 25

IX P10

IX P11

IX P12

IX P13

IX P14

IX P15

IX P16

IX P17

IX P18

IX P19

IX P20

IX P21

Figure 25. Vronda Tomb IX: pottery (**IX P10–IX P21**). Scale 1:3.

FIGURE 26

Figure 26. Vronda Tomb IX: pottery (**IX P22–IX P27**). Scale 1:3.

FIGURE 27

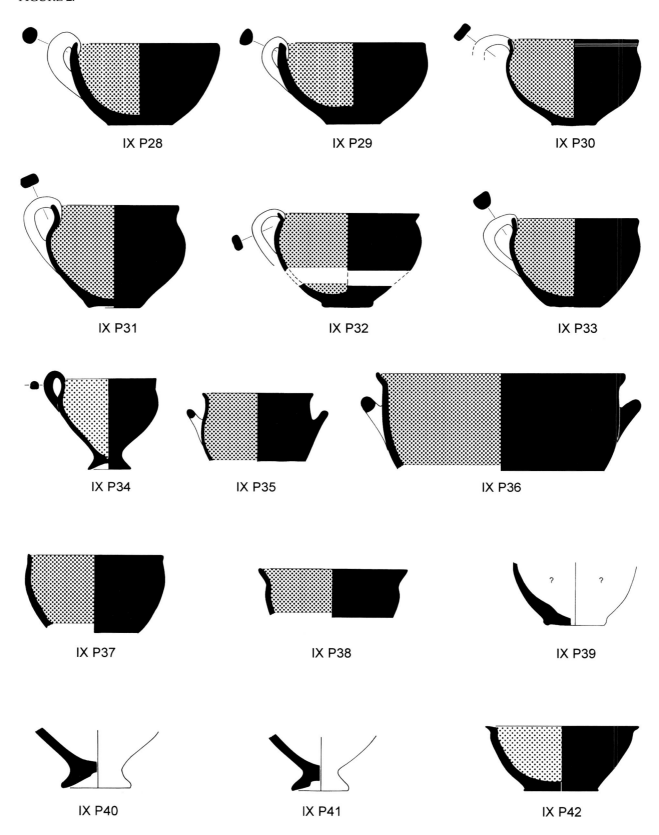

Figure 27. Vronda Tomb IX: pottery (**IX P28–IX P42**). Scale 1:3.

FIGURE 28

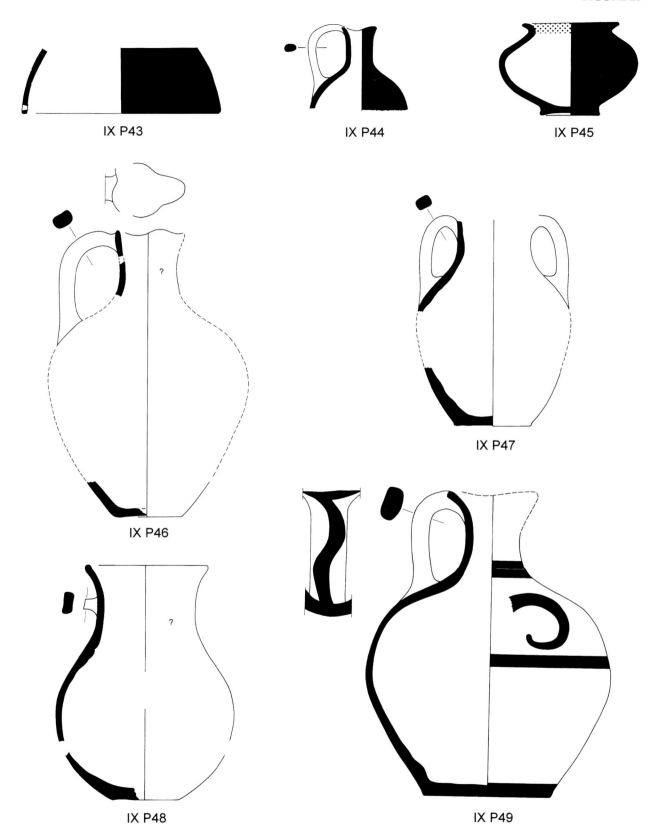

IX P43

IX P44

IX P45

IX P46

IX P47

IX P48

IX P49

Figure 28. Vronda Tomb IX: pottery (**IX P43–IX P49**). Scale 1:3.

FIGURE 29

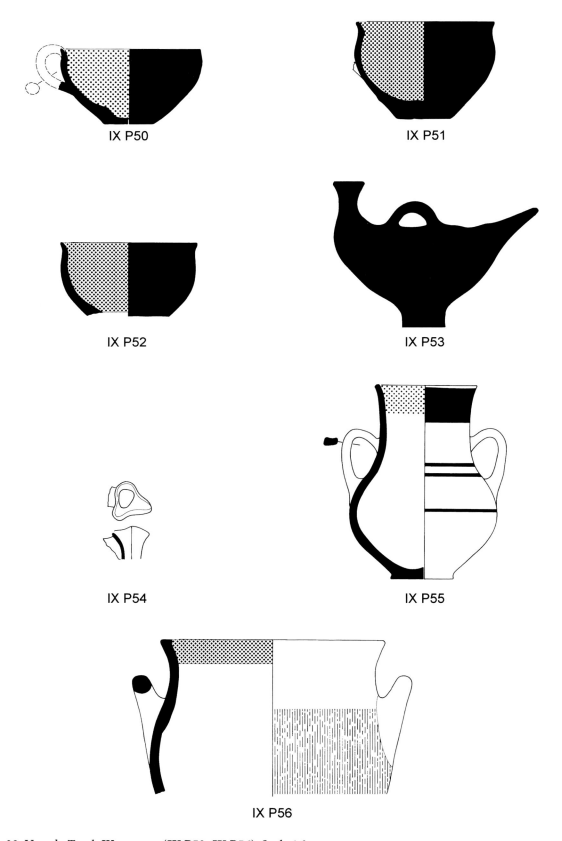

IX P50

IX P51

IX P52

IX P53

IX P54

IX P55

IX P56

Figure 29. Vronda Tomb IX: pottery (**IX P50–IX P56**). Scale 1:3.

FIGURE 30

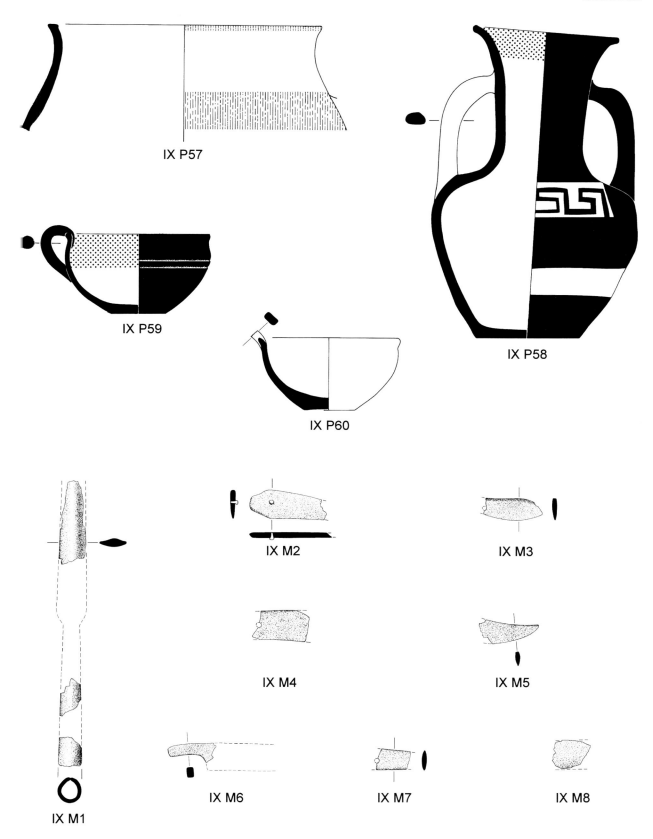

Figure 30. Vronda Tomb IX: pottery (**IX P57–IX P60**) and iron objects (**IX M1–IX M8**). Scale 1:3.

FIGURE 31

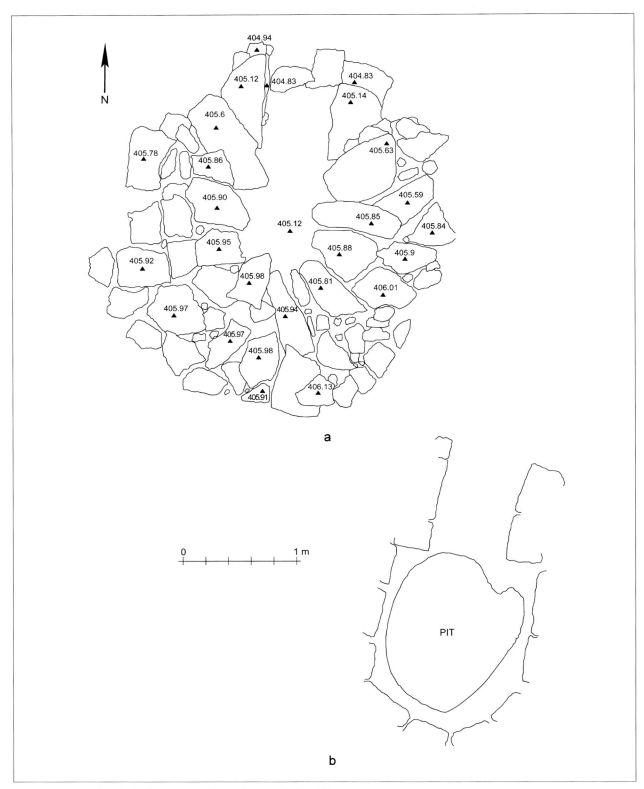

a

b

Figure 31. Vronda Tomb X: top plan (a) and ground plan (b).

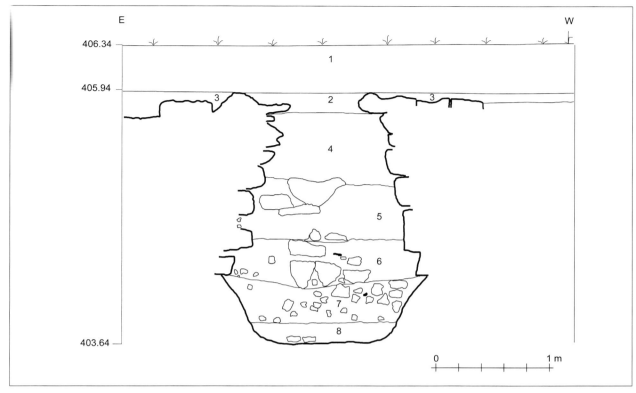

Figure 32. Vronda Tomb X: section. The composition of numbered levels is explained in the text (Ch. 2, p. 45).

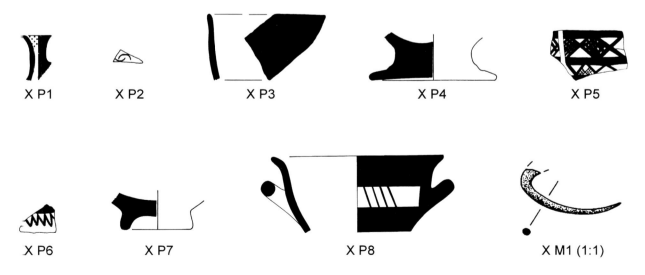

Figure 33. Vronda Tomb X: pottery (**X P1–X P8**) and bronze object (**X M1**). Scale 1:3 unless otherwise stated.

FIGURE 34

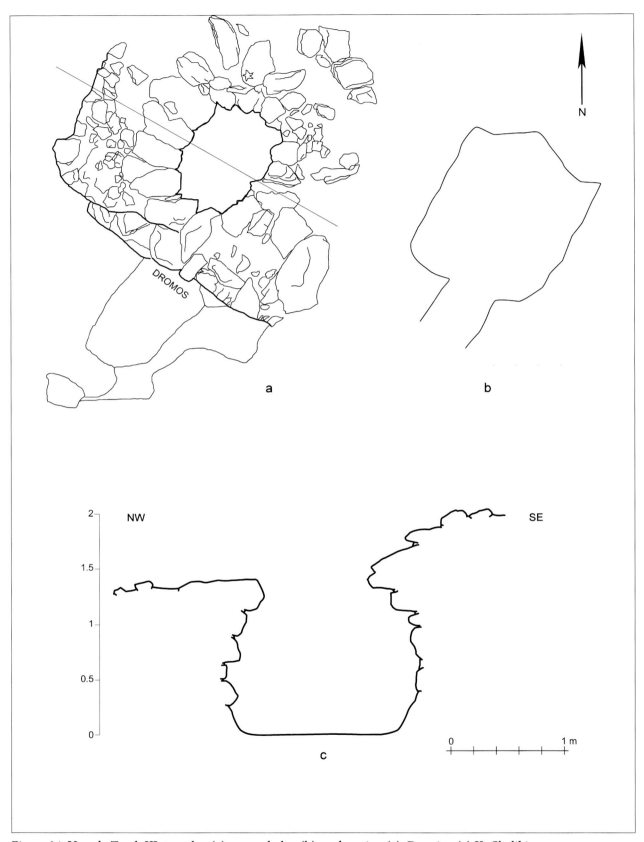

Figure 34. Vronda Tomb XI: top plan (a), ground plan (b), and section (c). Drawing (c) K. Chalikias.

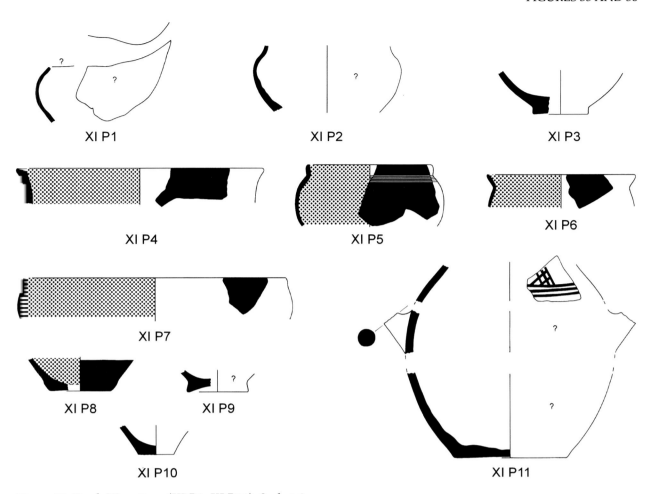

XI P1

XI P2

XI P3

XI P4

XI P5

XI P6

XI P7

XI P8

XI P9

XI P10

XI P11

Figure 35. Tomb XI: pottery (**XI P1–XI P11**). Scale 1:3.

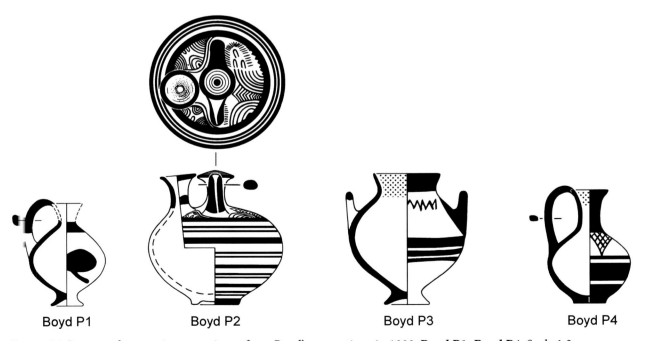

Boyd P1

Boyd P2

Boyd P3

Boyd P4

Figure 36. Pottery of uncertain provenience from Boyd's excavations in 1900: **Boyd P1–Boyd P4**. Scale 1:3.

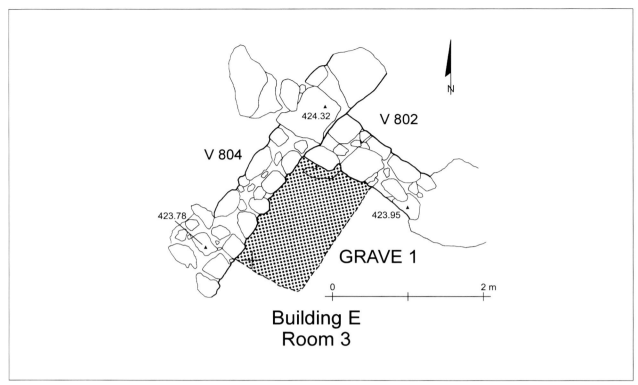

Figure 37. Plan of Grave 1.

Figure 38. Grave 1: pottery (**GR1 P1–GR1 P5**). Scale 1:3.

FIGURE 39

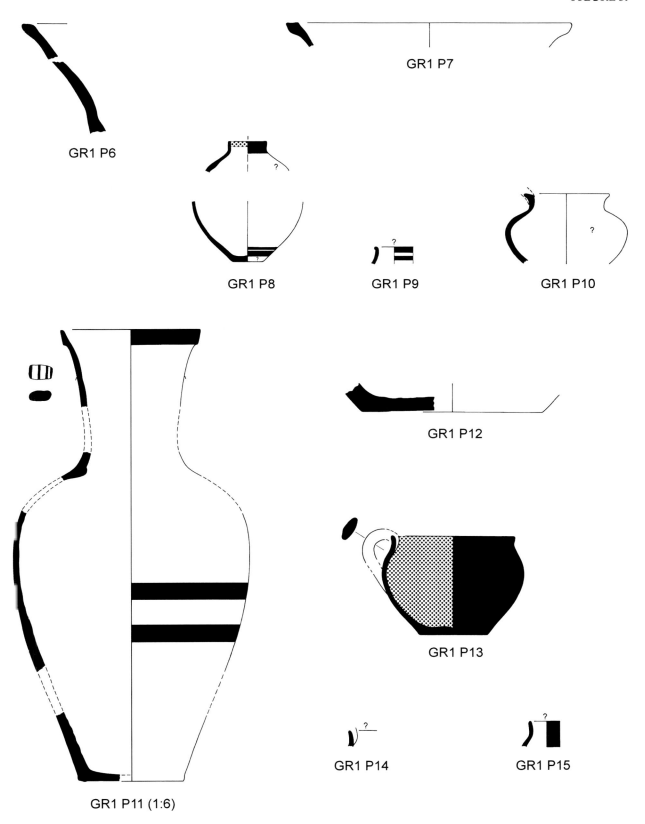

F gure 39. Grave 1: pottery (**GR1 P6–GR1 P15**). Scale 1:3 unless otherwise indicated.

FIGURE 40

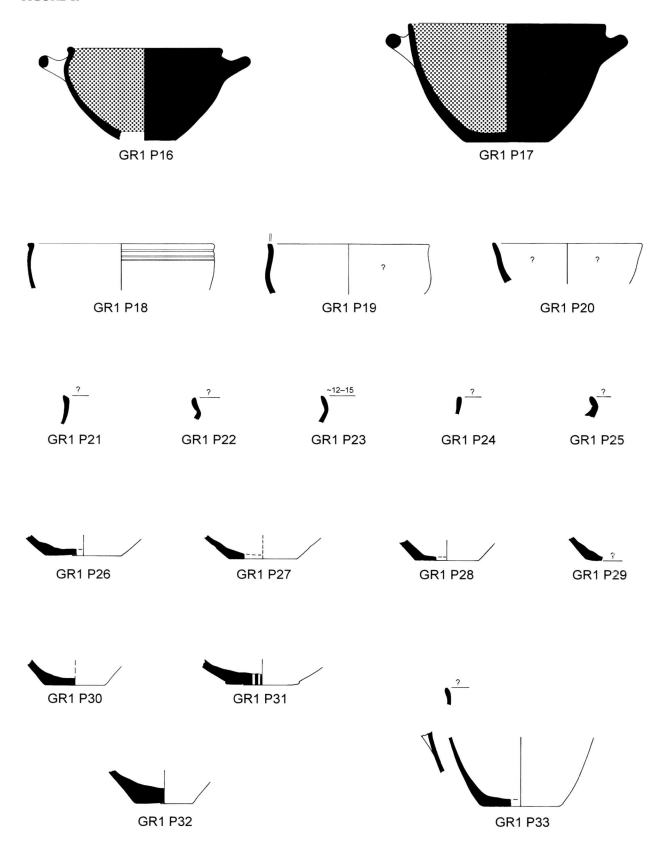

Figure 40. Grave 1: pottery (**GR1 P16–GR1 P33**). Scale 1:3.

FIGURE 41

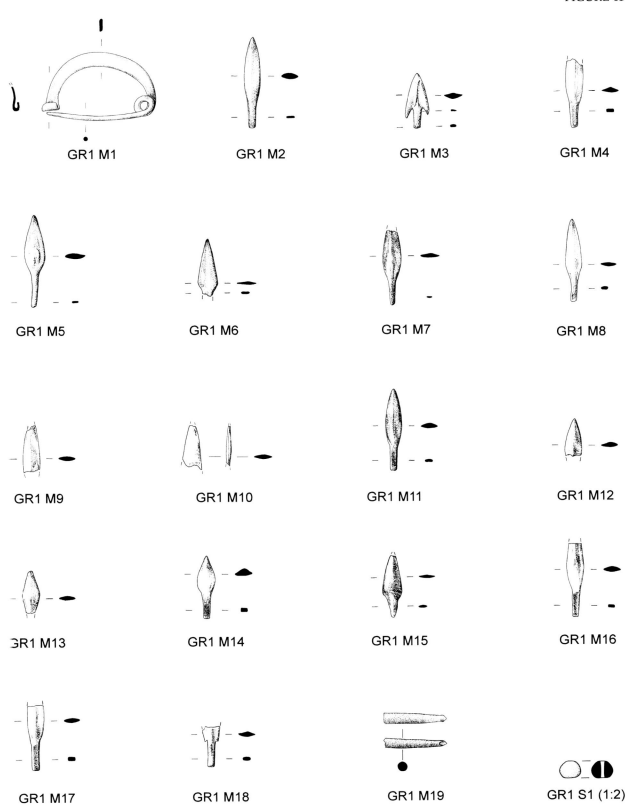

Figure 41. Grave 1: objects: bronze fibula (**GR1 M1**), iron arrowheads (**GR1 M2**–**GR1 M18**), iron awl (**GR1 M19**), and stone bead (**GR1 S1**). Scale 1:3 unless otherwise stated.

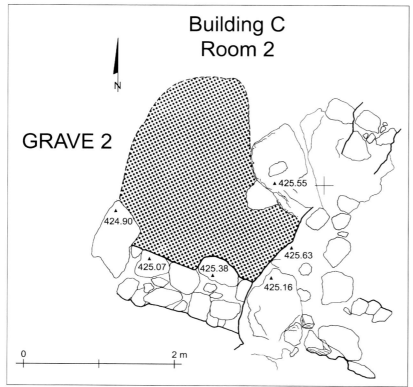

Figure 42. Plan of Grave 2.

Figure 43. Grave 2: pottery (**GR2 P1**, **GR2 P2**). Scale 1:3.

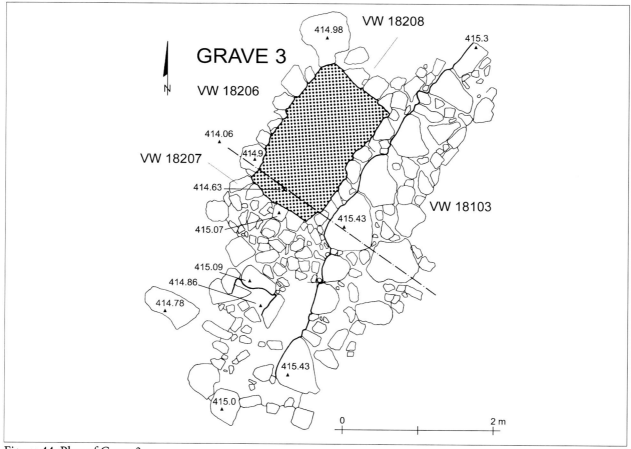

Figure 44. Plan of Grave 3.

FIGURE 45

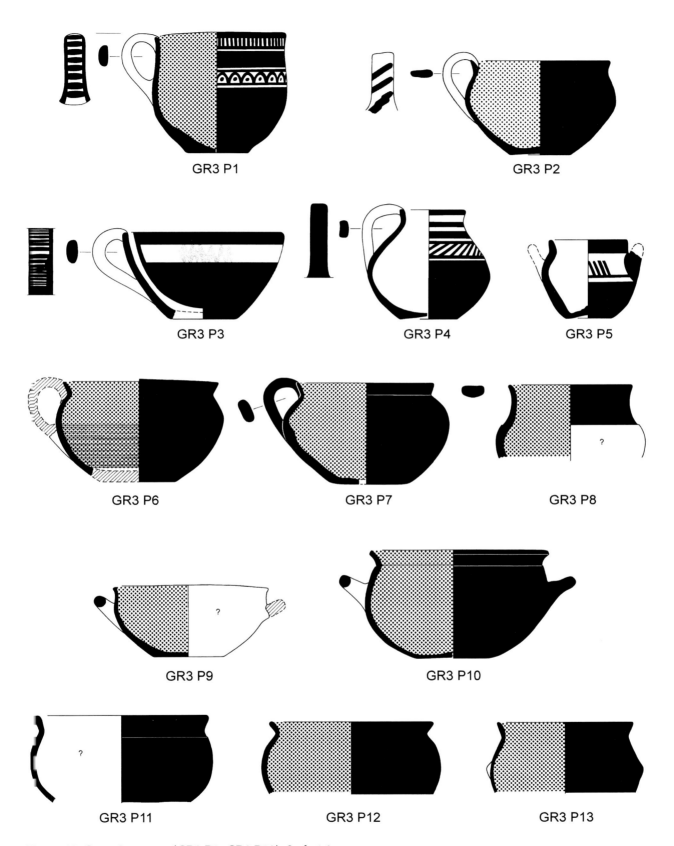

F gure 45. Grave 3: pottery (**GR3 P1–GR3 P13**). Scale 1:3.

FIGURE 46

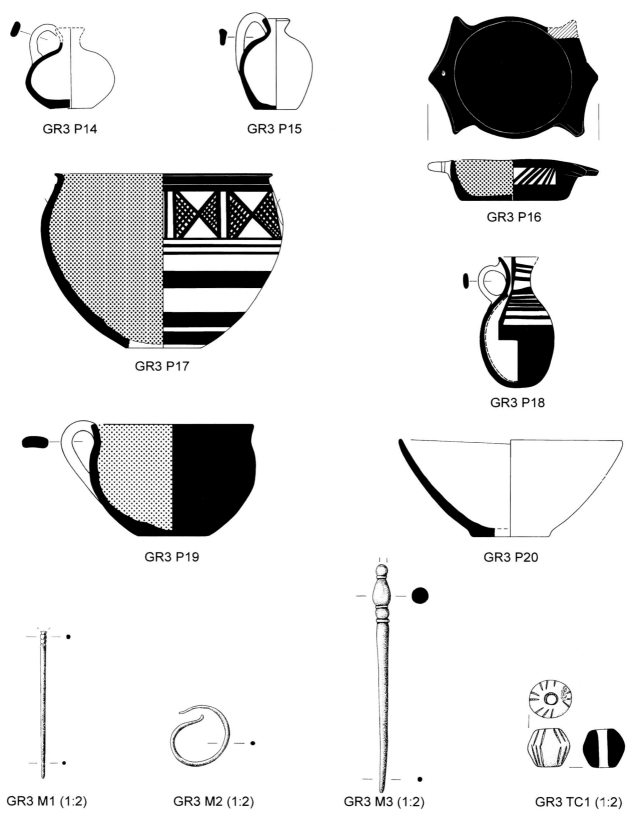

GR3 P14

GR3 P15

GR3 P16

GR3 P17

GR3 P18

GR3 P19

GR3 P20

GR3 M1 (1:2)

GR3 M2 (1:2)

GR3 M3 (1:2)

GR3 TC1 (1:2)

Figure 46. Grave 3: pottery (**GR3 P14–GR3 P20**), bronze objects (**GR3 M1, GR3 M2**), iron pin (**GR3 M3**), and terra-cotta bead (**GR3 TC1**). Scale 1:3 unless otherwise stated.

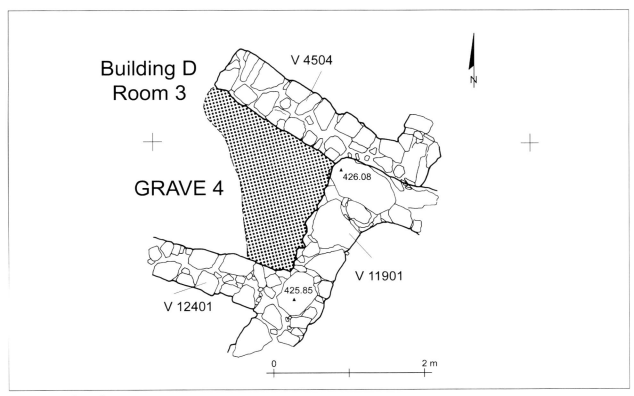

Figure 47. Plan of Grave 4.

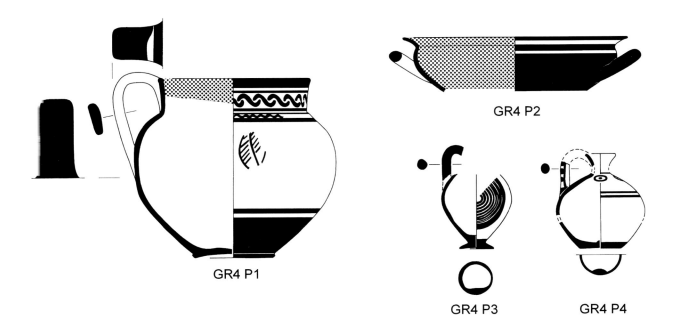

Figure 48. Grave 4: pottery (**GR4 P1–GR4 P4**). Scale 1:3.

FIGURE 49

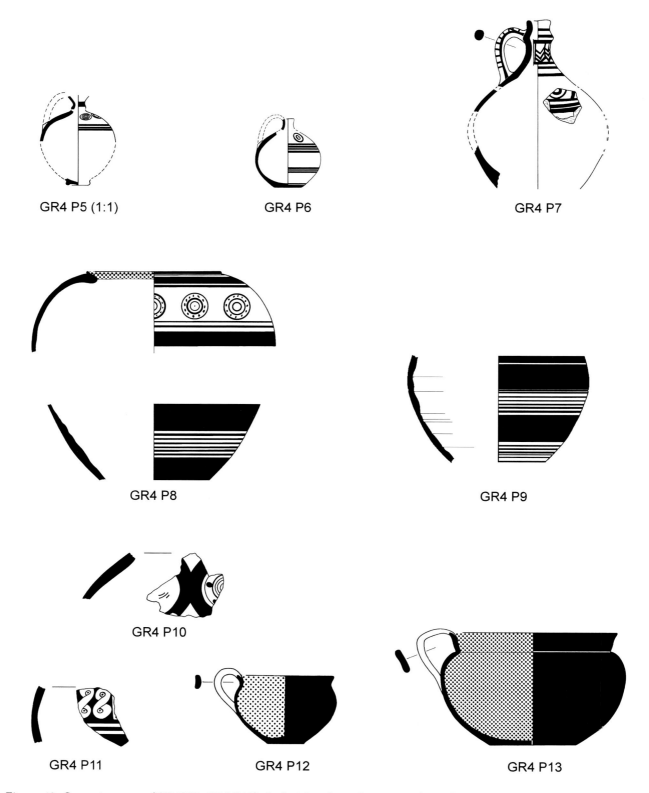

GR4 P5 (1:1)

GR4 P6

GR4 P7

GR4 P8

GR4 P9

GR4 P10

GR4 P11

GR4 P12

GR4 P13

Figure 49. Grave 4: pottery (**GR4 P5–GR4 P13**). Scale 1:3 unless otherwise indicated.

FIGURE 50

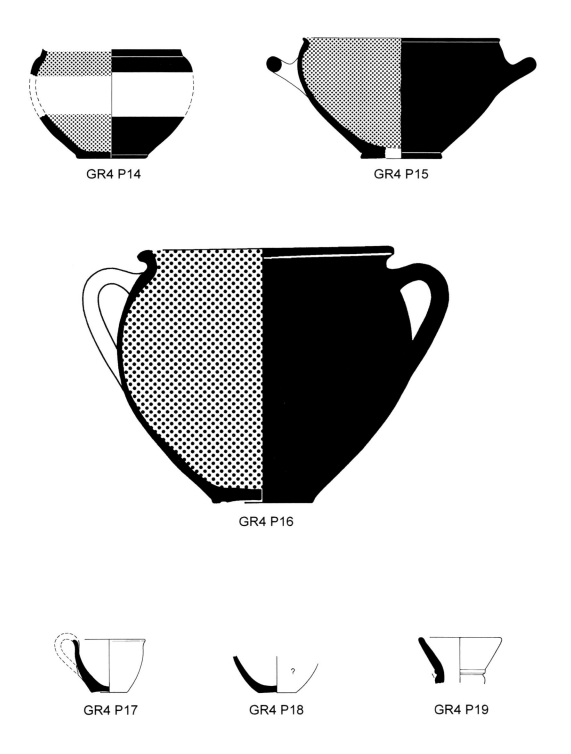

Figure 50. Grave 4: pottery (**GR4 P14–GR4 P19**). Scale 1:3.

FIGURE 51

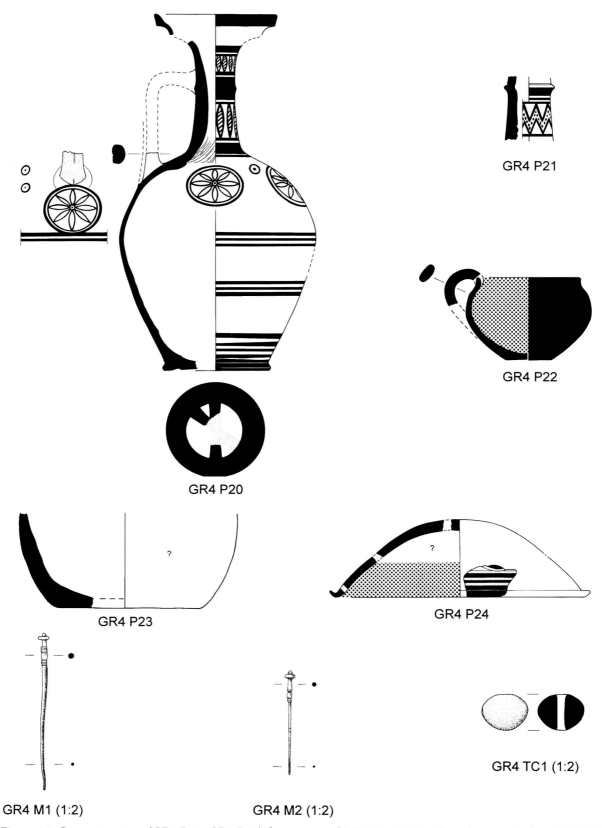

GR4 P21

GR4 P22

GR4 P20

GR4 P23

GR4 P24

GR4 M1 (1:2)

GR4 M2 (1:2)

GR4 TC1 (1:2)

Figure 51. Grave 4: pottery (**GR4 P20–GR4 P24**), bronze pins (**GR4 M1**, **GR4 M2**), and terracotta bead (**GR4 TC1**). Scale 1:3 unless otherwise stated.

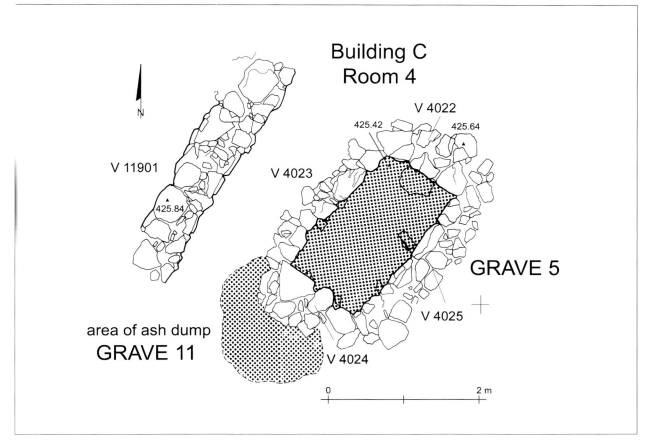

Figure 52. Plan of Graves 5 and 11.

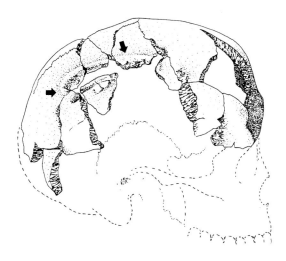

Figure 53. Grave 5: Reconstructed cranial vault
of Burial 1 showing trepanation. Not to scale.
Drawing G. Houston.

FIGURE 54

Figure 54. Grave 5: pottery (**GR5 P1**–**GR5 P7**). Scale 1:3.

FIGURE 55

GR5 P8

GR5 P9

GR5 P10

~13

GR5 P11

GR5 P12

GR5 P13

GR5 P14

GR5 P15

GR5 P16

GR5 P17

Figure 55. Grave 5: pottery (**GR5 P8–GR5 P17**). Scale 1:3.

FIGURE 56

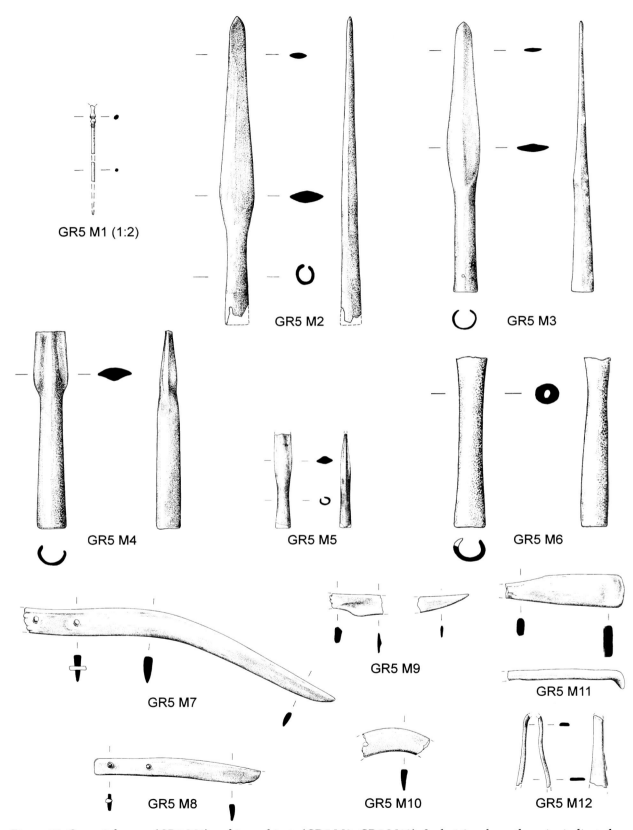

Figure 56. Grave 5: bronze (**GR5 M1**) and iron objects (**GR5 M2–GR5 M12**). Scale 1:3 unless otherwise indicated.

FIGURE 57

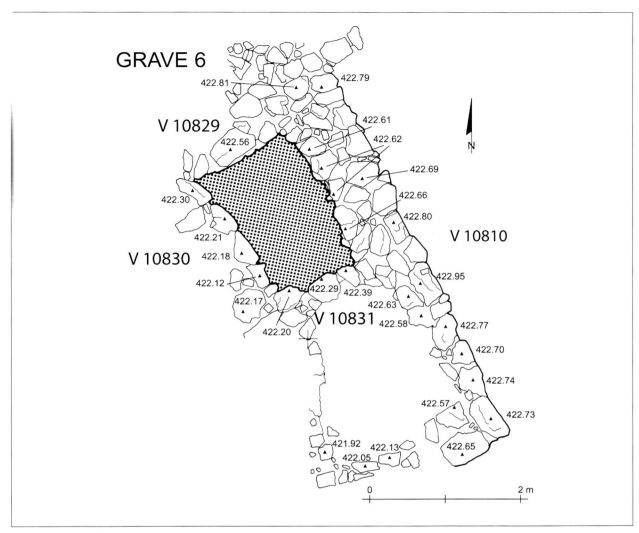

Figure 57. Plan of Grave 6.

FIGURE 58

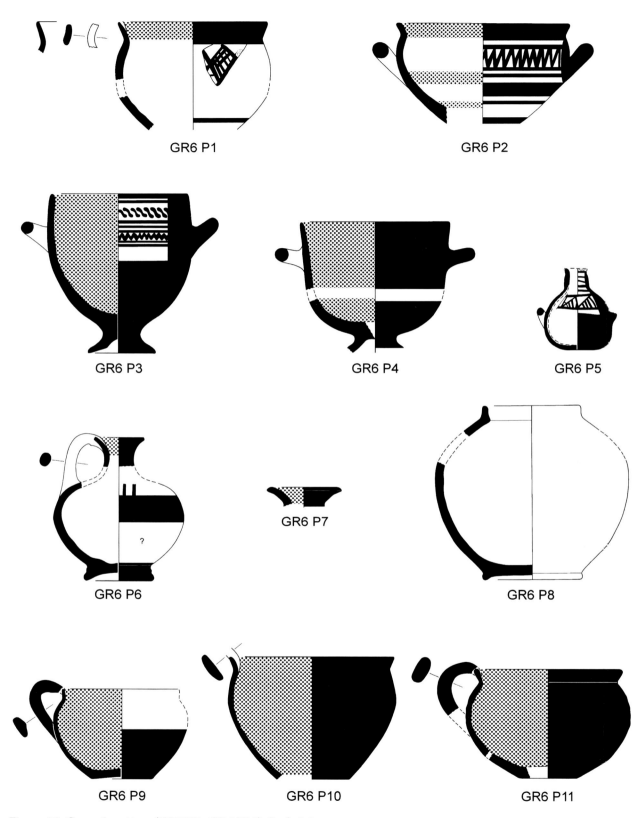

Figure 58. Grave 6: pottery (**GR6 P1–GR6 P11**). Scale 1:3.

FIGURE 59

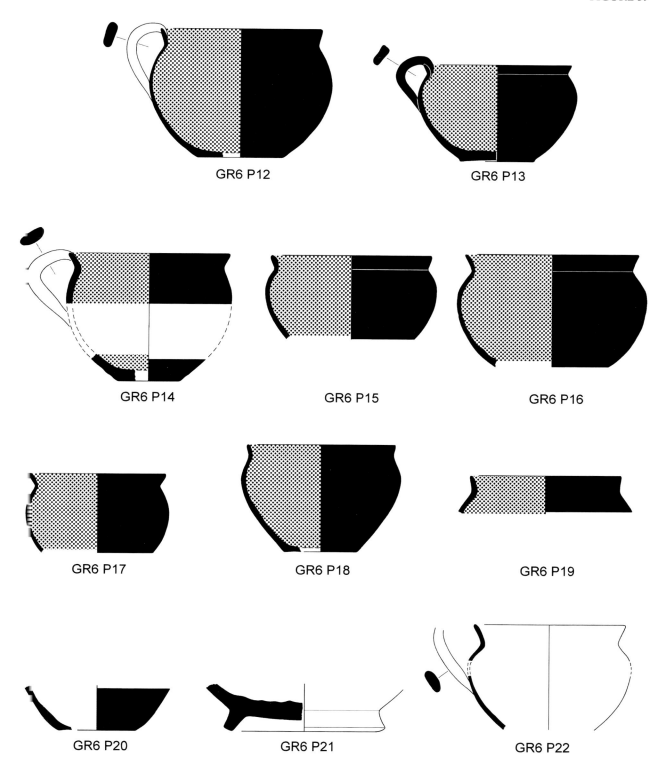

Figure 59. Grave 6: pottery (**GR6 P12–GR6 P22**). Scale 1:3.

FIGURE 60

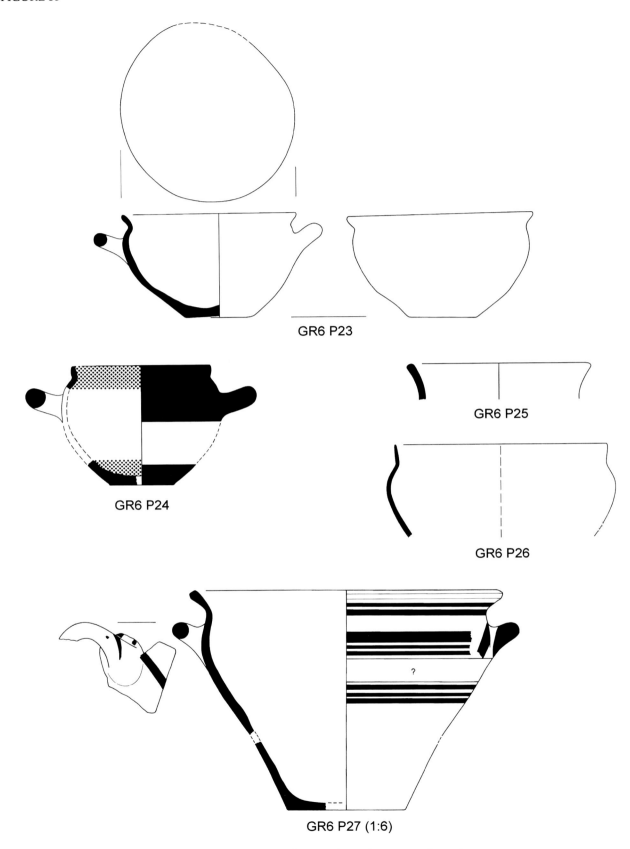

GR6 P23

GR6 P24

GR6 P25

GR6 P26

GR6 P27 (1:6)

Figure 60. Grave 6: pottery (**GR6 P23–GR6 P27**). Scale 1:3 unless otherwise indicated.

FIGURE 61

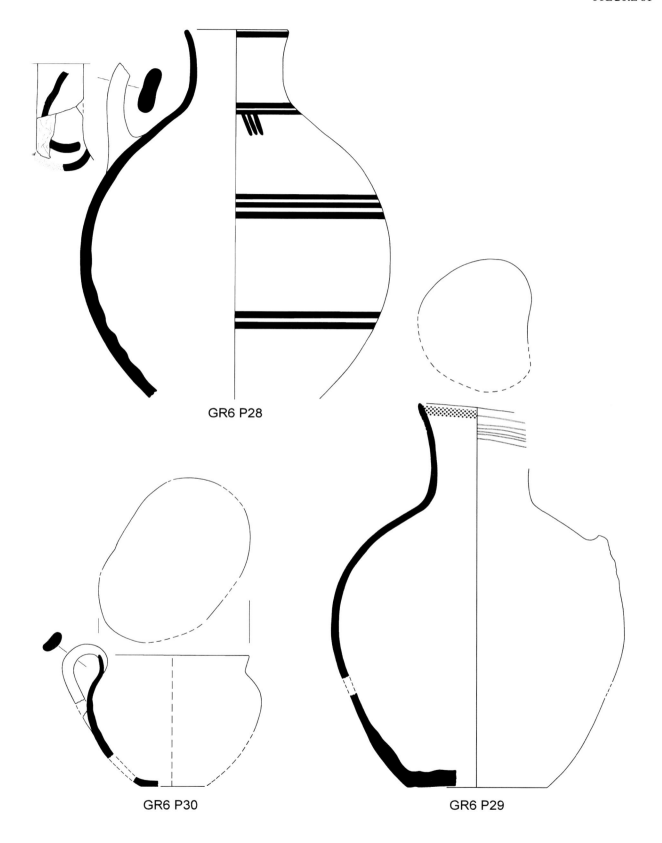

GR6 P28

GR6 P30

GR6 P29

Figure 61. Grave 6: pottery (**GR6 P28–GR6 P30**). Scale 1:3.

FIGURE 62

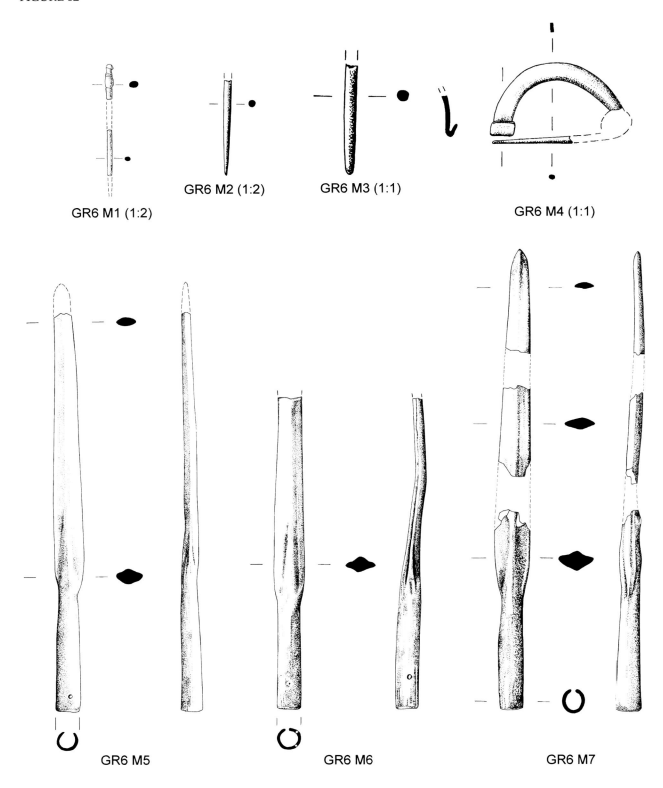

GR6 M1 (1:2)

GR6 M2 (1:2)

GR6 M3 (1:1)

GR6 M4 (1:1)

GR6 M5

GR6 M6

GR6 M7

Figure 62. Grave 6: iron jewelry (**GR6 M1–GR6 M4**) and spearheads (**GR6 M5–GR6 M7**). Scale 1:3 unless otherwise indicated.

FIGURE 63

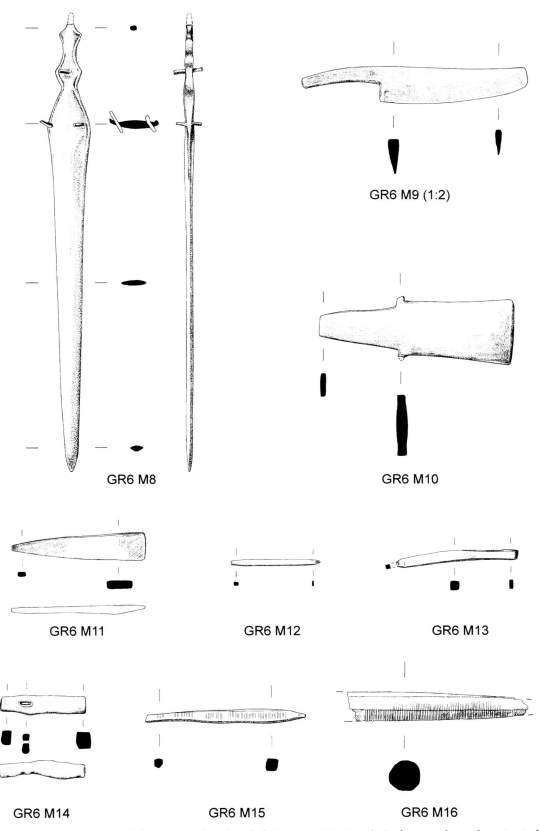

GR6 M9 (1:2)

GR6 M8

GR6 M10

GR6 M11

GR6 M12

GR6 M13

GR6 M14

GR6 M15

GR6 M16

Figure 63. Grave 6: iron dirk (**GR6 M8**) and tools (**GR6 M9–GR6 M16**). Scale 1:3 unless otherwise indicated.

FIGURE 64

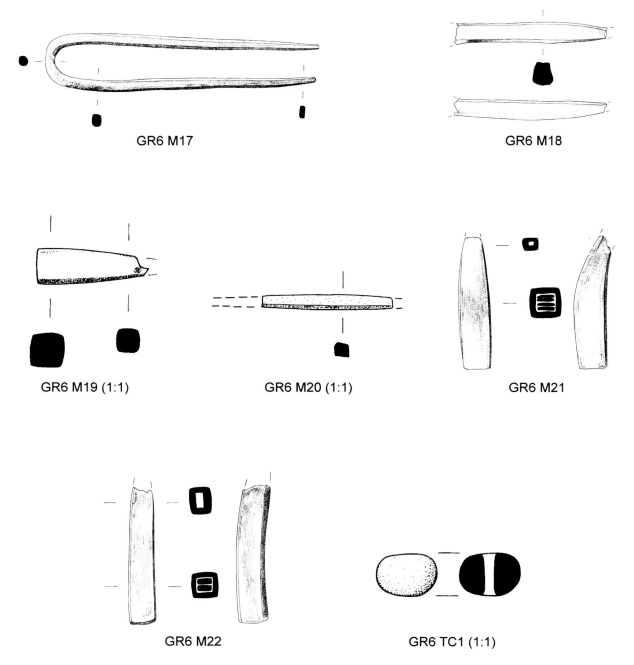

Figure 64. Grave 6: iron tools (**GR6 M17–GR6 M22**) and terracotta bead (**GR6 TC1**). Scale 1:3 unless otherwise indicated.

FIGURE 65

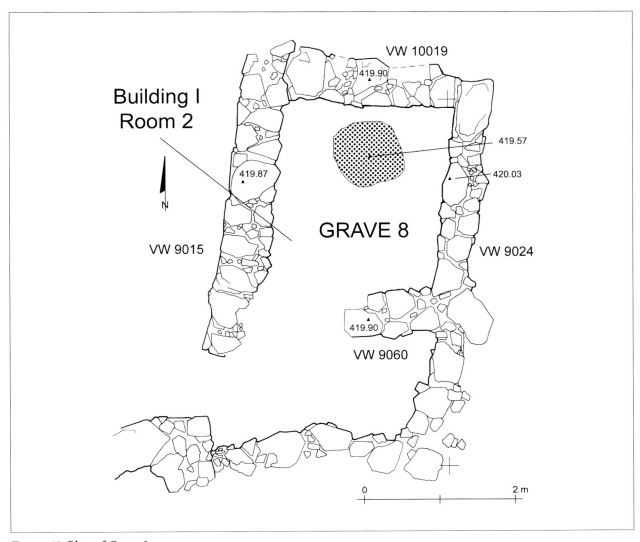

Figure 65. Plan of Grave 8.

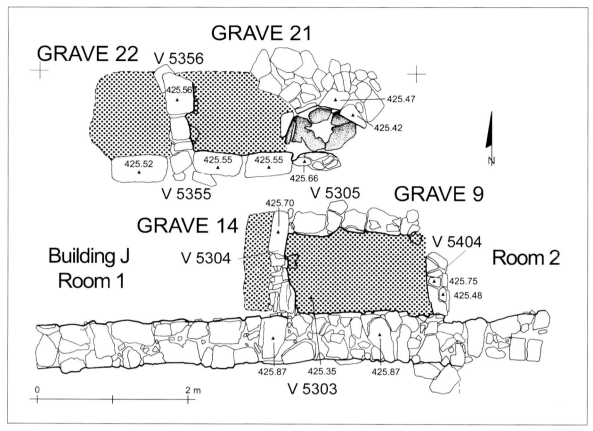

Figure 66. Plan of Graves 9, 14, 21, and 22.

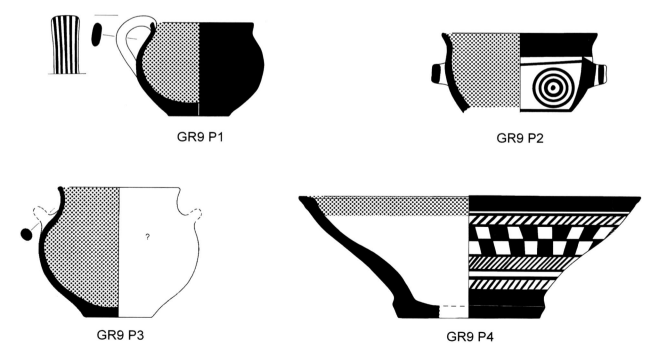

Figure 67. Grave 9: pottery (**GR9 P1–GR9 P4**). Scale 1:3.

FIGURE 68

Figure 68. Grave 9: pottery (**GR9 P5–GR9 P14**). Scale 1:3 unless otherwise indicated.

FIGURE 69

Figure 69. Grave 9: pottery (**GR9 P15–GR9 P24**). Scale 1:3.

FIGURE 70

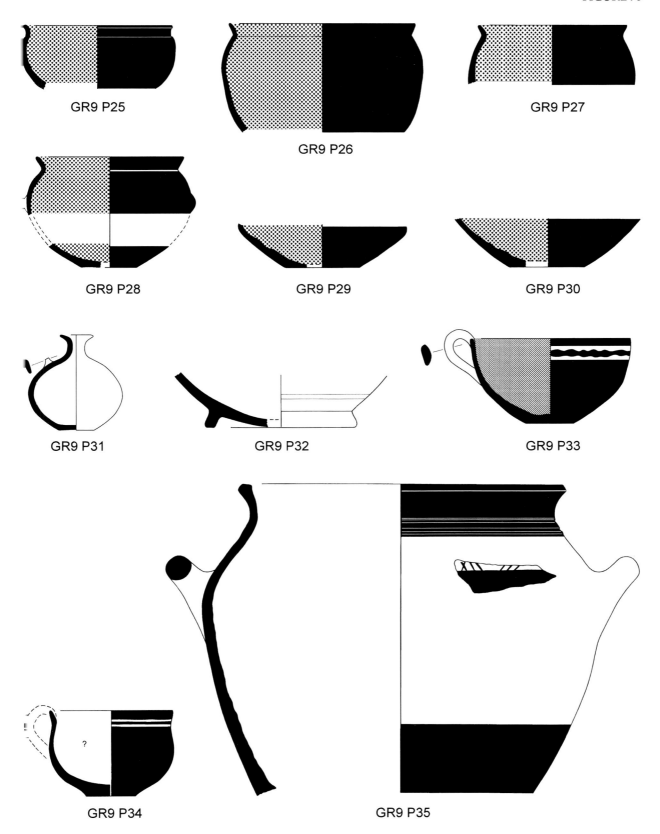

Figure 70. Grave 9: pottery (**GR9 P25–GR9 P35**). Scale 1:3.

FIGURE 71

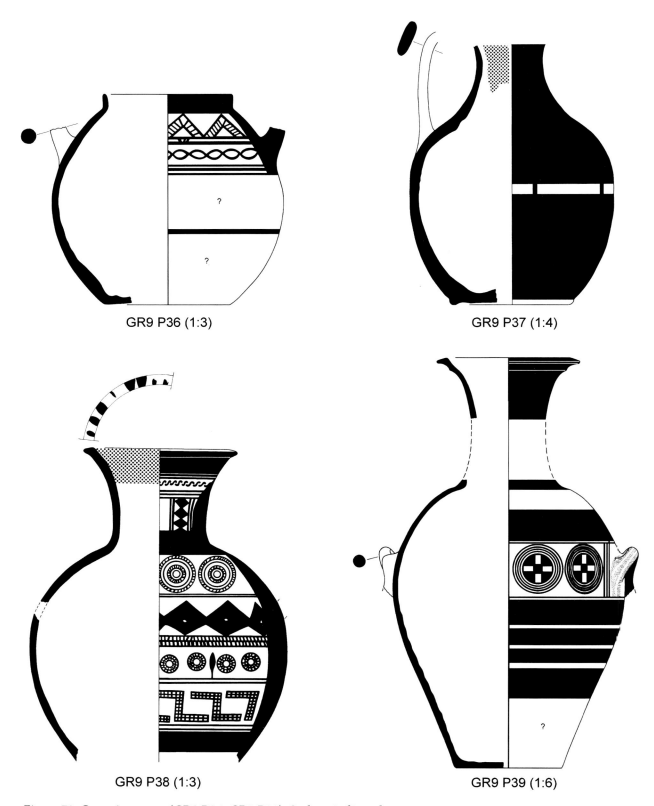

GR9 P36 (1:3)

GR9 P37 (1:4)

GR9 P38 (1:3)

GR9 P39 (1:6)

Figure 71. Grave 9: pottery (**GR9 P36–GR9 P39**). Scale as indicated.

FIGURE 72

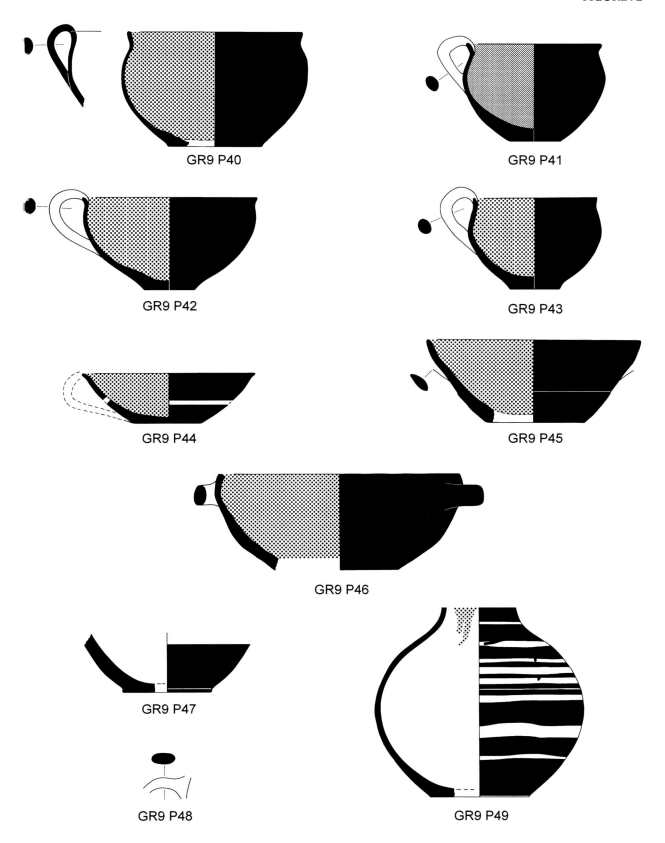

GR9 P40

GR9 P41

GR9 P42

GR9 P43

GR9 P44

GR9 P45

GR9 P46

GR9 P47

GR9 P48

GR9 P49

Figure 72. Grave 9: pottery (**GR9 P40–GR9 P49**). Scale 1:3.

FIGURE 73

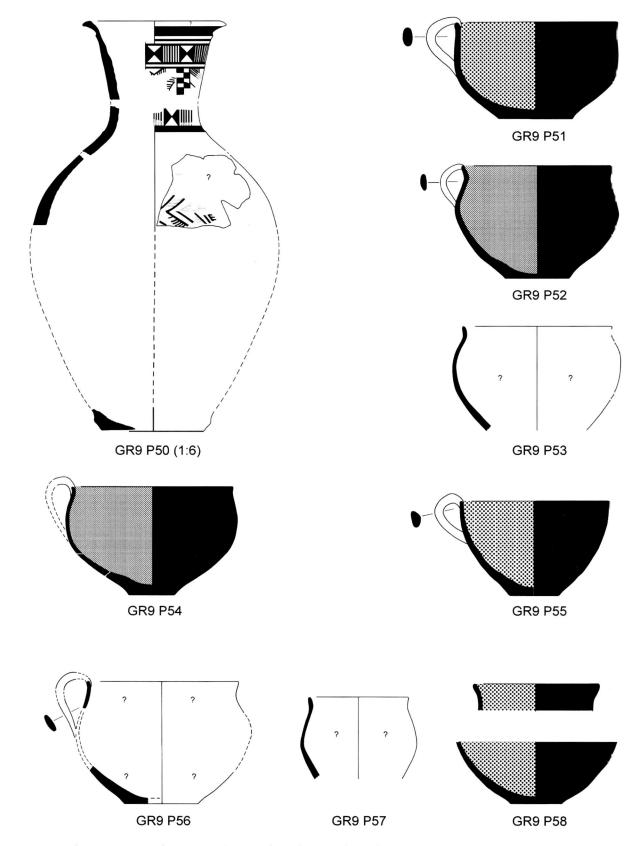

Figure 73. Grave 9: pottery (**GR9 P50–GR9 P58**). Scale 1:3 unless otherwise indicated.

FIGURE 74

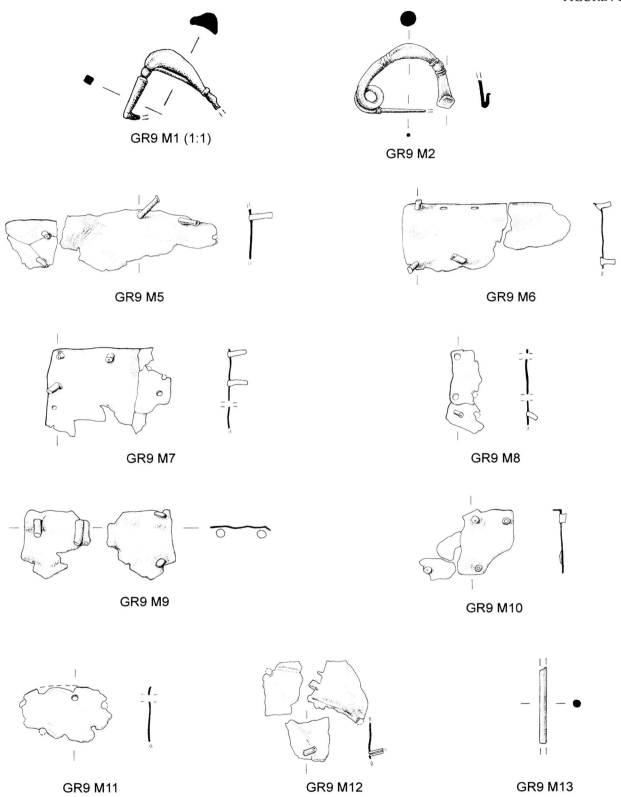

GR9 M1 (1:1)

GR9 M2

GR9 M5

GR9 M6

GR9 M7

GR9 M8

GR9 M9

GR9 M10

GR9 M11

GR9 M12

GR9 M13

Figure 74. Grave 9: bronze objects (**GR9 M1**, **GR9 M2**, **GR9 M5–GR9 M12**) and iron pin (**GR9 M13**). Scale 1:2 unless otherwise indicated.

FIGURE 75

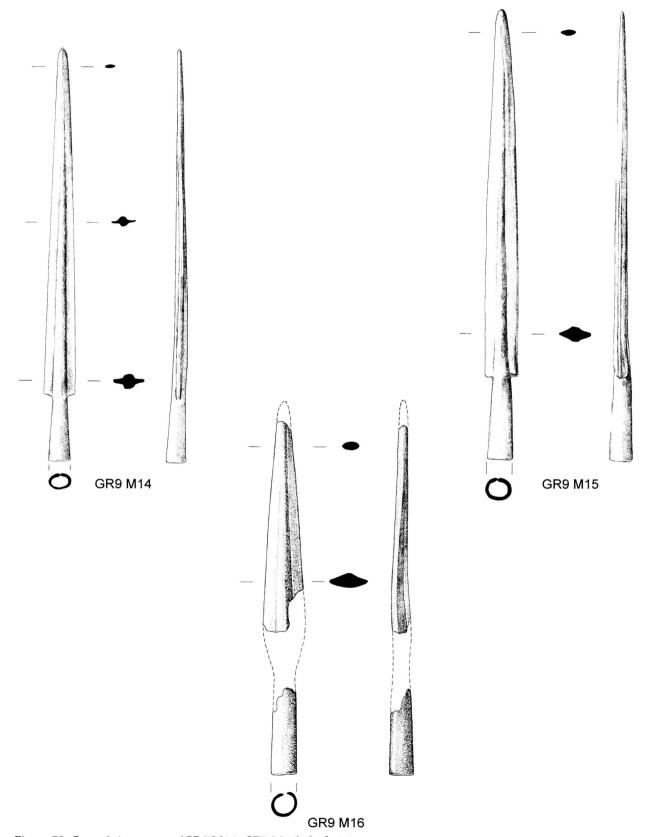

GR9 M14

GR9 M15

GR9 M16

Figure 75. Grave 9: iron spears (**GR9 M14–GR9 M16**). Scale 1:3.

FIGURE 76

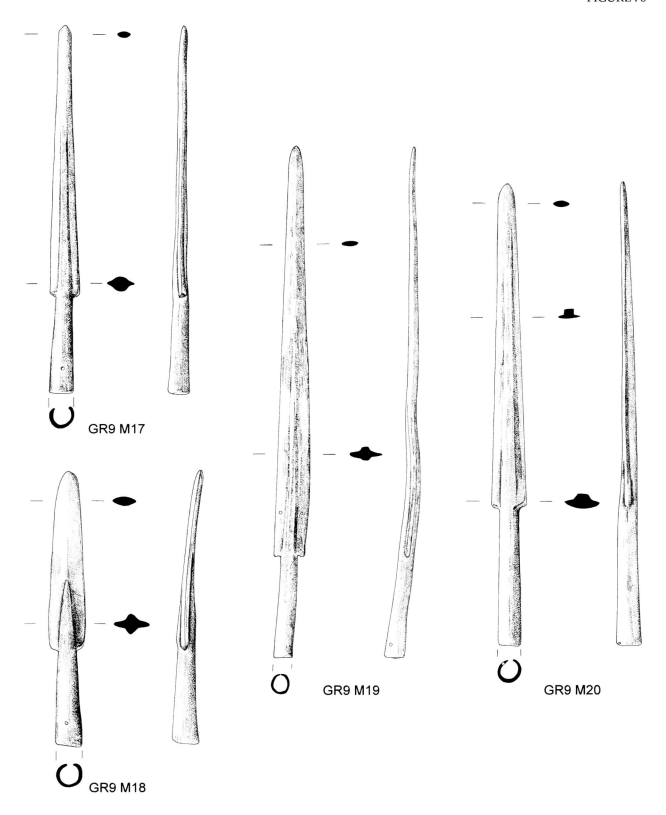

GR9 M17

GR9 M18

GR9 M19

GR9 M20

Figure 76. Grave 9: iron spears (**GR9 M17–GR9 M20**). Scale 1:3.

FIGURE 77

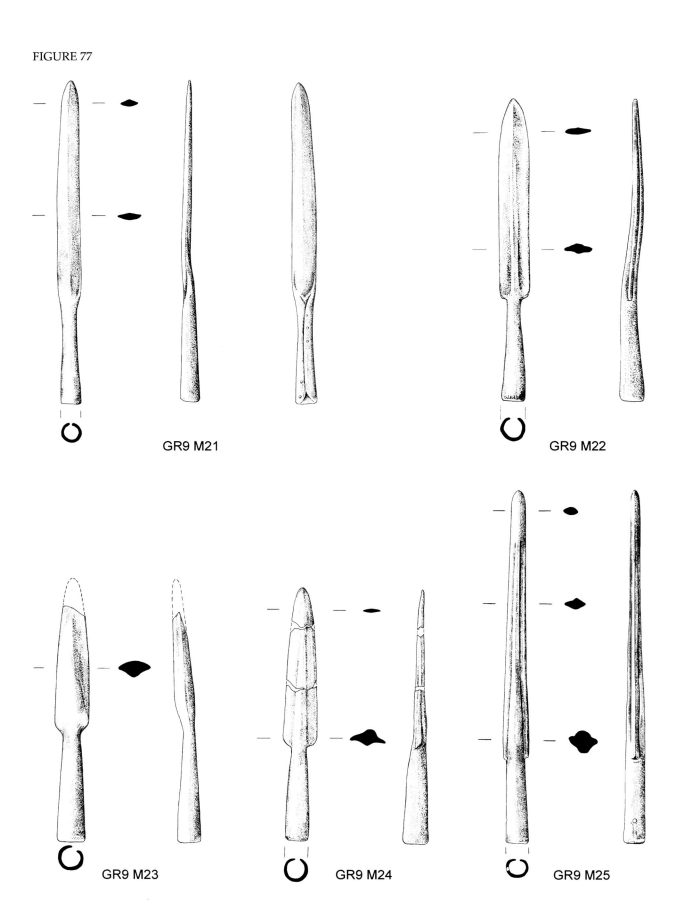

GR9 M21

GR9 M22

GR9 M23

GR9 M24

GR9 M25

Figure 77. Grave 9: iron spears (**GR9 M21–GR9 M25**). Scale 1:3.

FIGURE 78

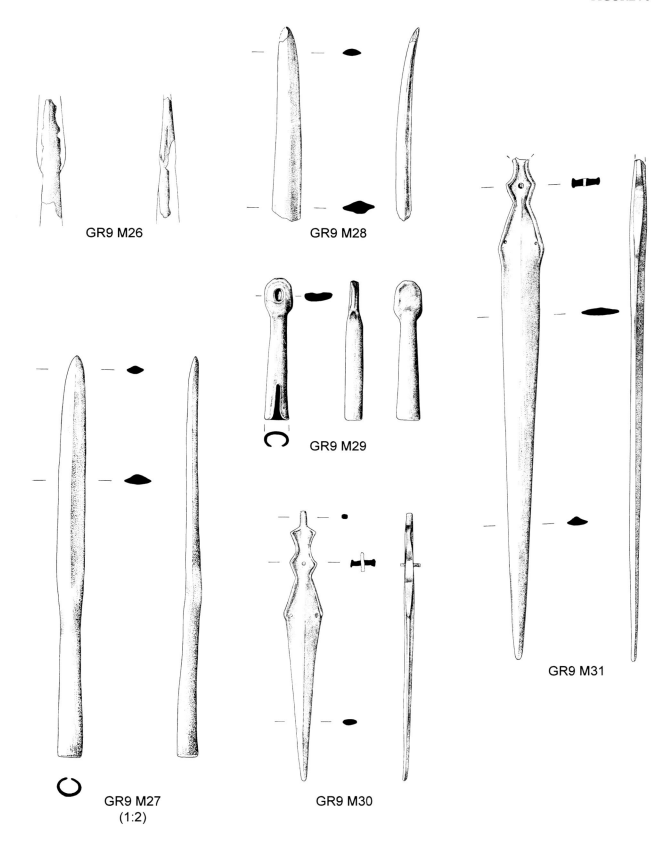

GR9 M26

GR9 M28

GR9 M29

GR9 M27
(1:2)

GR9 M30

GR9 M31

Figure 78. Grave 9: iron spears (**GR9 M26–GR9 M29**) and dirks or daggers (**GR9 M30**, **GR9 M31**). Scale 1:3 unless otherwise indicated.

FIGURE 79

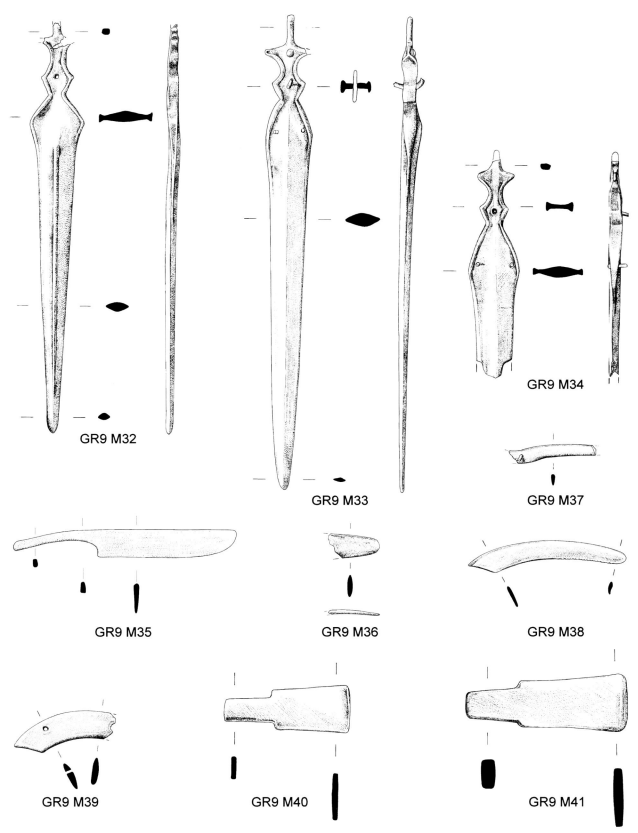

GR9 M32

GR9 M33

GR9 M34

GR9 M37

GR9 M35

GR9 M36

GR9 M38

GR9 M39

GR9 M40

GR9 M41

Figure 79. Grave 9: iron dirks or daggers (**GR9 M32–GR9 M34**), knives (**GR9 M35–GR9 M39**), and axes (**GR9 M40, GR9 M41**). Scale 1:3.

FIGURE 80

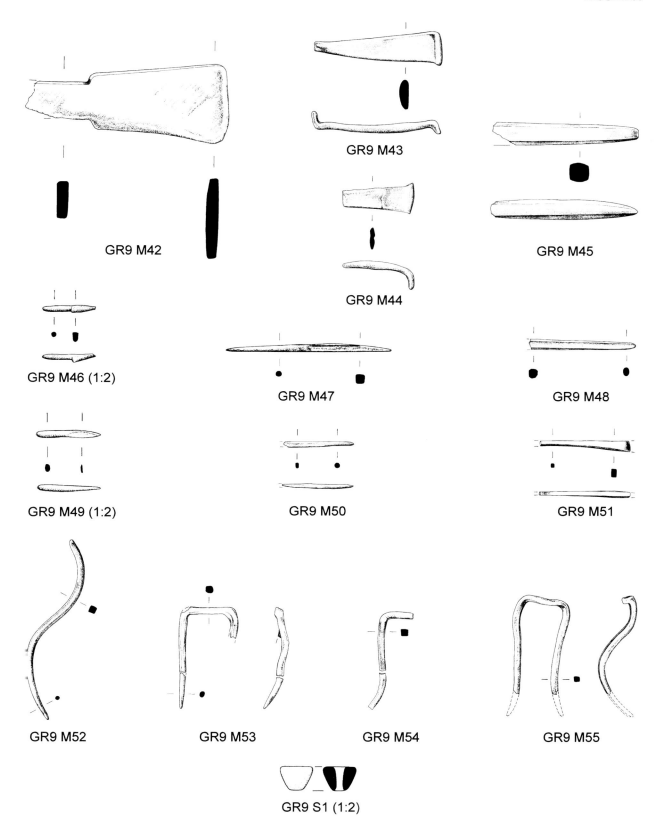

GR9 M42

GR9 M43

GR9 M44

GR9 M45

GR9 M46 (1:2)

GR9 M47

GR9 M48

GR9 M49 (1:2)

GR9 M50

GR9 M51

GR9 M52

GR9 M53

GR9 M54

GR9 M55

GR9 S1 (1:2)

F gure 80. Grave 9: iron axe (**GR9 M42**), scrapers (**GR9 M43**, **GR9 M44**), tools (**GR9 M45–GR9 M55**), and stone bead (**GR9 S1**). Scale 1:3 unless otherwise indicated.

FIGURE 81

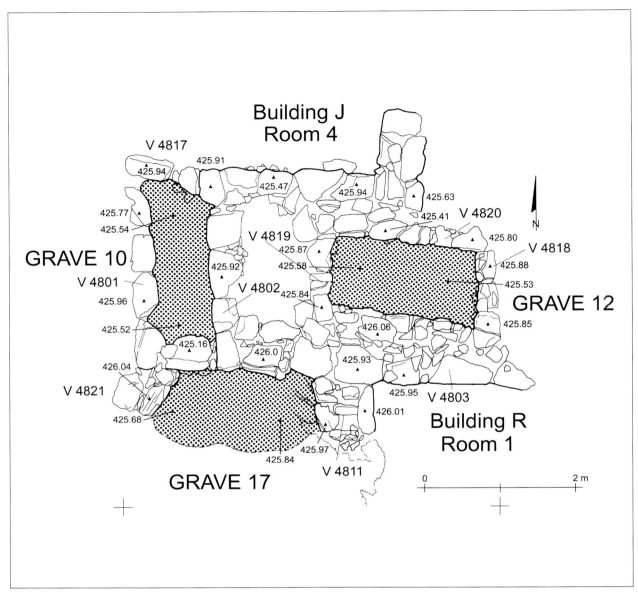

Figure 81. Plan of Graves 10, 12, and 17.

FIGURE 82

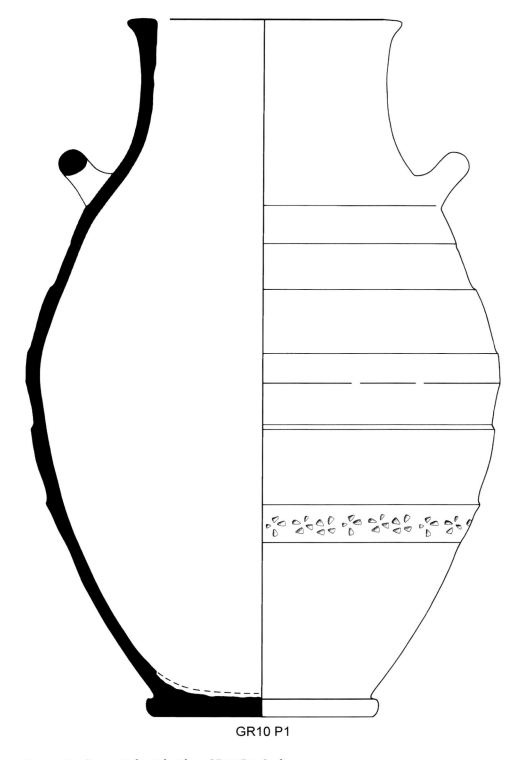

GR10 P1

Figure 82. Grave 10, burial pithos **GR10 P1**. Scale 1:4.

FIGURE 83

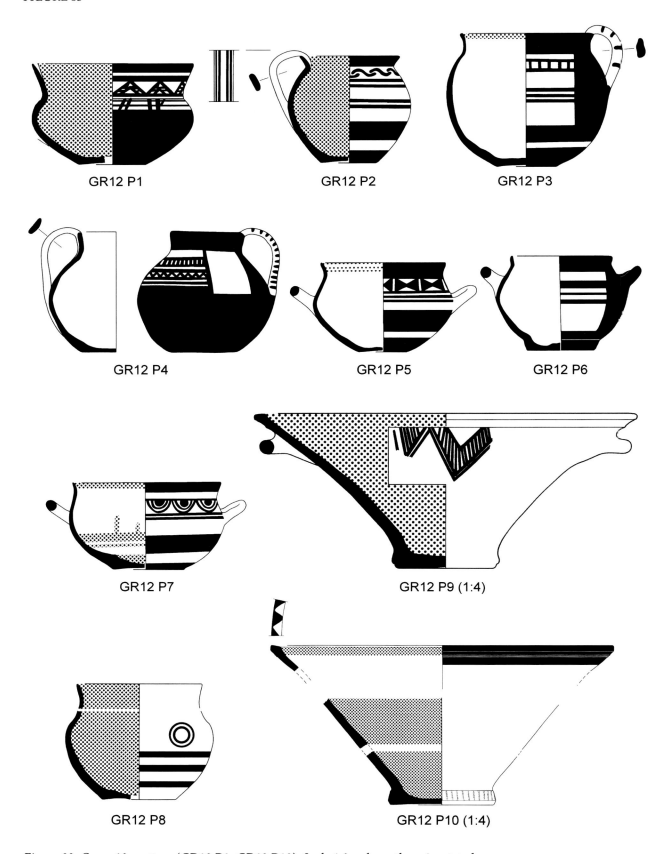

Figure 83. Grave 12: pottery (**GR12 P1–GR12 P10**). Scale 1:3 unless otherwise stated.

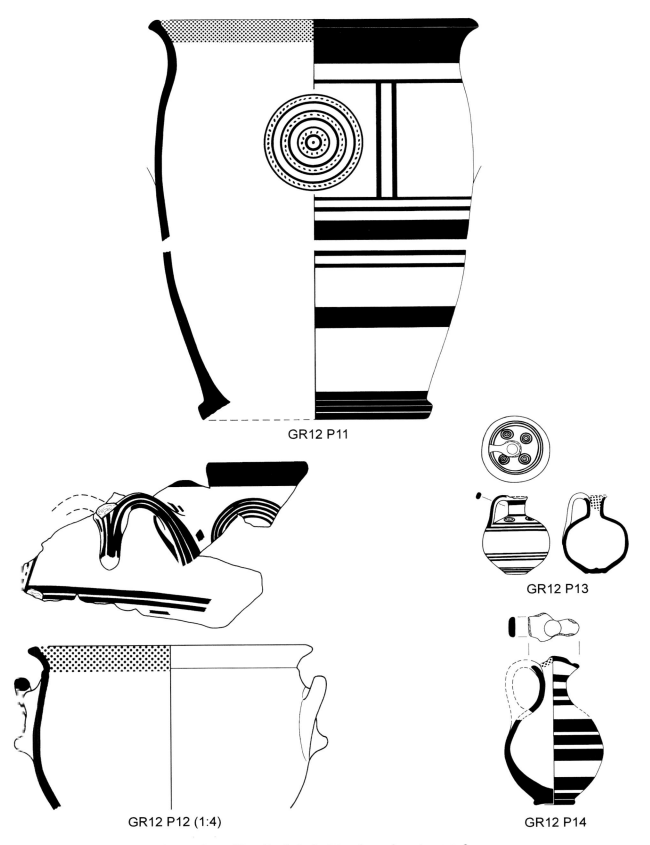

FIGURE 84

GR12 P11

GR12 P13

GR12 P12 (1:4)

GR12 P14

Figure 84. Grave 12: pottery (**GR12 P11–GR12 P14**). Scale 1:3 unless otherwise stated.

FIGURE 85

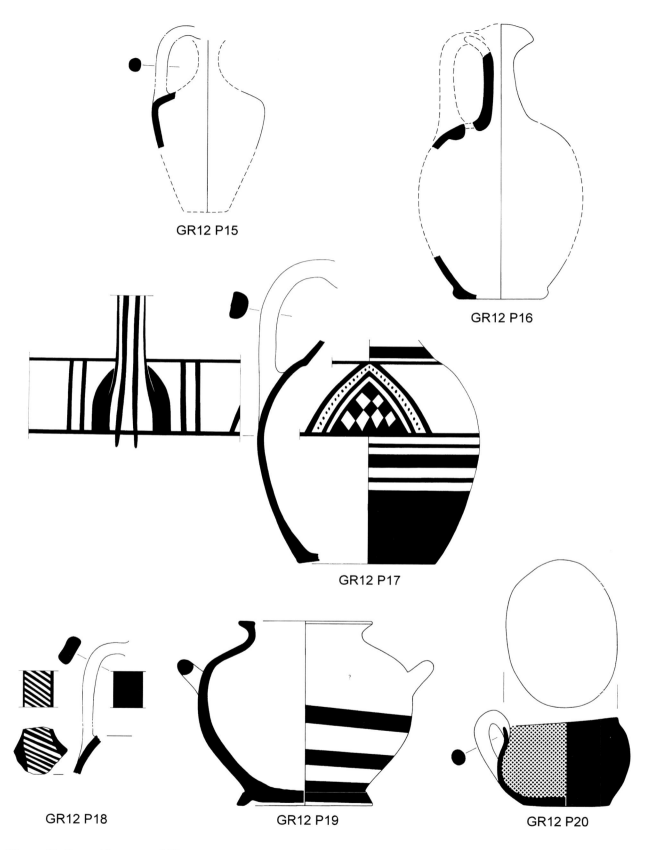

GR12 P15

GR12 P16

GR12 P17

GR12 P18

GR12 P19

GR12 P20

Figure 85. Grave 12: pottery (**GR12 P15–GR12 P20**). Scale 1:3.

FIGURE 86

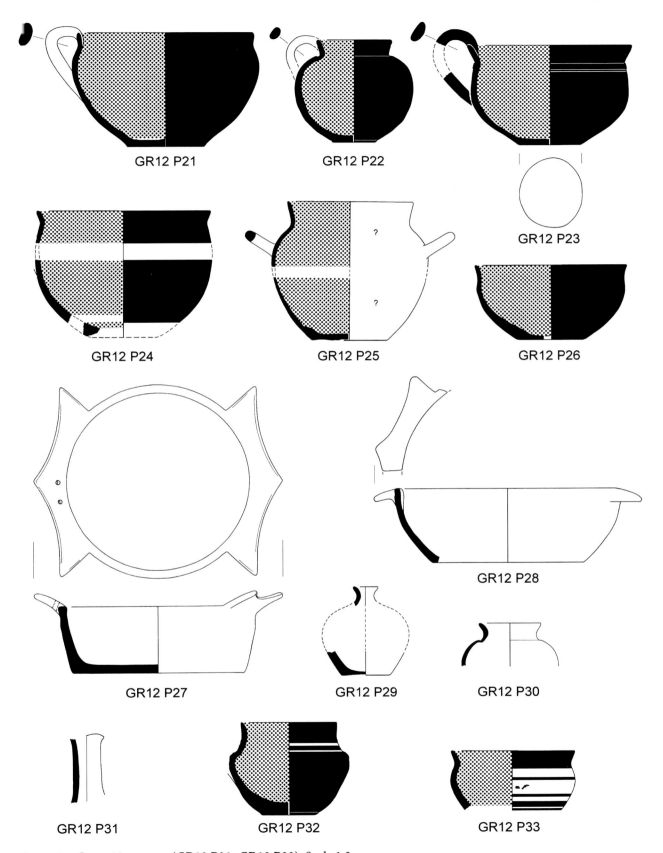

GR12 P21

GR12 P22

GR12 P23

GR12 P24

GR12 P25

GR12 P26

GR12 P27

GR12 P28

GR12 P29

GR12 P30

GR12 P31

GR12 P32

GR12 P33

F gure 86. Grave 12: pottery (**GR12 P21–GR12 P33**). Scale 1:3.

FIGURE 87

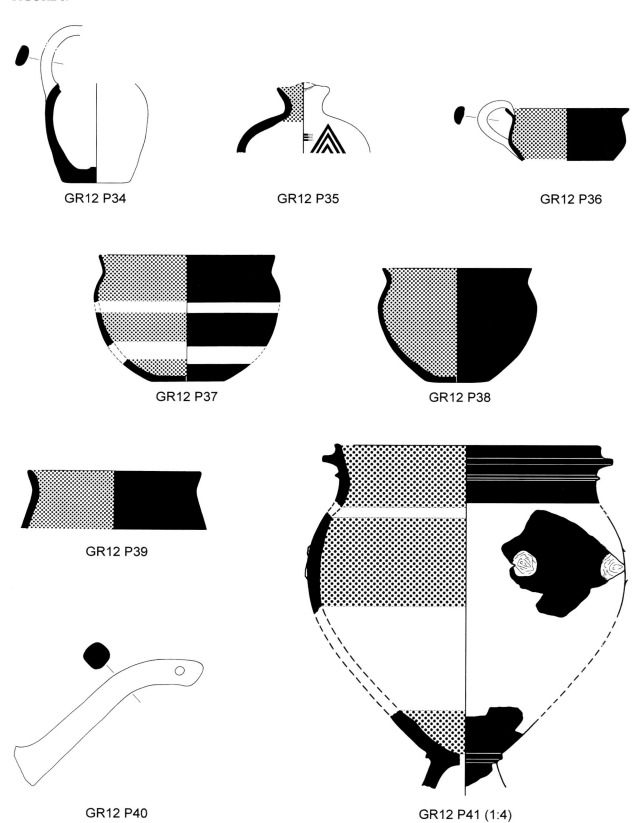

GR12 P34

GR12 P35

GR12 P36

GR12 P37

GR12 P38

GR12 P39

GR12 P40

GR12 P41 (1:4)

Figure 87. Grave 12: pottery (**GR12 P34–GR12 P41**). Scale 1:3 unless otherwise stated.

FIGURE 88

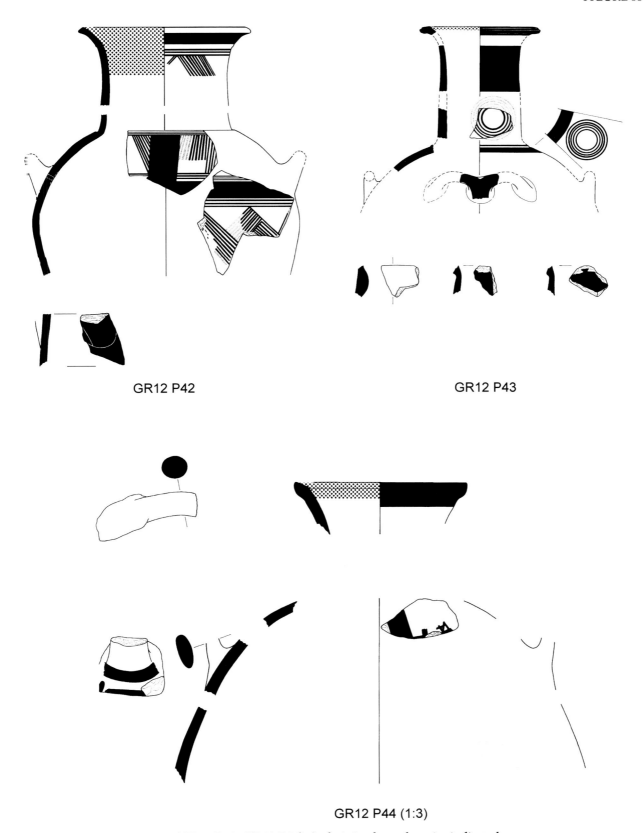

GR12 P42

GR12 P43

GR12 P44 (1:3)

Figure 88. Grave 12: pottery (**GR12 P42–GR12 P44**). Scale 1:6 unless otherwise indicated.

FIGURE 89

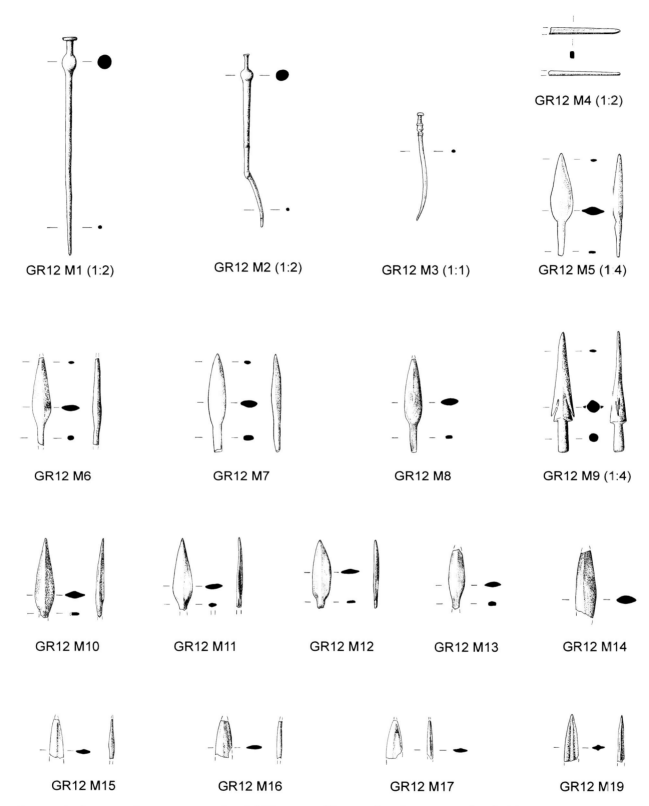

Figure 89. Grave 12: bronze pins and awl (**GR12 M1–GR12 M4**) and iron arrowheads (**GR12 M5–GR12 M17**, **GR12 M19**). Scale 1:3 unless otherwise indicated.

FIGURE 90

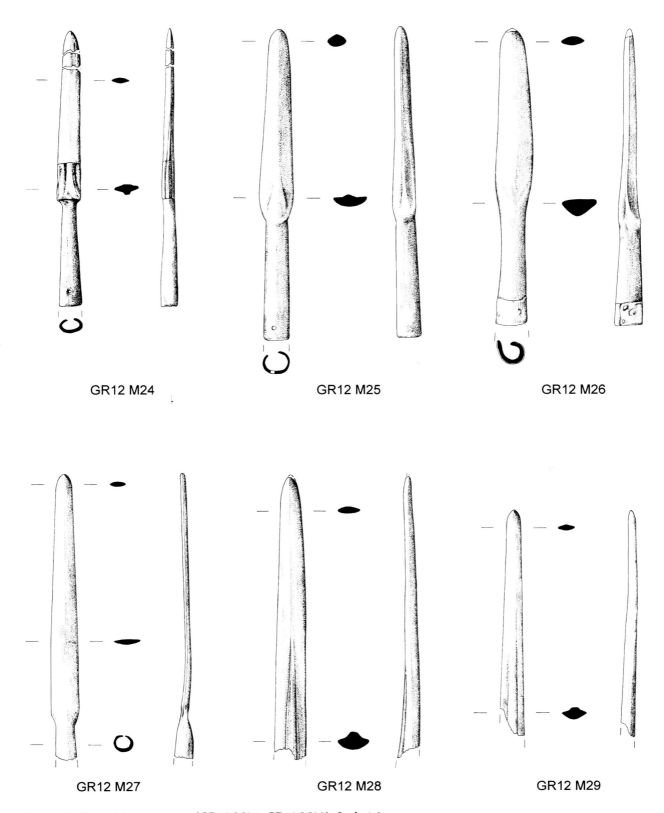

GR12 M24

GR12 M25

GR12 M26

GR12 M27

GR12 M28

GR12 M29

Figure 90. Grave 12: iron spears (**GR12 M24–GR12 M29**). Scale 1:3.

FIGURE 91

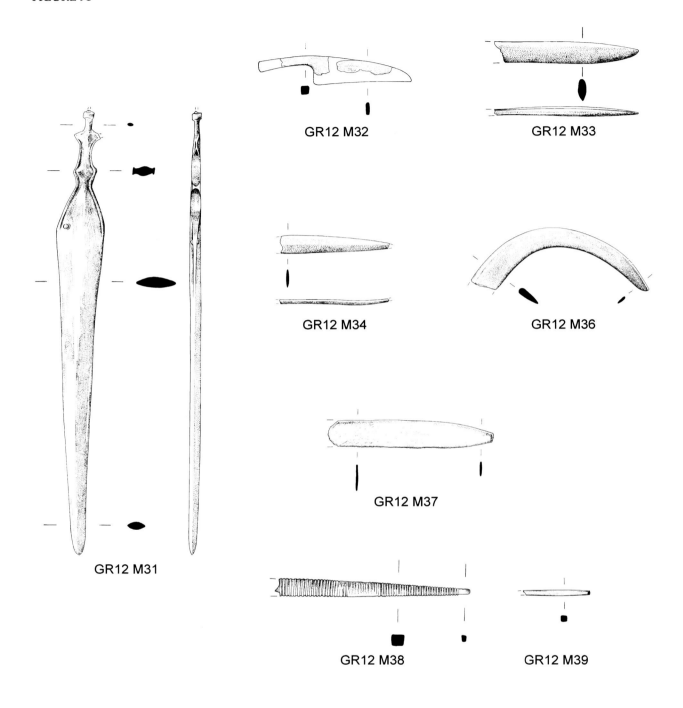

GR12 M32

GR12 M33

GR12 M34

GR12 M36

GR12 M37

GR12 M31

GR12 M38

GR12 M39

Figure 91. Grave 12: iron dirk (**GR12 M31**) and tools (**GR12 M32–GR12 M34, GR12 M36–GR 12 M39**). Scale 1:3.

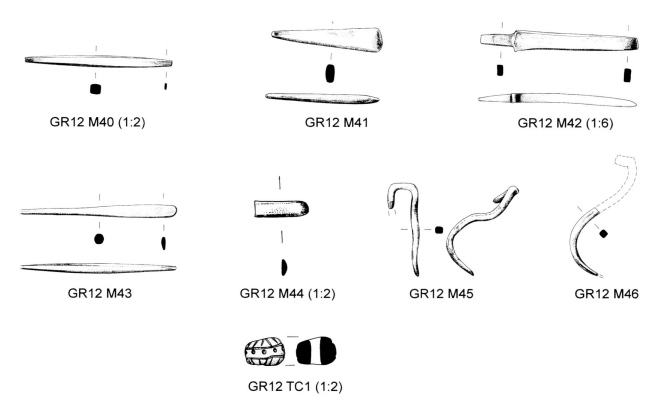

GR12 M40 (1:2)

GR12 M41

GR12 M42 (1:6)

GR12 M43

GR12 M44 (1:2)

GR12 M45

GR12 M46

GR12 TC1 (1:2)

Figure 92. Grave 12: iron tools (**GR12 M40–GR12 M46**) and terracotta bead (**GR12 TC1**). Scale 1:3 unless otherwise stated.

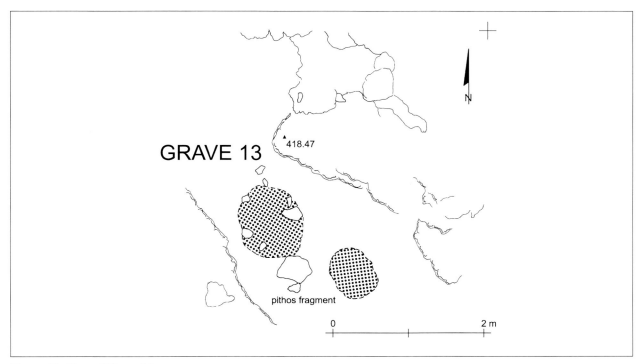

GRAVE 13

▲ 418.47

pithos fragment

0   2 m

Figure 93. Plan of Grave 13.

FIGURE 94

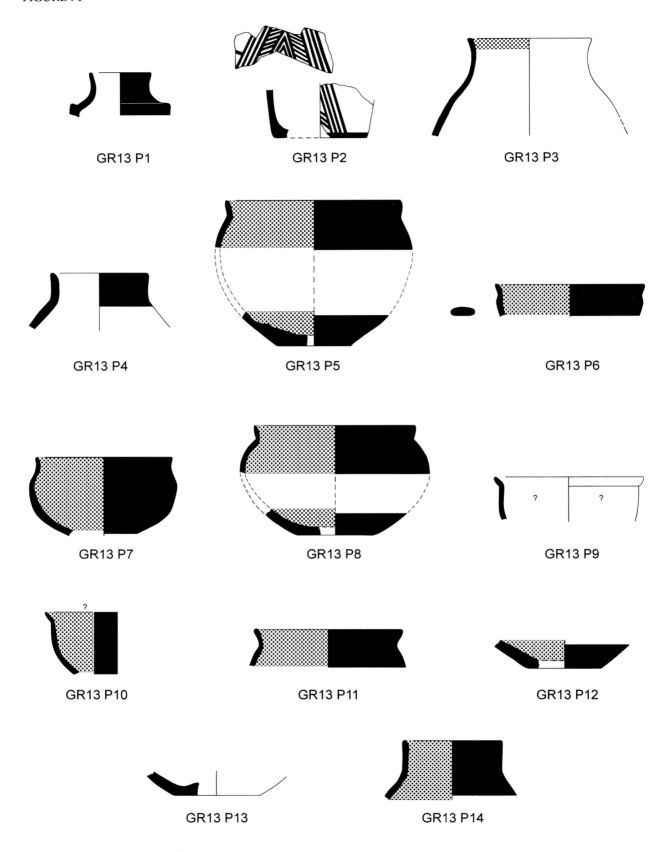

Figure 94. Grave 13: pottery (**GR13 P1–GR13 P14**). Scale 1:3.

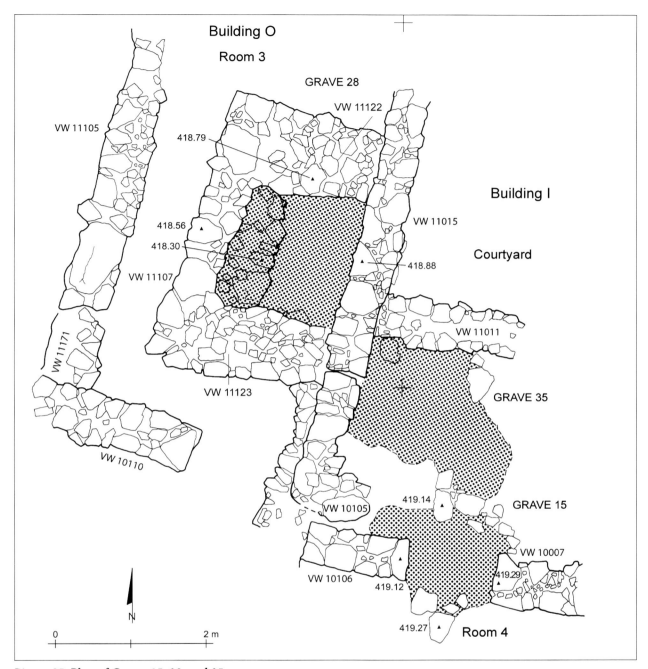

Figure 95. Plan of Graves 15, 28, and 35.

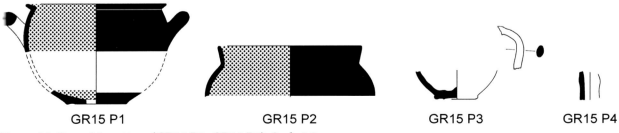

Figure 96. Grave 15: pottery (**GR15 P1–GR15 P4**). Scale 1:3.

FIGURE 97

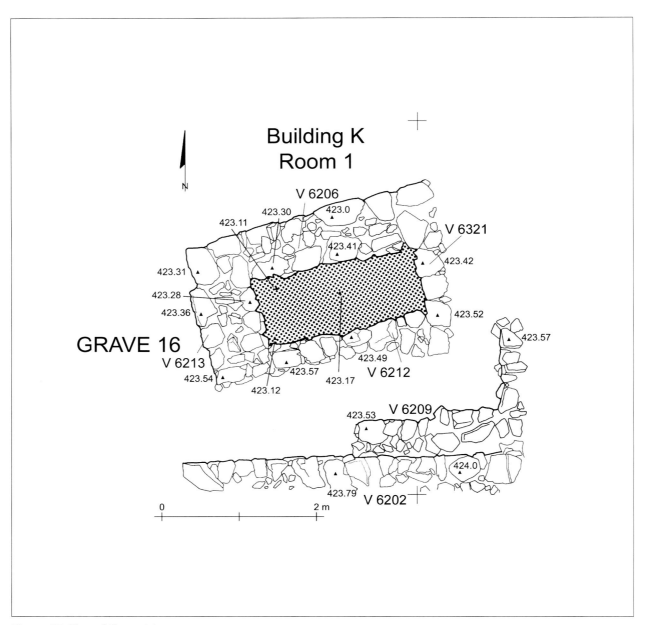

Figure 97. Plan of Grave 16.

FIGURE 98

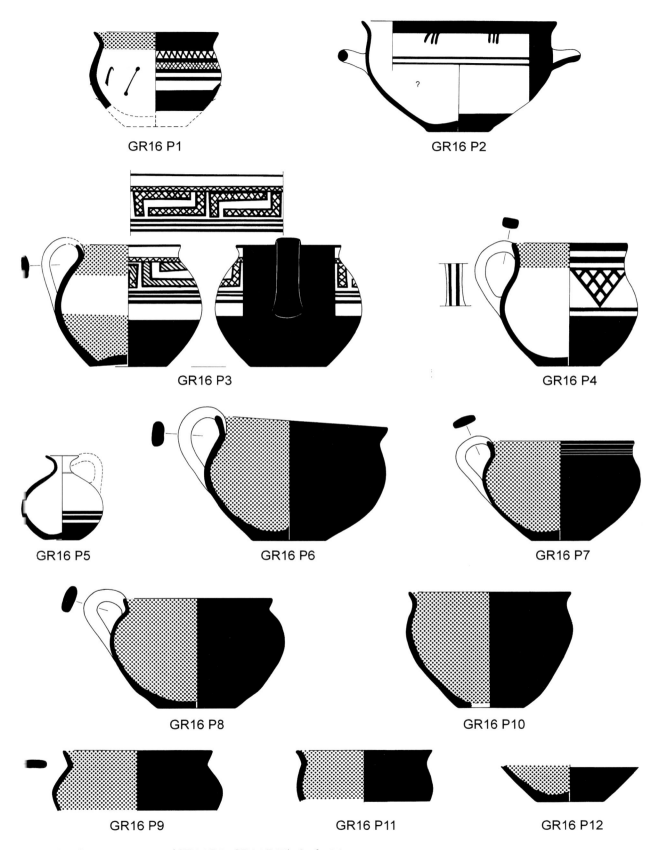

Figure 98. Grave 16: pottery (**GR16 P1–GR16 P12**). Scale 1:3.

FIGURE 99

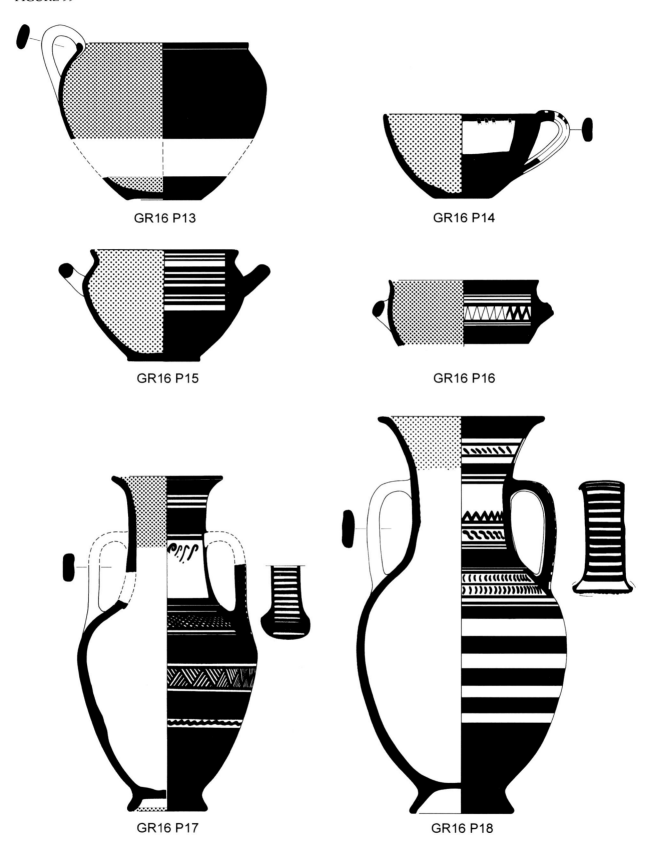

GR16 P13

GR16 P14

GR16 P15

GR16 P16

GR16 P17

GR16 P18

Figure 99. Grave 16: pottery (**GR16 P13–GR16 P18**). Scale 1:3.

FIGURE 100

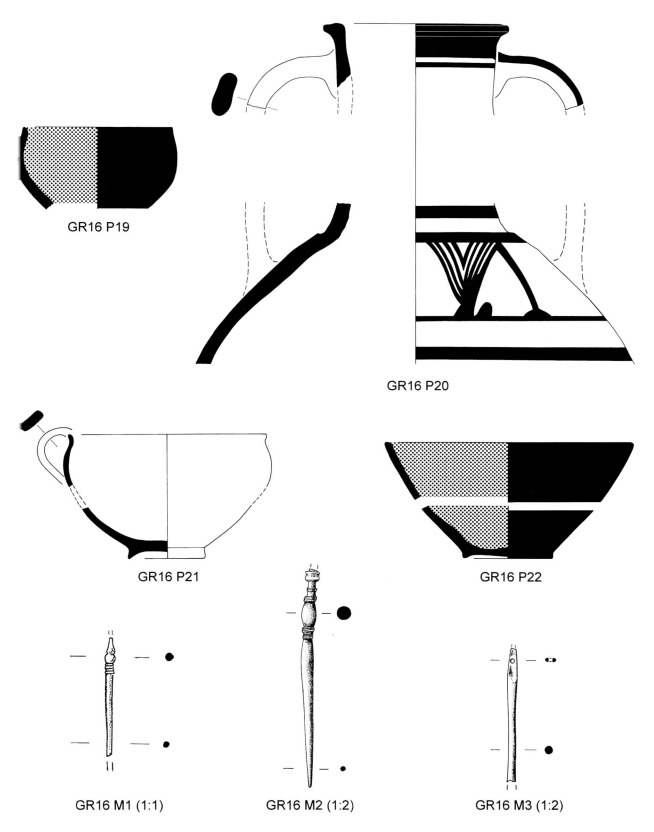

GR16 P19

GR16 P20

GR16 P21

GR16 P22

GR16 M1 (1:1)

GR16 M2 (1:2)

GR16 M3 (1:2)

Figure 100. Grave 16: pottery (**GR16 P19–GR16 P22**), bronze pin (**GR16 M1**), iron pin (**GR16 M2**), and iron needle (**GR16 M3**). Scale 1:3 unless otherwise indicated.

FIGURE 101

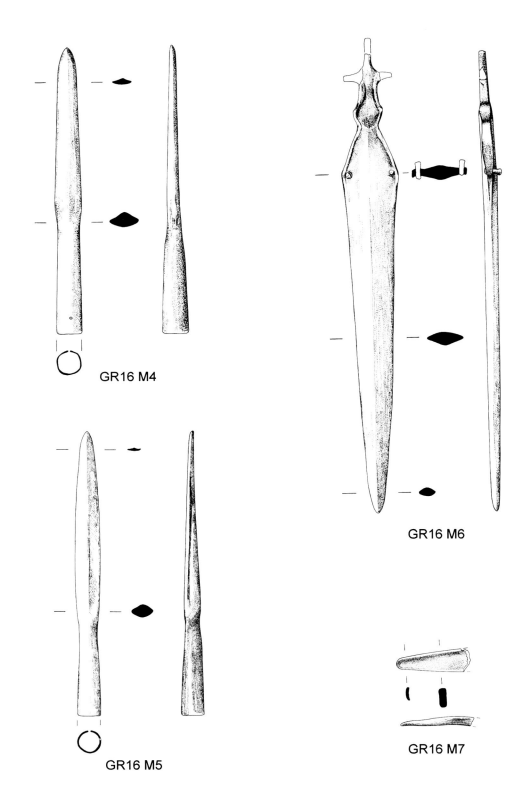

Figure 101. Grave 16, iron objects: spearheads (**GR16 M4**, **GR16 M5**), dagger (**GR16 M6**), and chisel (**GR16 M7**). Scale 1:3.

FIGURE 102

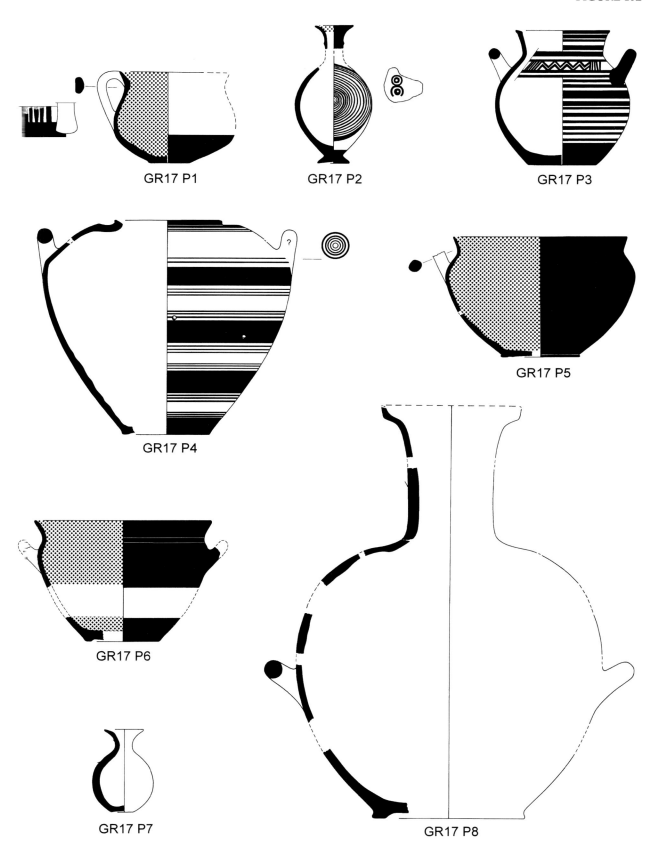

GR17 P1

GR17 P2

GR17 P3

GR17 P4

GR17 P5

GR17 P6

GR17 P7

GR17 P8

Figure 102. Grave 17: pottery (**GR17 P1–GR17 P8**). Scale 1:3.

FIGURE 103

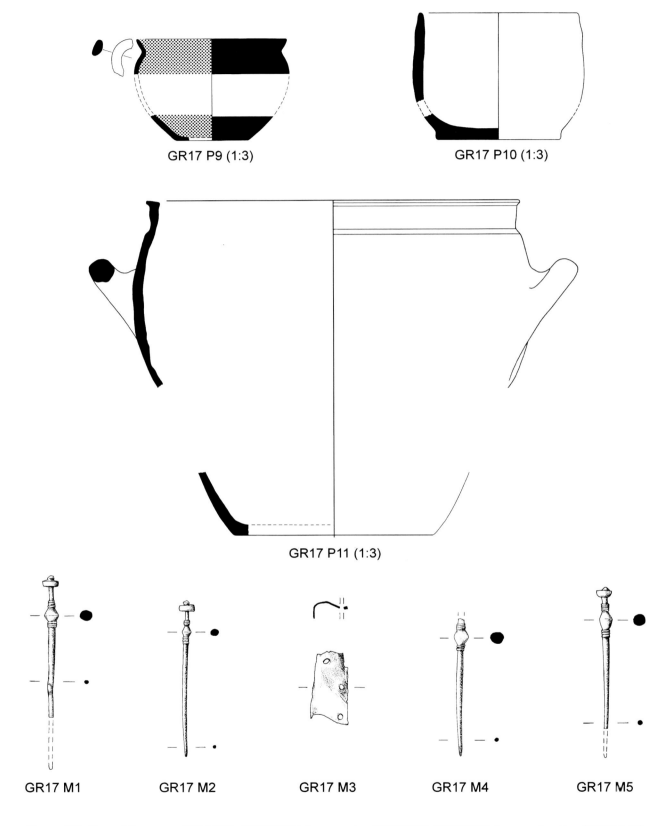

GR17 P9 (1:3)

GR17 P10 (1:3)

GR17 P11 (1:3)

GR17 M1   GR17 M2   GR17 M3   GR17 M4   GR17 M5

Figure 103. Grave 17: pottery (**GR17 P9–GR17 P11**), bronze pins (**GR17 M1, GR17 M2**), bronze sheeting (**GR17 M3**), and iron pins (**GR17 M4, GR17 M5**). Scale 1:2 unless otherwise indicated.

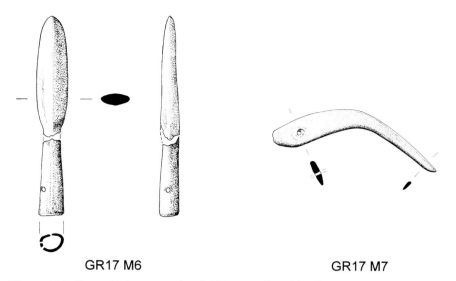

GR17 M6   GR17 M7

Figure 104. Grave 17: iron spearhead (**GR17 M6**) and knife (**GR17 M7**). Scale 1:3.

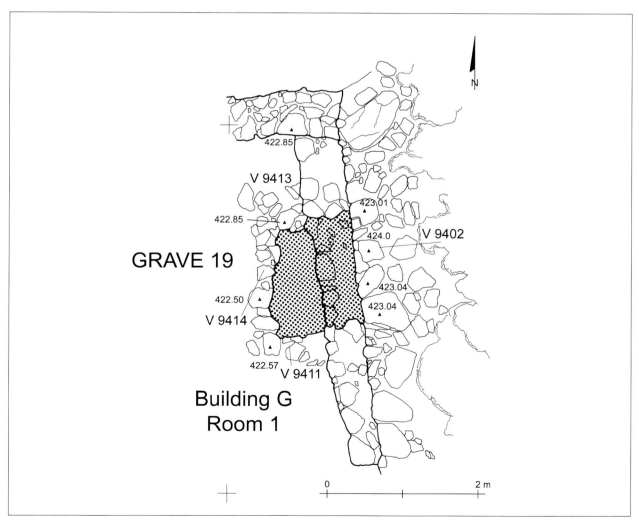

Figure 105. Plan of Grave 19.

FIGURE 106

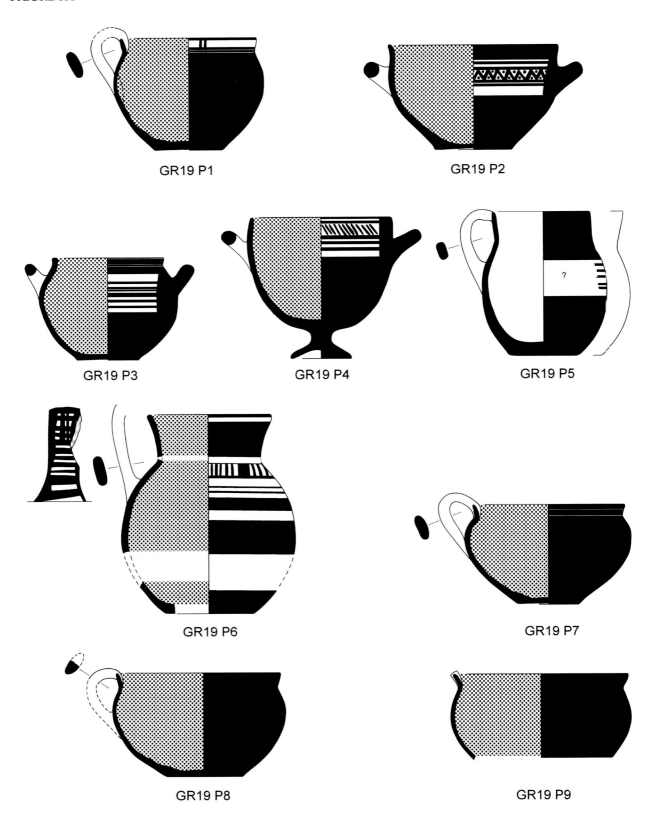

Figure 106. Grave 19: pottery (**GR19 P1–GR19 P9**). Scale 1:3.

FIGURE 107

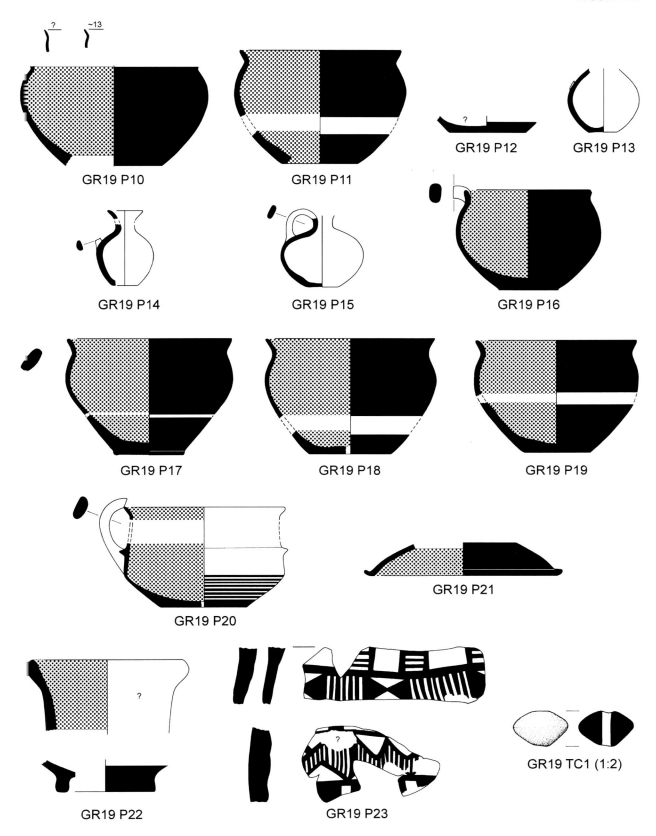

F gure 107. Grave 19: pottery (**GR19 P10–GR19 P23**) and terracotta object (**GR19 TC1**). Scale 1:3 unless otherwise indicated.

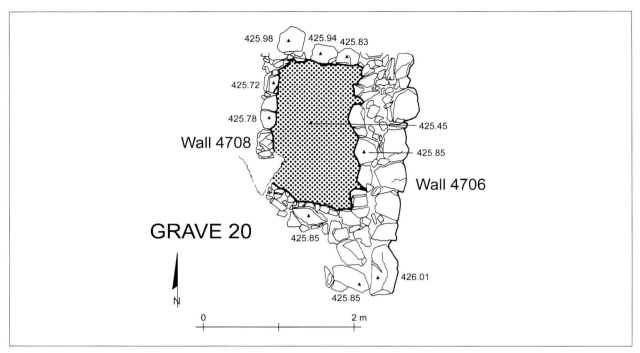

Figure 108. Plan of Grave 20.

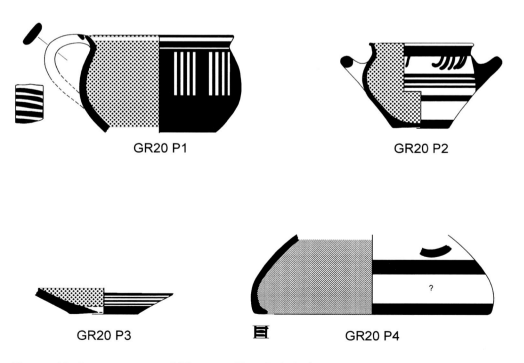

Figure 109. Grave 20: pottery (**GR20 P1–GR19 P4**). Scale 1:3.

FIGURE 110

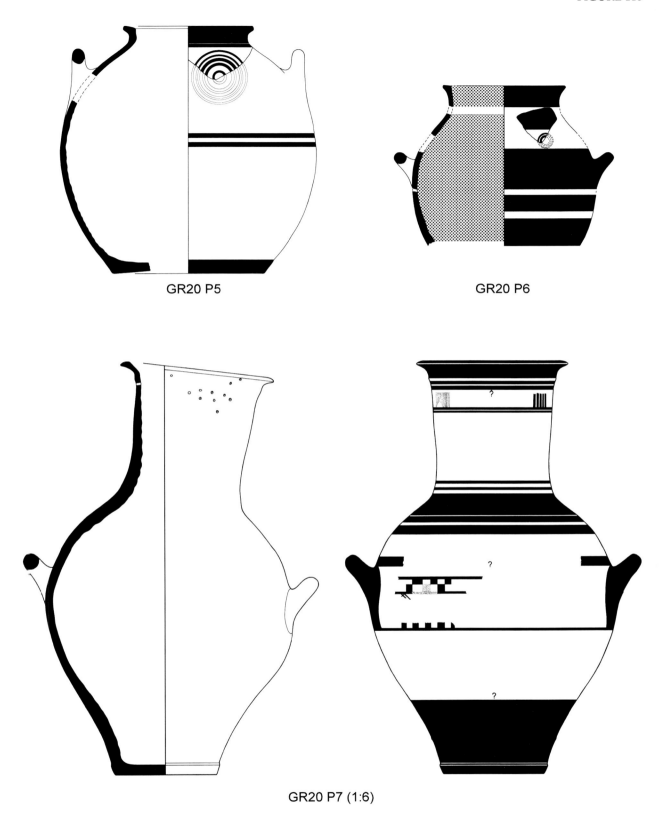

GR20 P5

GR20 P6

GR20 P7 (1:6)

Figure 110. Grave 20: pottery (**GR20 P5–GR19 P7**). Scale 1:4 unless otherwise stated.

FIGURE 111

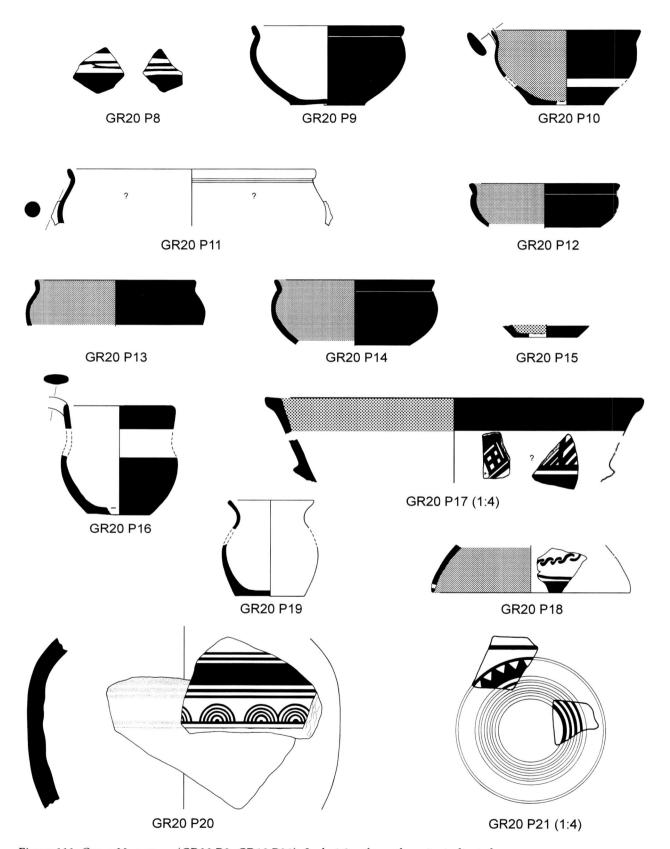

Figure 111. Grave 20: pottery (**GR20 P8–GR19 P21**). Scale 1:3 unless otherwise indicated.

FIGURE 112

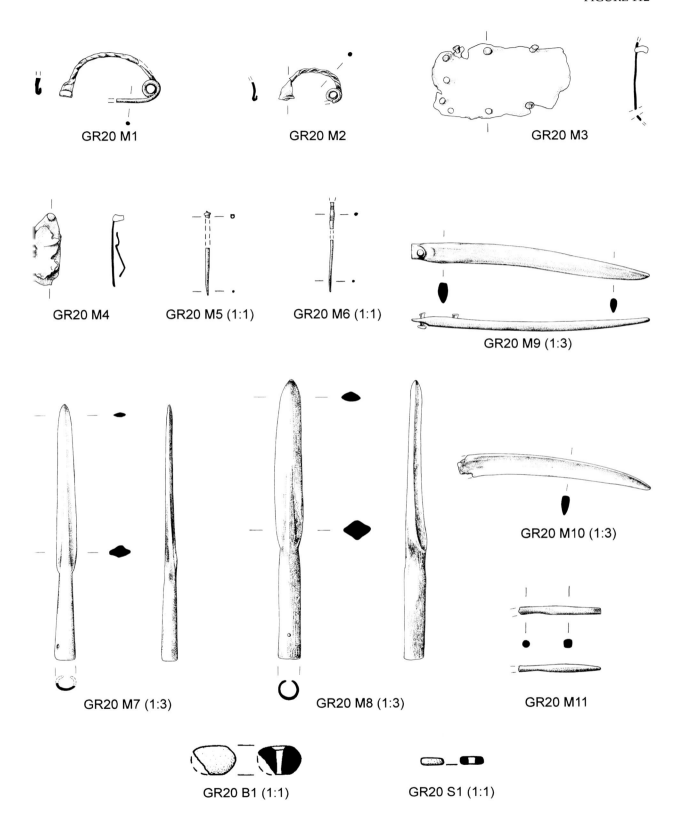

GR20 M1

GR20 M2

GR20 M3

GR20 M4

GR20 M5 (1:1)

GR20 M6 (1:1)

GR20 M9 (1:3)

GR20 M7 (1:3)

GR20 M8 (1:3)

GR20 M10 (1:3)

GR20 M11

GR20 B1 (1:1)

GR20 S1 (1:1)

Figure 112. Grave 20: bronze fibulae (**GR20 M1**, **GR20 M2**), bronze sheeting (**GR20 M3**, **GR19 M4**), iron pins (**GR20 M5**, **GR19 M6**), iron spearheads (**GR20 M7**, **GR19 M8**), iron knives (**GR20 M9**, **GR19 M10**), iron tool (**GR20 M11**), ivory or bone bead (**GR20 B1**), and stone bead (**GR20 S1**). Scale 1:2 unless otherwise indicated.

FIGURE 113

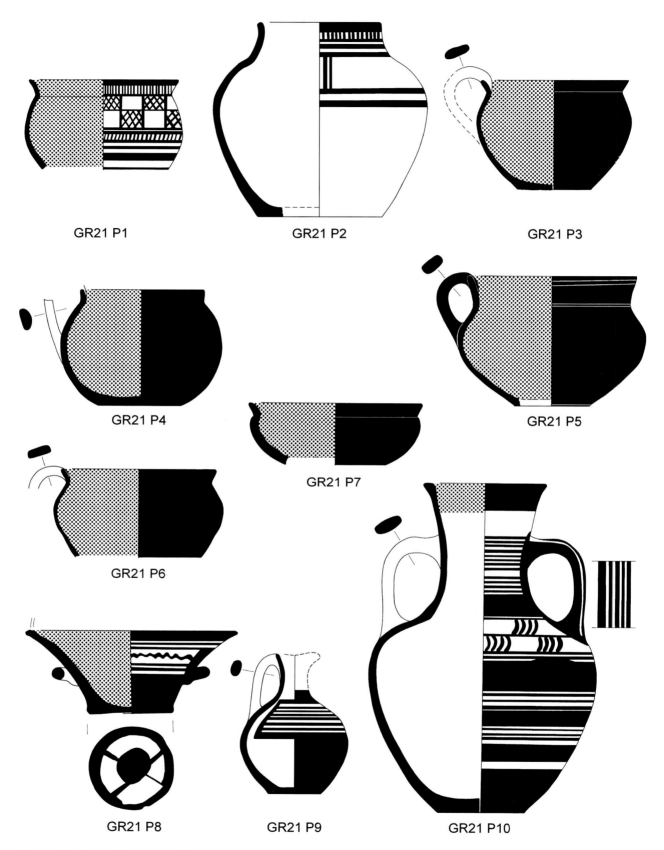

GR21 P1

GR21 P2

GR21 P3

GR21 P4

GR21 P5

GR21 P6

GR21 P7

GR21 P8

GR21 P9

GR21 P10

Figure 113. Grave 21: pottery (**GR21 P**1–**GR19 P10**). Scale 1:3.

FIGURE 114

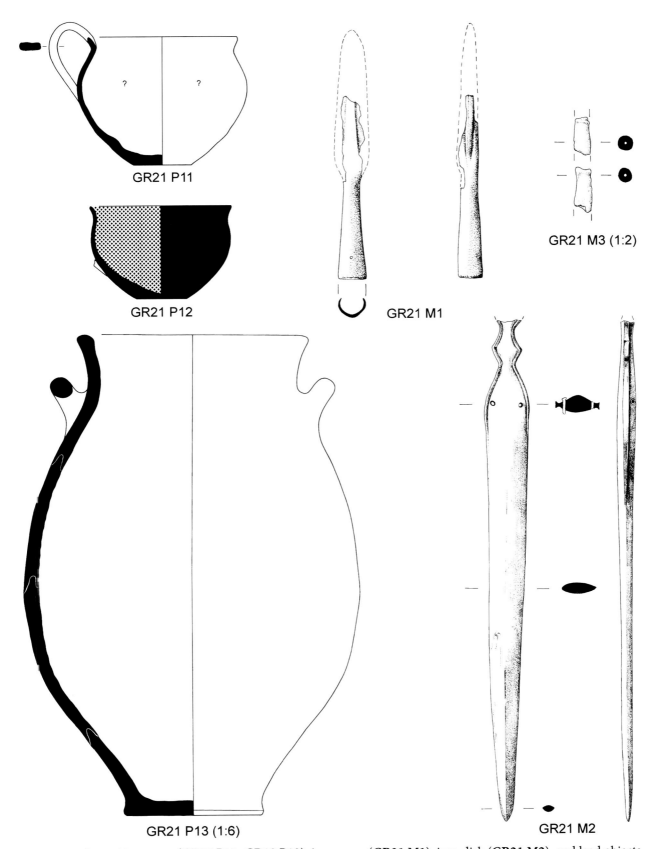

GR21 P11

GR21 P12

GR21 P13 (1:6)

GR21 M1

GR21 M3 (1:2)

GR21 M2

Figure 114. Grave 21: pottery (**GR21 P11**–**GR19 P13**), iron spear (**GR21 M1**), iron dirk (**GR21 M2**), and lead objects (**GR21 M3**). Scale 1:3 unless otherwise indicated.

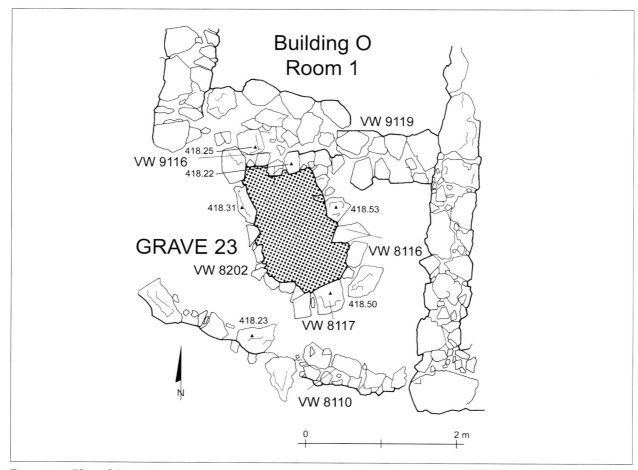

Figure 115. Plan of Grave 23.

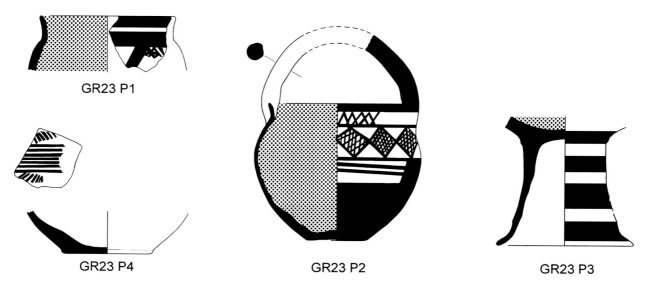

Figure 116. Grave 23: pottery (**GR23 P1–GR23 P4**). Scale 1:3.

FIGURE 117

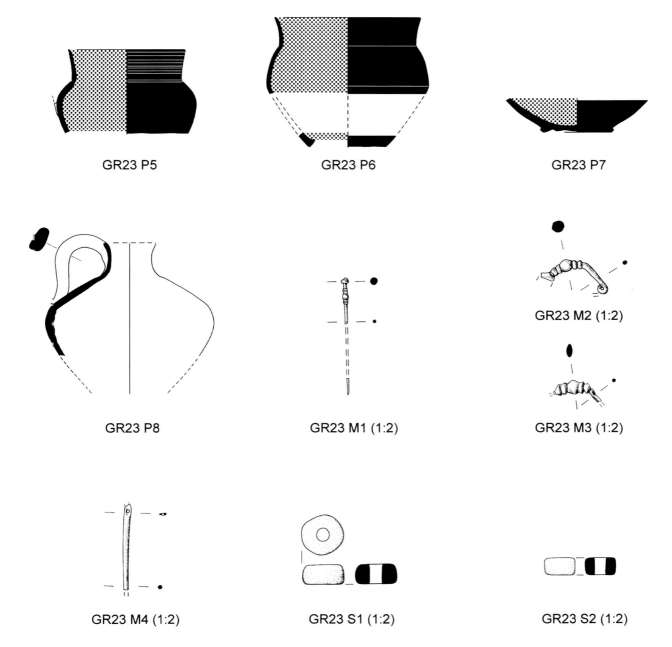

GR23 P5

GR23 P6

GR23 P7

GR23 P8

GR23 M1 (1:2)

GR23 M2 (1:2)

GR23 M3 (1:2)

GR23 M4 (1:2)

GR23 S1 (1:2)

GR23 S2 (1:2)

Figure 117. Grave 23: pottery (**GR23 P5–GR23 P8**) and bronze (**GR23 M1–GR23 M3**), iron (**GR23 M4**), and stone (**GR23 S1, GR23 S2**) objects. Scale 1:3 unless otherwise indicated.

FIGURE 118

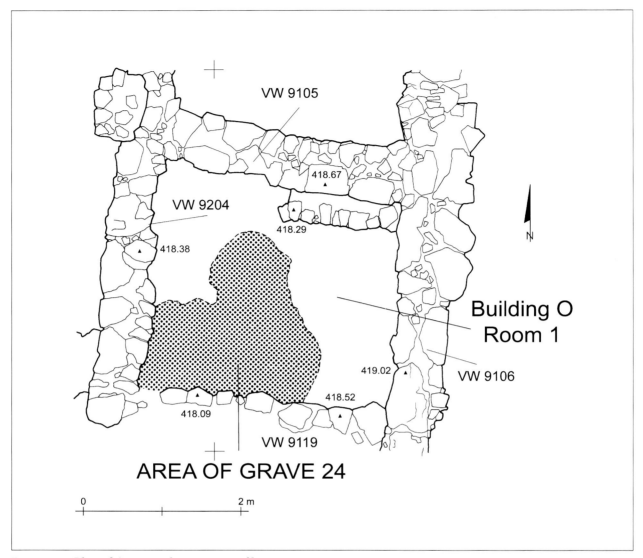

Figure 118. Plan of Grave 24 showing area of human remains.

FIGURE 119

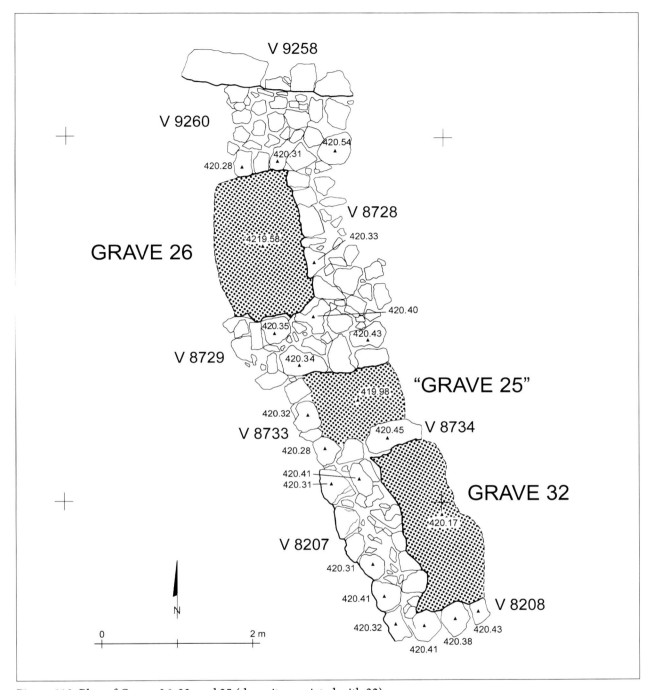

Figure 119. Plan of Graves 26, 32, and 25 (deposit associated with 32).

FIGURE 120

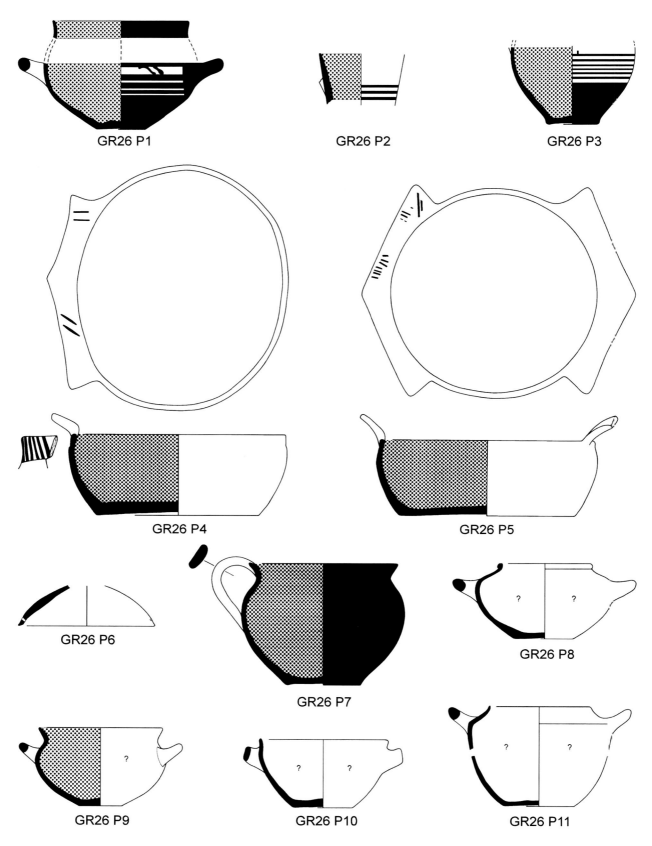

Figure 120. Grave 26: pottery (**GR26 P1–GR26 P11**). Scale 1:3.

FIGURE 121

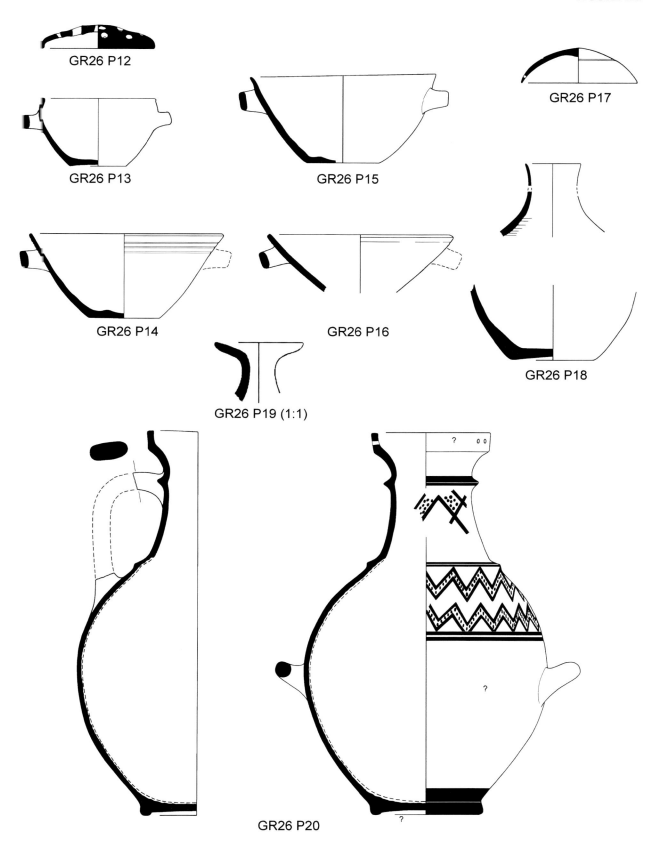

Figure 121. Grave 26: pottery (**GR26 P12–GR26 P20**). Scale 1:3.

FIGURE 122

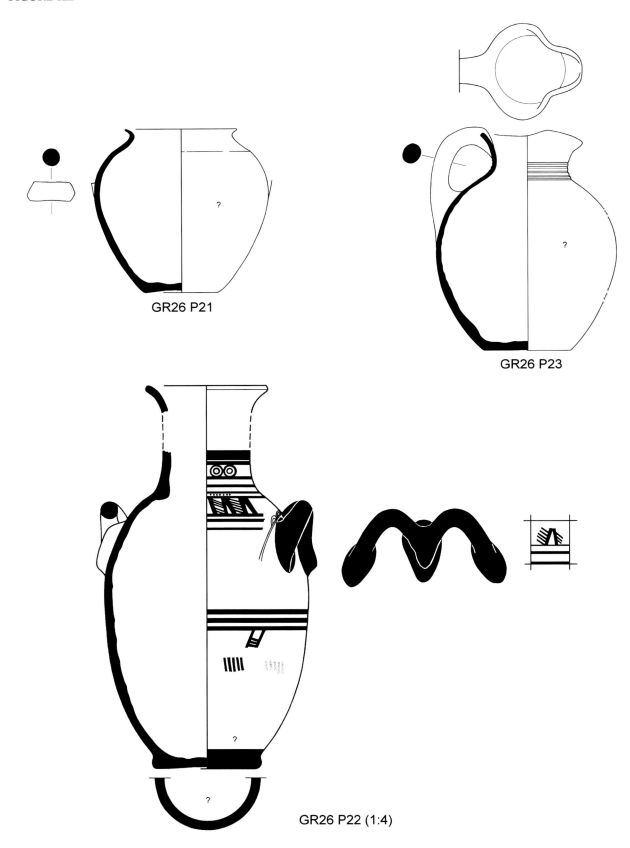

GR26 P21

GR26 P23

GR26 P22 (1:4)

Figure 122. Grave 26: pottery (**GR26 P21**–**GR26 P23**). Scale 1:3 unless otherwise indicated.

FIGURE 123

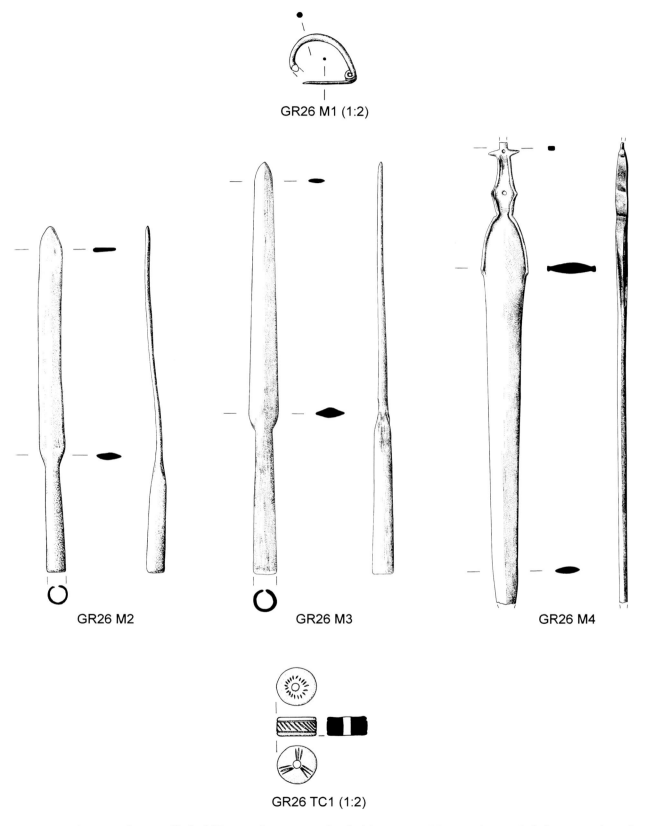

GR26 M1 (1:2)

GR26 M2

GR26 M3

GR26 M4

GR26 TC1 (1:2)

F gure 123. Grave 26: bronze fibula (**GR26 M1**), iron spearheads (**GR26 M2**, **GR26 M3**), iron dirk (**GR26 M4**), and terracotta bead (**GR26 TC1**). Scale 1:3 unless otherwise indicated.

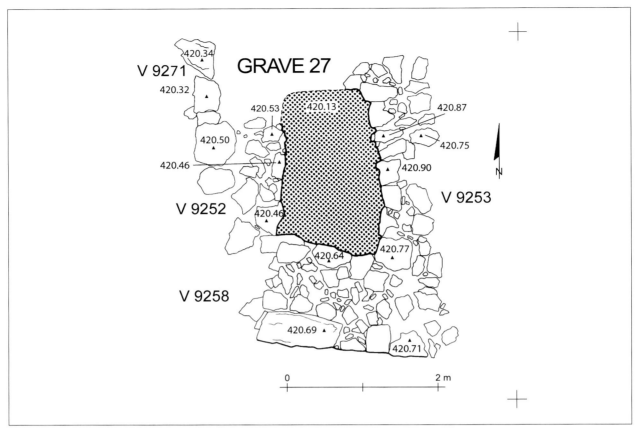

Figure 124. Plan of Grave 27.

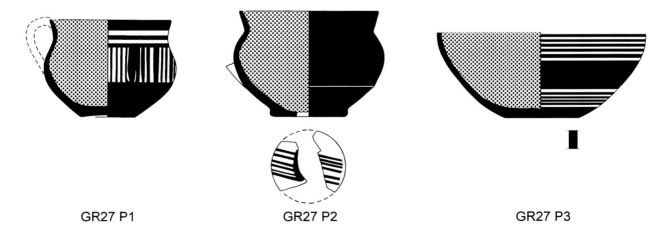

GR27 P1　　　　GR27 P2　　　　GR27 P3

Figure 125. Grave 27: pottery (**GR27 P1–GR27 P3**). Scale 1:3.

FIGURE 126

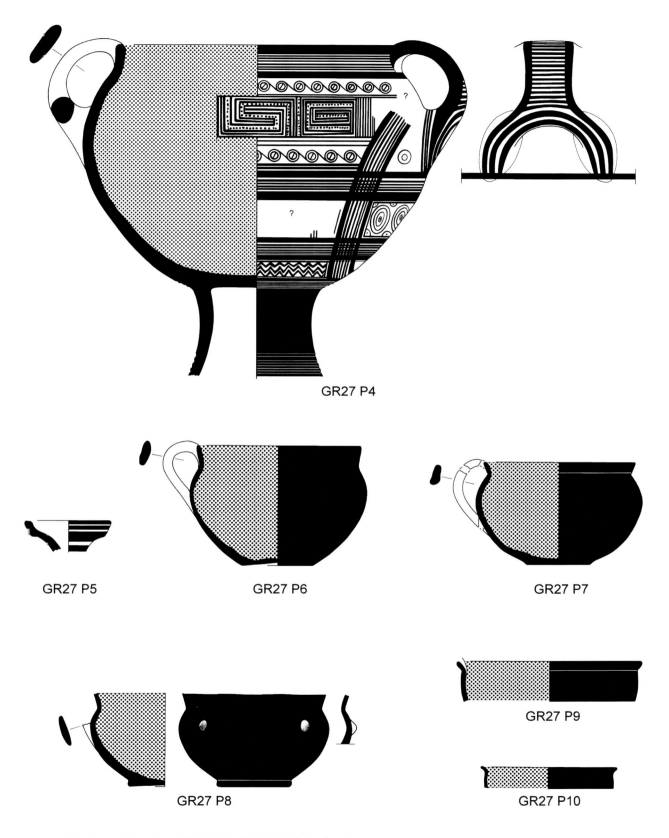

GR27 P4

GR27 P5

GR27 P6

GR27 P7

GR27 P8

GR27 P9

GR27 P10

F gure 126. Grave 27: pottery (**GR27 P4–GR27 P10**). Scale 1:3.

FIGURE 127

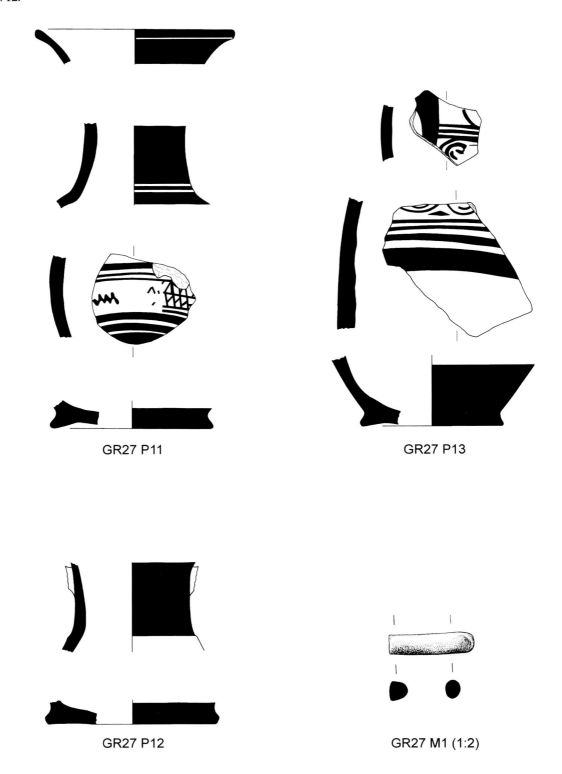

GR27 P11

GR27 P13

GR27 P12

GR27 M1 (1:2)

Figure 127. Grave 27: pottery (**GR27 P11**–**GR27 P13**) and iron object (**GR27 M1**). Scale 1:3 unless otherwise indicated.

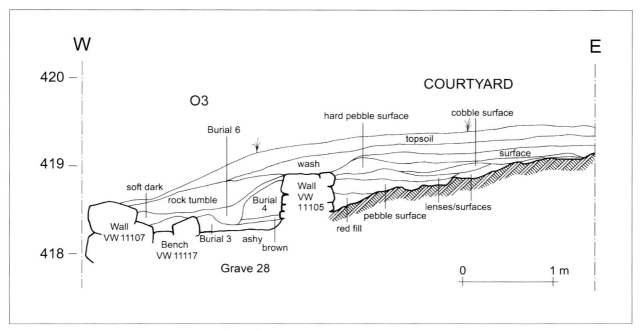

Figure 128. Grave 28: east–west section through grave.

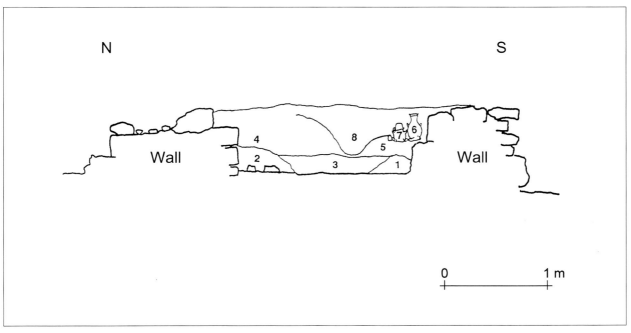

Figure 129. Grave 28: schematic north–south section showing locations of Burials 1–8.

FIGURE 130

GR28 P1

GR28 P2

GR28 P3

GR28 P4

GR28 P5

GR28 P6

GR28 P7

GR28 P8

Figure 130. Grave 28: pottery (**GR28 P1–GR28 P8**). Scale 1:3.

FIGURE 131

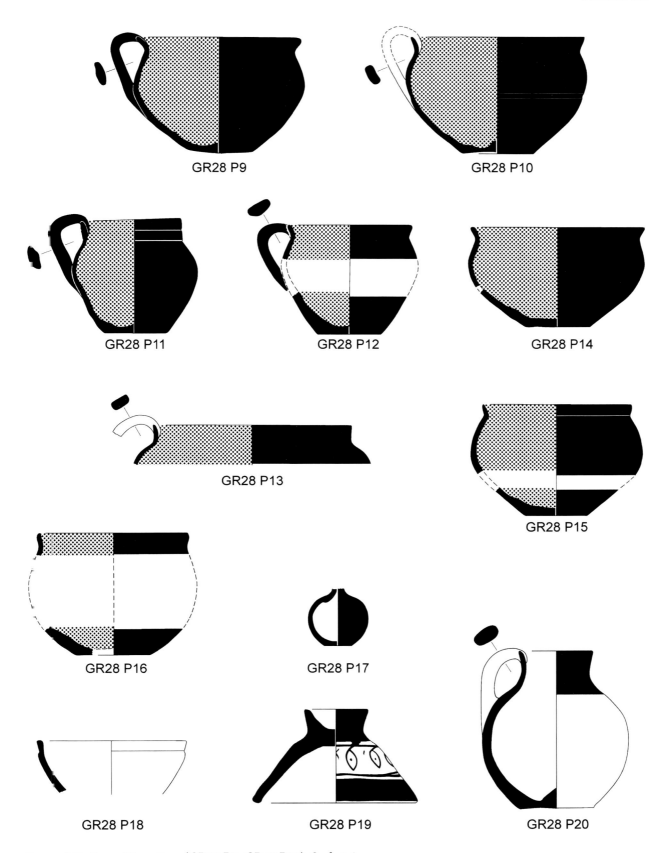

GR28 P9

GR28 P10

GR28 P11

GR28 P12

GR28 P14

GR28 P13

GR28 P15

GR28 P16

GR28 P17

GR28 P18

GR28 P19

GR28 P20

Figure 131. Grave 28: pottery (**GR28 P9–GR28 P20**). Scale 1:3.

FIGURE 132

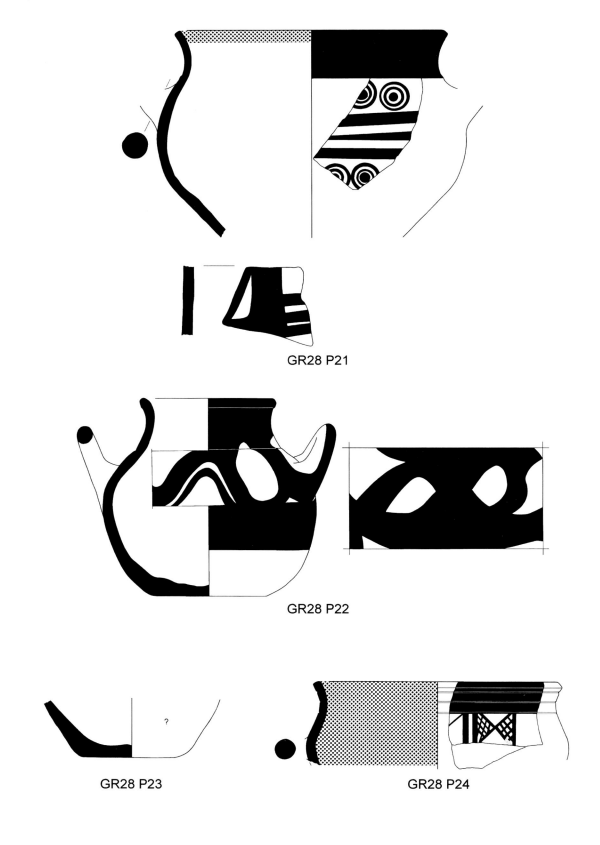

GR28 P21

GR28 P22

GR28 P23

GR28 P24

Figure 132. Grave 28: pottery (**GR28 P21–GR28 P24**). Scale 1:3.

FIGURE 133

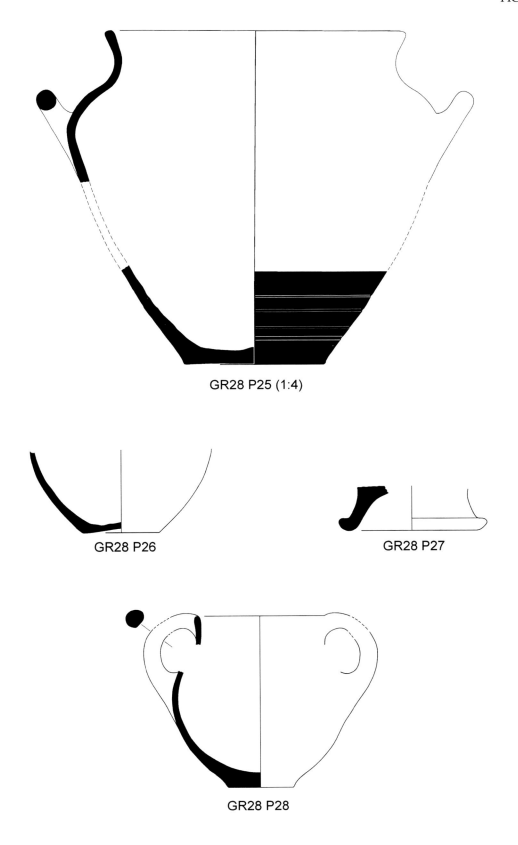

GR28 P25 (1:4)

GR28 P26

GR28 P27

GR28 P28

Figure 133. Grave 28: pottery (**GR28 P25–GR28 P28**). Scale 1:3 unless otherwise indicated.

FIGURE 134

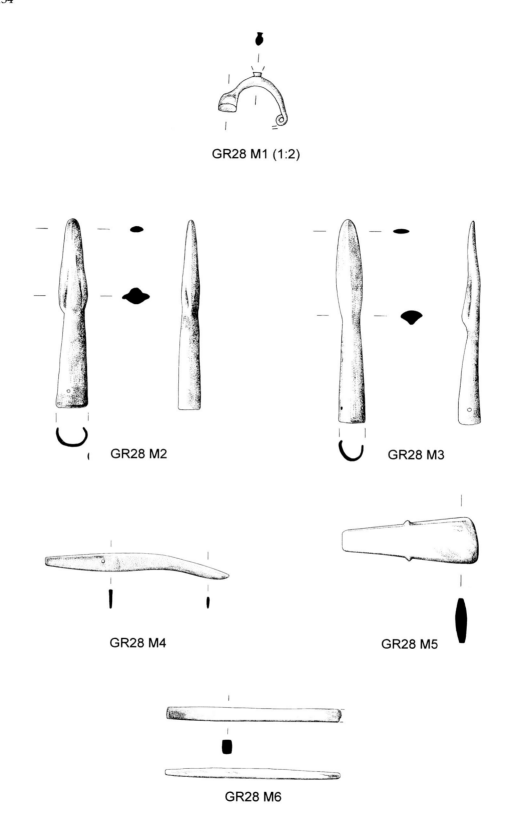

GR28 M1 (1:2)

GR28 M2

GR28 M3

GR28 M4

GR28 M5

GR28 M6

Figure 134. Grave 28: bronze fibula (**GR28 M1**), iron spearheads (**GR28 M2**, **GR28 M3**), and iron tools (**GR28 M4–GR28 M6**). Scale 1:3 unless otherwise indicated.

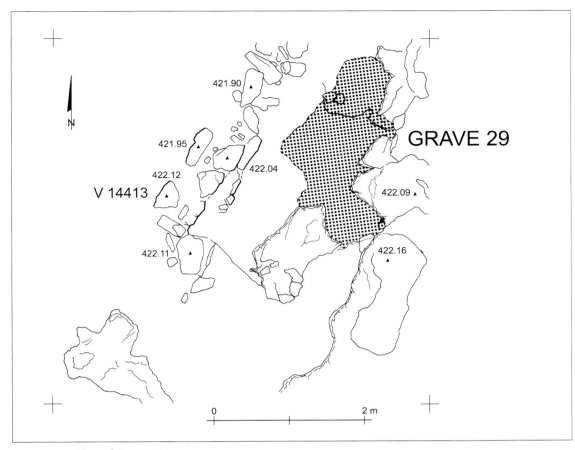

Figure 135. Plan of Grave 29.

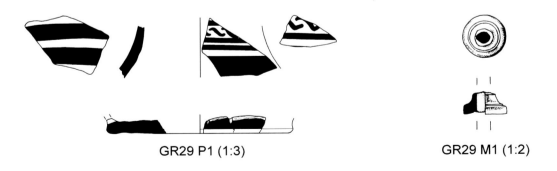

GR29 P1 (1:3)

GR29 M1 (1:2)

Figure 136. Grave 29: pottery (**GR29 P1**) and lead button (**GR29 M1**). Scale as indicated.

FIGURE 137

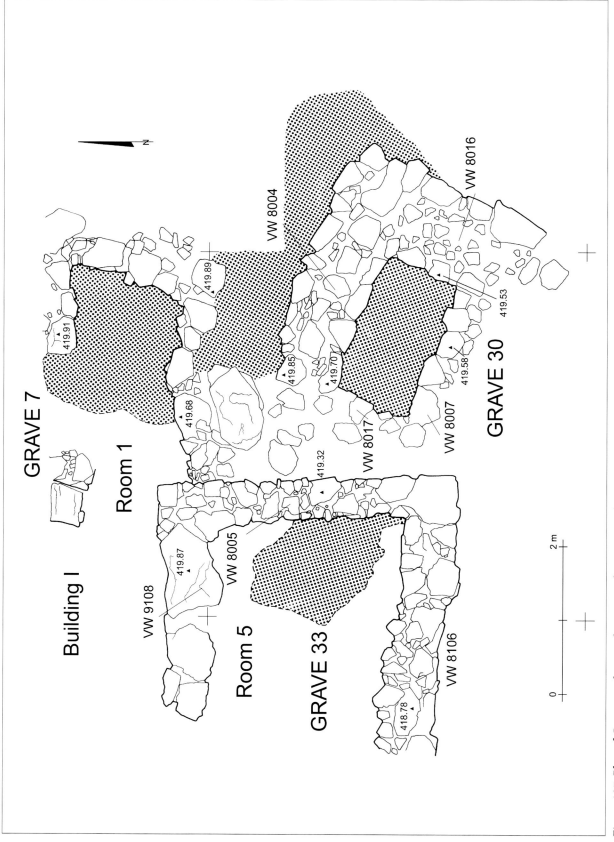

Figure 137. Plan of Grave 30, showing locations of Graves 7 and 33.

FIGURE 138

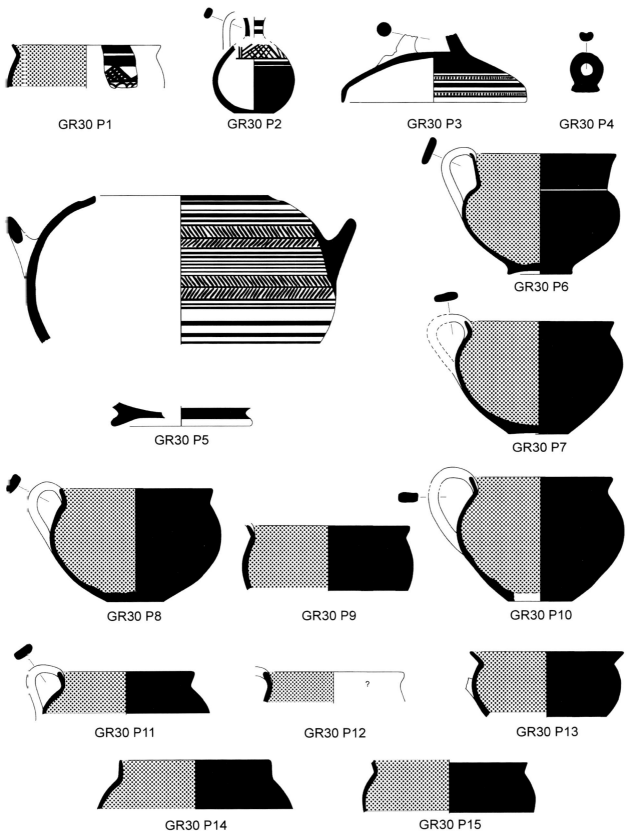

Figure 138. Grave 30: pottery (**GR30 P1–GR30 P15**). Scale 1:3.

FIGURE 139

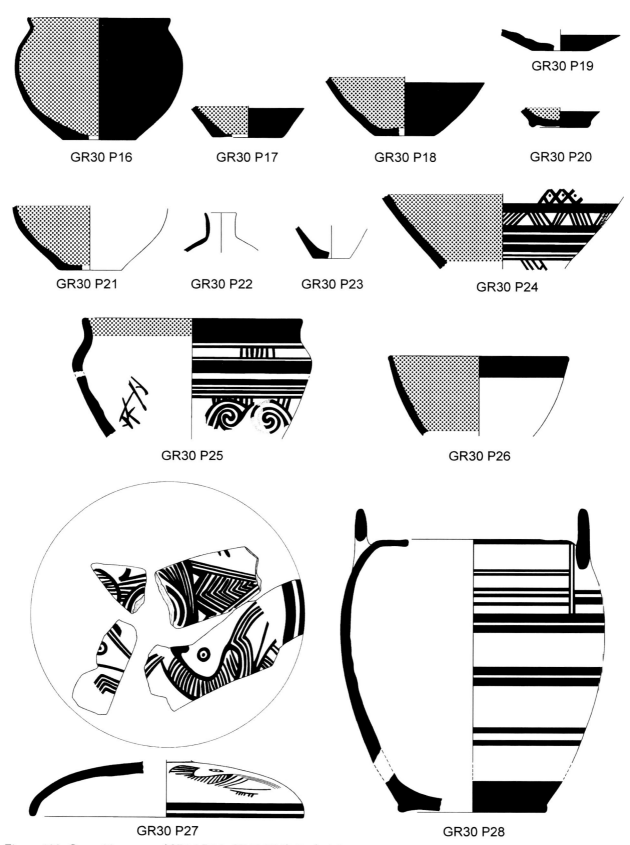

GR30 P16

GR30 P17

GR30 P18

GR30 P19

GR30 P20

GR30 P21

GR30 P22

GR30 P23

GR30 P24

GR30 P25

GR30 P26

GR30 P27

GR30 P28

Figure 139. Grave 30: pottery (**GR30 P16–GR30 P28**). Scale 1:3.

FIGURE 140

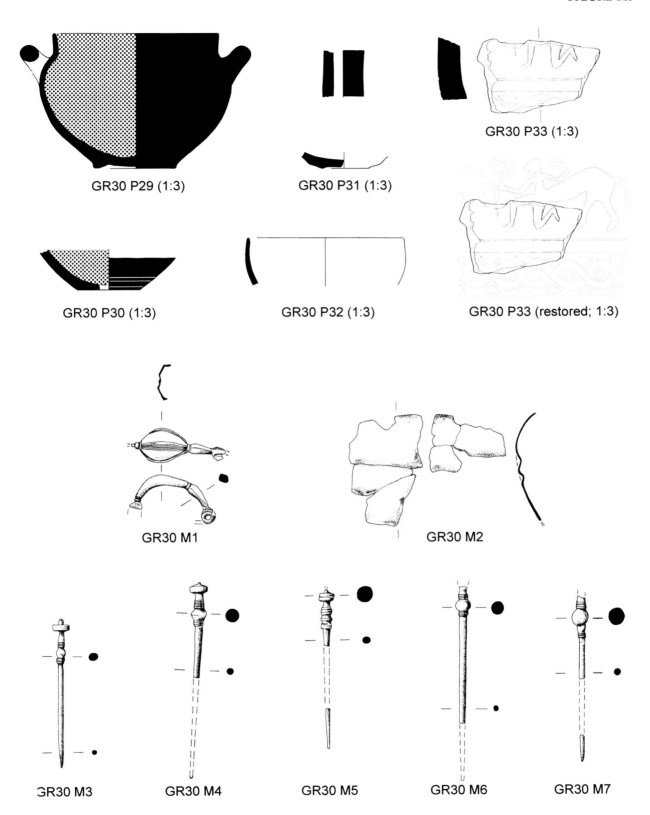

GR30 P29 (1:3)

GR30 P31 (1:3)

GR30 P33 (1:3)

GR30 P30 (1:3)

GR30 P32 (1:3)

GR30 P33 (restored; 1:3)

GR30 M1

GR30 M2

GR30 M3

GR30 M4

GR30 M5

GR30 M6

GR30 M7

Figure 140. Grave 30: pottery (**GR30 P29–GR30 P33**), bronze fibula (**GR30 M1**) and sheeting (**GR30 M2**), and iron pins (**GR30 M3–GR30 M7**). Scale 1:2 unless otherwise indicated.

FIGURE 141

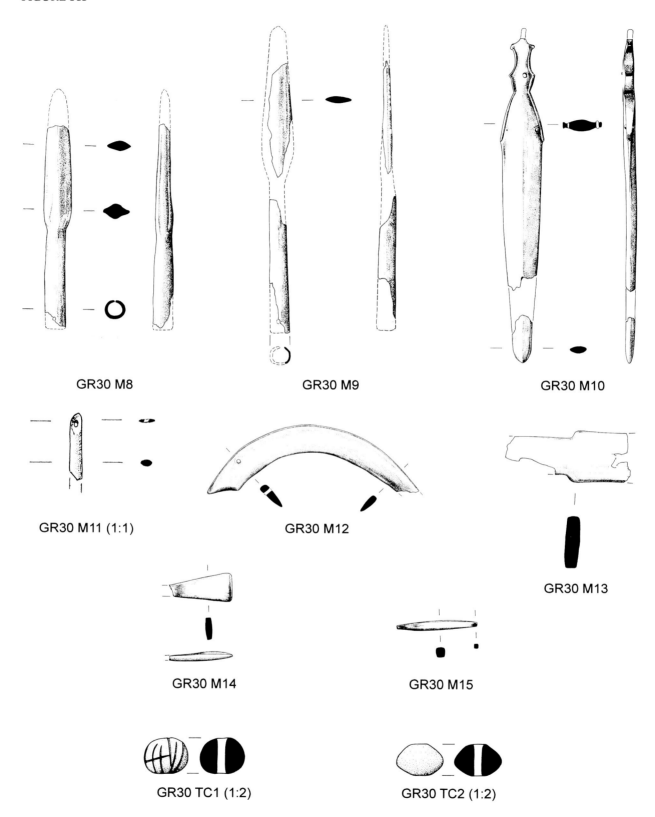

GR30 M8

GR30 M9

GR30 M10

GR30 M11 (1:1)

GR30 M12

GR30 M13

GR30 M14

GR30 M15

GR30 TC1 (1:2)

GR30 TC2 (1:2)

Figure 141. Grave 30: iron spearheads (**GR30 M8**, **GR30 M9**), dagger (**GR30 M10**), needle (**GR30 M11**), sickle (**GR30 M12**), axe-head (**GR30 M13**), chisel (**GR30 M14**), and tool (**GR30 M15**); and terracotta beads (**GR30 TC1**, **GR30 TC2**). Scale 1:3 unless otherwise indicated.

FIGURE 142

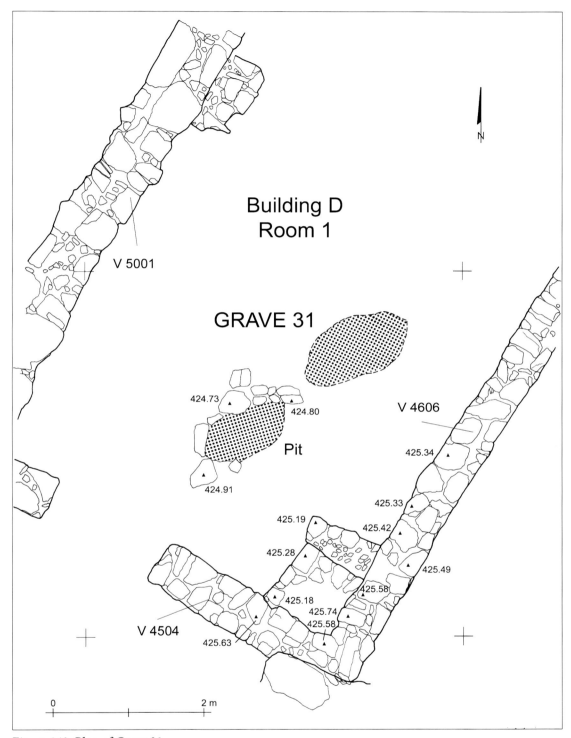

Figure 142. Plan of Grave 31.

FIGURE 143

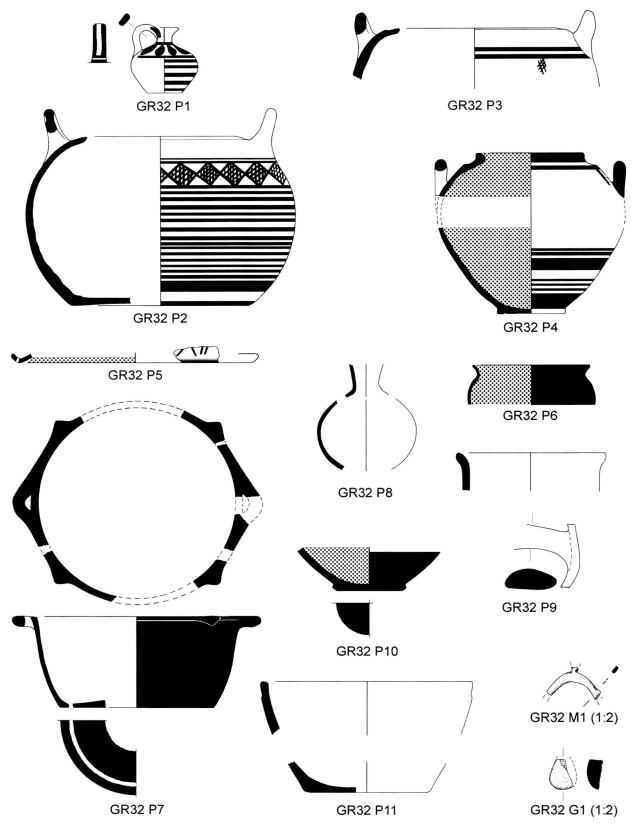

Figure 143. Grave 32: pottery (**GR32 P1–GR32 P11**), bronze fibula (**GR32 M1**), and glass bead (**GR32 G1**). Scale 1:3 unless otherwise indicated.

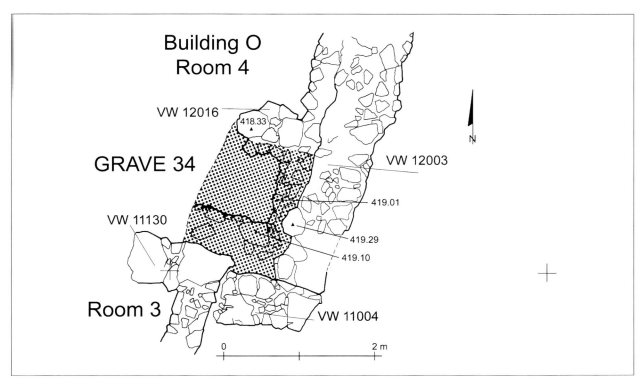

Figure 144. Plan of Grave 34.

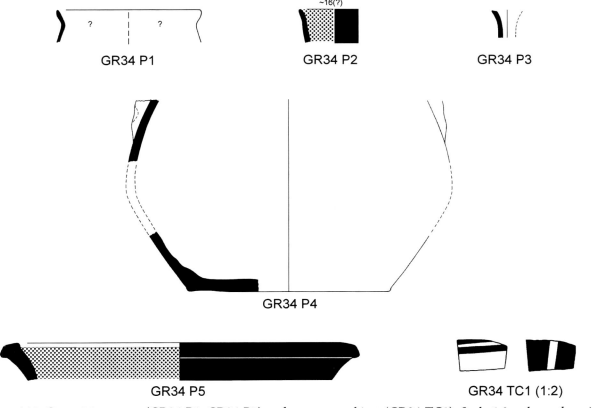

Figure 145. Grave 34: pottery (**GR34 P1–GR34 P5**) and terracotta object (**GR34 TC1**). Scale 1:3 unless otherwise indicated.

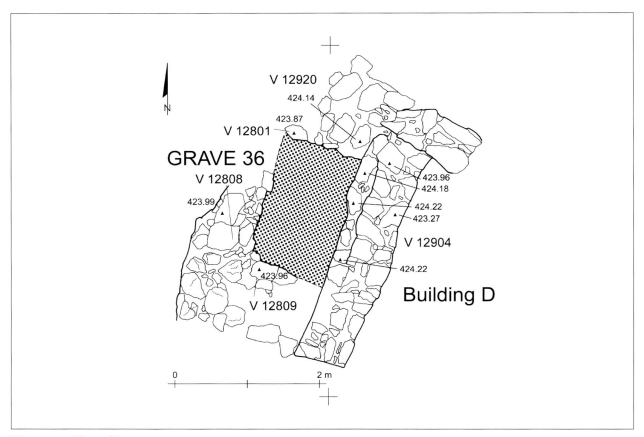

Figure 146. Plan of Grave 36.

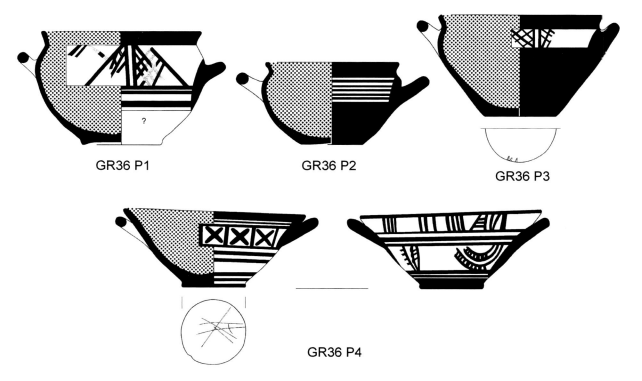

Figure 147. Grave 36: pottery (**GR36 P1–GR36 P4**). Scale 1:3.

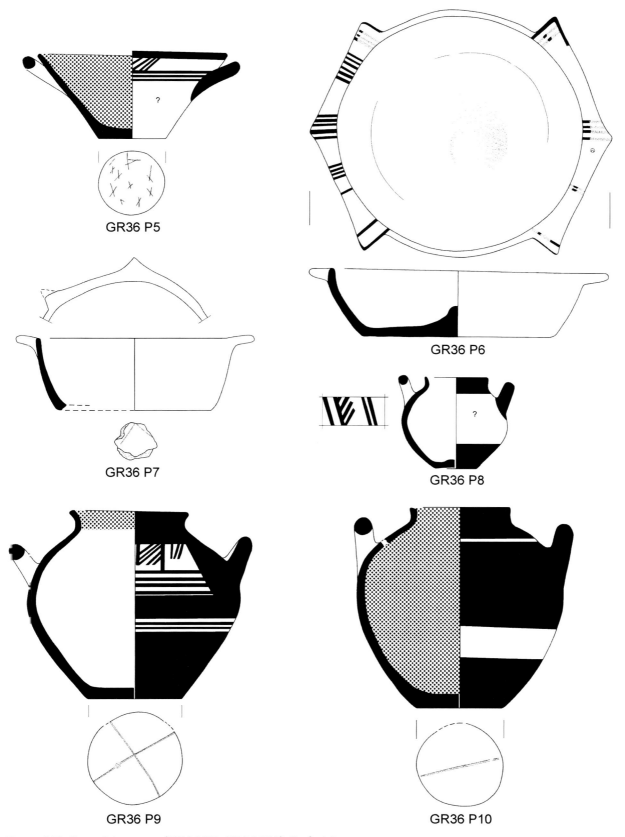

FIGURE 148

GR36 P5

GR36 P6

GR36 P7

GR36 P8

GR36 P9

GR36 P10

Figure 148. Grave 36: pottery (**GR36 P5–GR36 P10**). Scale 1:3.

FIGURE 149

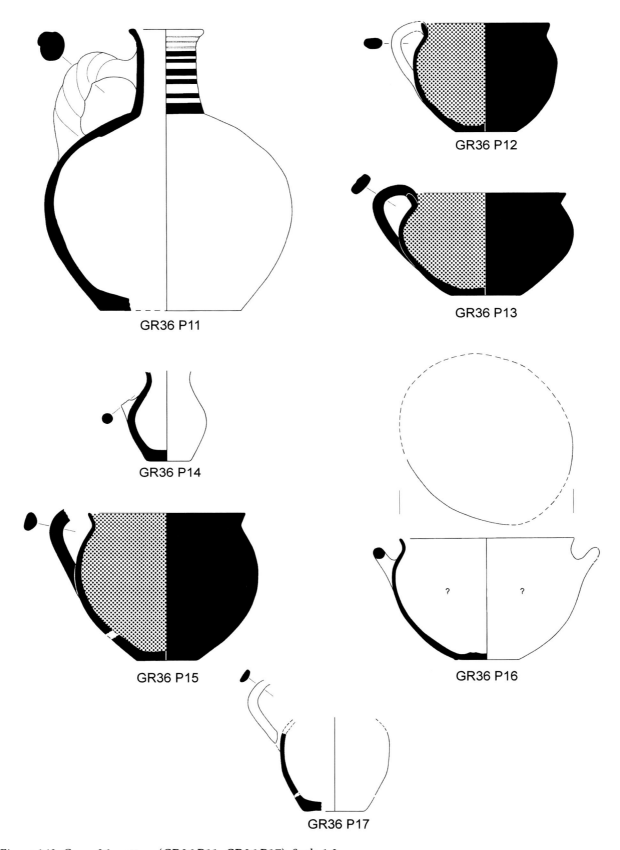

Figure 149. Grave 36: pottery (**GR36 P11–GR36 P17**). Scale 1:3.

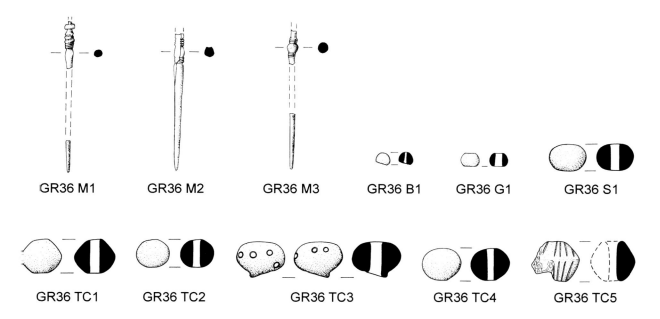

GR36 M1   GR36 M2   GR36 M3   GR36 B1   GR36 G1   GR36 S1

GR36 TC1   GR36 TC2   GR36 TC3   GR36 TC4   GR36 TC5

Figure 150. Grave 36: iron pins (**GR36 M1–GR36 M3**); beads of various materials: ivory (**GR36 B1**), glass (**GR36 G1**), rock crystal (**GR36 S1**), terracotta (**GR36 TC1–GR36 TC5**). Scale 1:2.

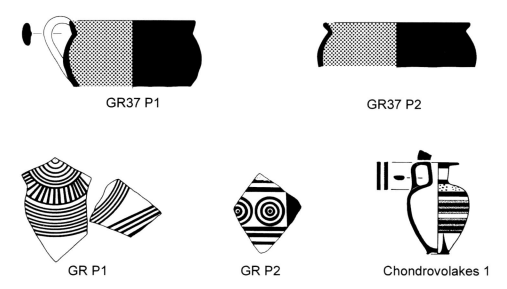

GR37 P1   GR37 P2

GR P1   GR P2   Chondrovolakes 1

Figure 151. Pottery from Grave 37 (**GR37 P1**, **GR37 P2**), surface finds not associated with any particular grave (**GR P1**, **GR P2**), and aryballos from Chondrovolakes (**Chondrovolakes 1**). Scale 1:3.

FIGURE 152

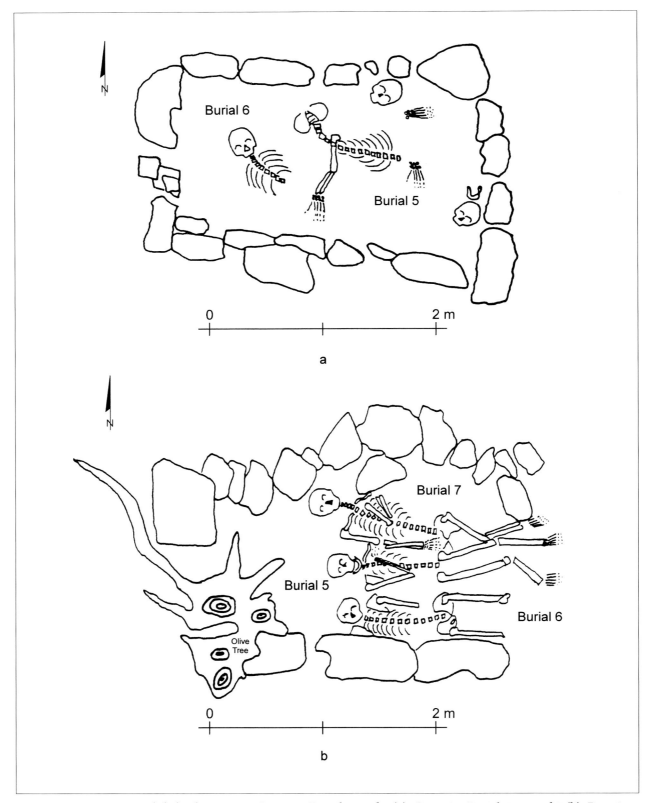

Figure 152. Reconstructed skeletal positions: Grave 12, Burials 5 and 6 (a); Grave 21, Burials 5, 6, and 7 (b). Drawings T. Faulkner.

FIGURE 153

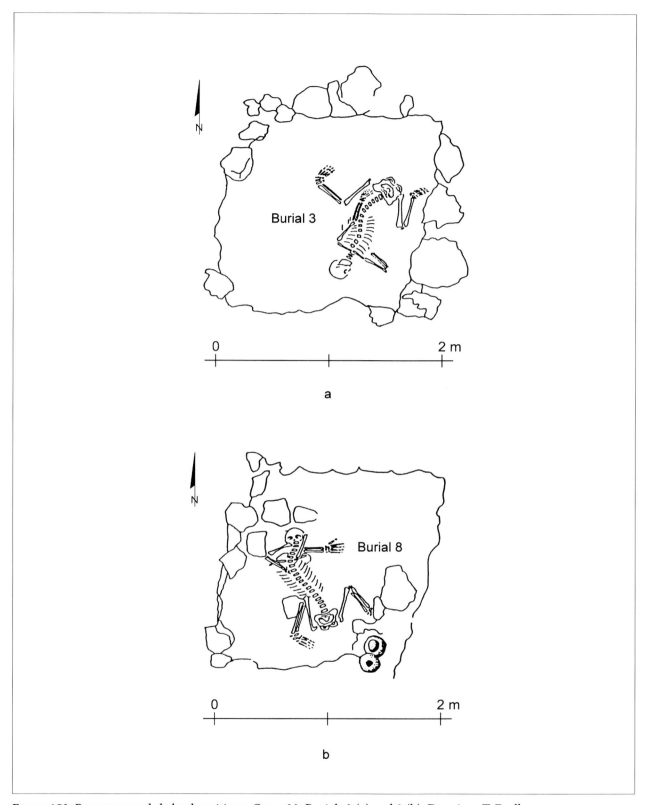

F gure 153. Reconstructed skeletal positions: Grave 28, Burials 3 (a) and 8 (b). Drawings T. Faulkner.

FIGURE 154

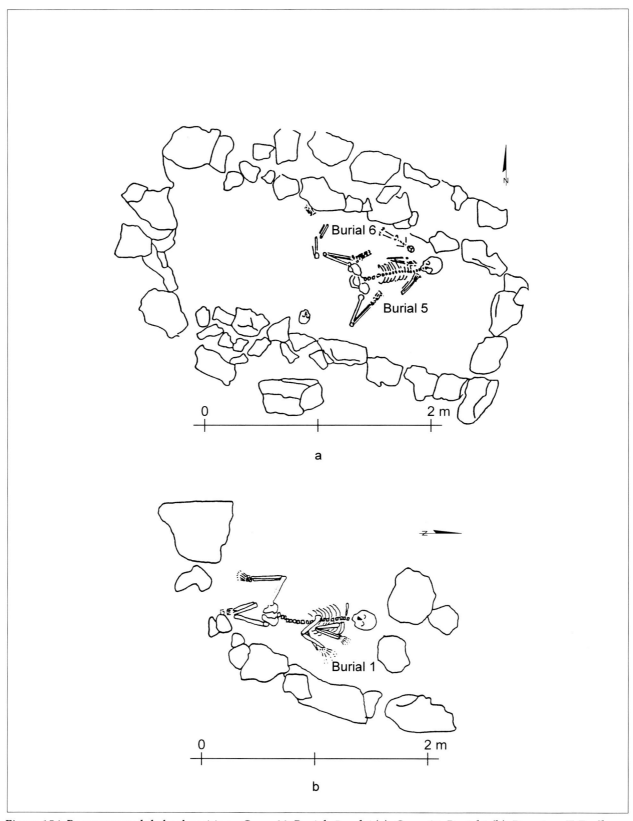

Figure 154. Reconstructed skeletal positions: Grave 30, Burials 5 and 6 (a); Grave 34, Burial 1 (b). Drawings T. Faulkner.

FIGURE 155

```
                KAVOUSI GRAVES DATA            GRAVE_____  BURIAL_____    LETTER_____

GRAVE_____  BURIAL_____  LETTER_____      FRONTAL CREST_____  TEMP SQUAMA_____
AREA_____  TRENCH_____  EXCAVATOR_____      FRONTAL SQUAMA_____  MASTIOD_____
LOCI_____      FRONTAL ORBIT_____  PETROUS_____
TOTAL_____  COMMINGLE_____      PARIETAL SAGIT_____  TEMP ZYG BAS_____
LOCATION_____  DATE_____      PARIETAL BREGMA_____  TEMP ZYG PROC_____
STRUCTURE_____  LONG AXIS_____  TYPE_____      PARIETAL OTHER_____  ZYG FRONTAL_____
DEPOSITION_____  CONTAINER_____      OCCIPITAL SQUAMA_____  ZYG TEMP PROC_____
POSITION_____HEAD_____      OCCIPITAL LATERL_____  ZYG MAX PROC_____
WEAPONS                                     OCCIPITAL BASAL_____

POTTERY                                     MAX NASAL_____  TOOTH CROWNS_____
                                            MAX ALVEOL_____
BRONZE                                      MAX BODY_____  TOOTH ROOTS SGL_____
                                            NASAL_____
TOOLS                                       MAN CONDYLE_____  TOOTH ROOTS DBL_____
                                            MAN RAM/GON_____
OTHER GIFTS                                 MAN CORANOID_____  TOOTH ROOTS MOLAR_____
                                            MAN ALVEOL_____
AGE_____                                MAN SYMPH_____  CARIES_____

                                            CLAV SHAFT_____  HUM HEAD_____
                                            CLAV LAT_____  HUM SHAFT_____
SEX_____                                CLAV MED_____  HUM DIST_____
                                            SCAP SPINE_____  RAD HEAD_____
                                            SCAP CORAC_____  RAD TUBER_____
                                            SCAP ACROM_____  RAD SHAFT_____
                                            SCAP LATERAL_____  RAD DIST_____
MNI_____
                                            ULNA NOTCH_____  CARPALS_____
                                            ULNA SHAFT_____  METACARP_____
                                            ULNA DIST_____  PHALANGES_____
PATHOLOGY
                                            STERNUM_____  THORACIC_____
                                            RIB HEADS_____  LUMBAR_____
                                            RIB FRAGS_____  UNID BODY_____
                                            ATLAS_____  SACRUM_____
ANOMALY                                     AXIS_____
                                            OTHER CERV_____

                                            ILIUM_____  FEM HEAD_____
CREMATION                                   ISCHIUM_____  FEM NECK_____
                                            PUBIS_____  TROCHANTER_____
                                            PUB SYMPH_____  SHAFT FRAGS_____
                                            SCIATIC_____  DIST FEMUR_____

                                            TIBIA PROX_____  PATELLA_____
MUNSEL_____     TIBIA DIST_____  TALUS_____
                                            TIBIA SHAFT_____  CALCANEUS_____
                                            FIB PROX_____  OTHER TARSAL_____
                                            FIB DIST_____  METATARSAL_____
                                            FIB SHAFT_____  PHALANGES_____
```

Figure 155. Specialized recording form for cremation burials.

FIGURE 156

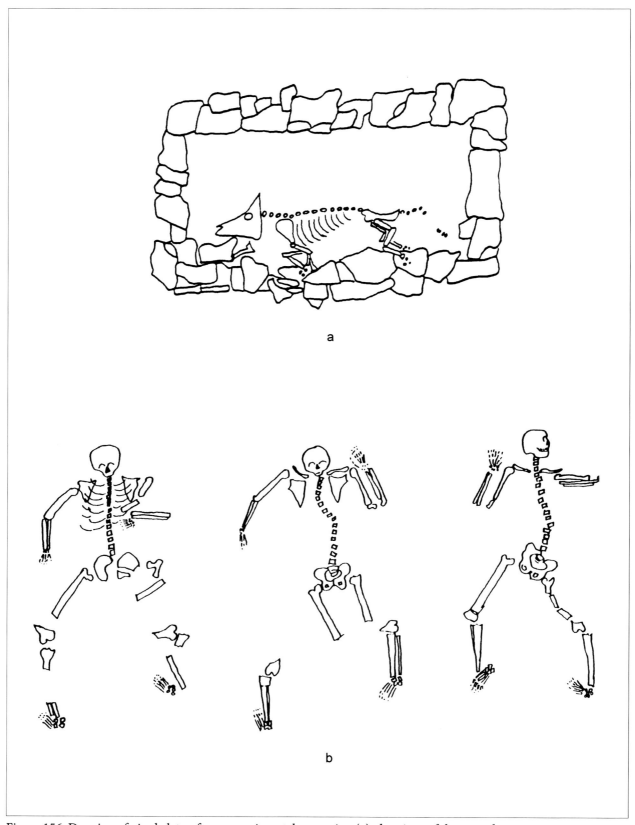

Figure 156. Drawing of pig skeleton from experimental cremation (a); drawings of three modern mortuary cremations (b). Not to scale. Drawings T. Faulkner.

FIGURE 157

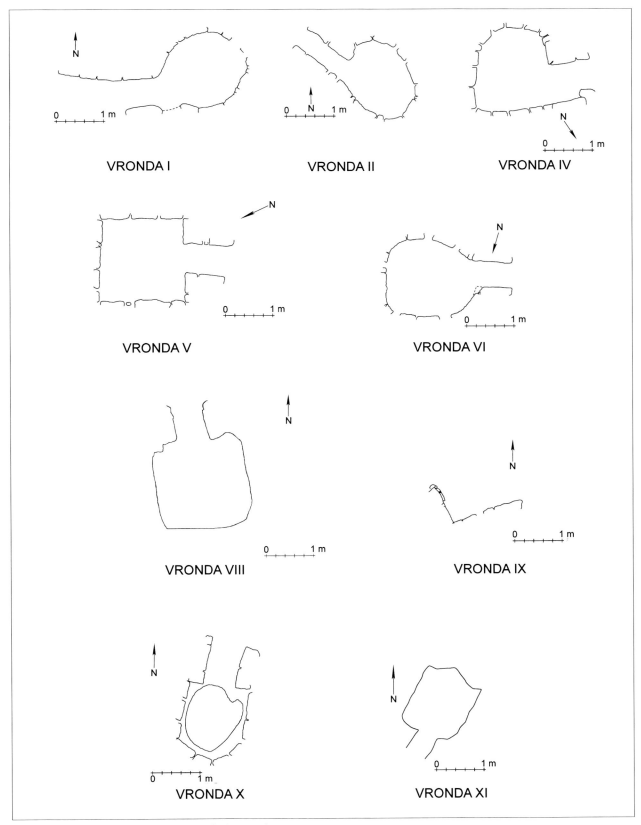

Figure 157. Ground plans of Vronda tholos tombs.

FIGURE 158

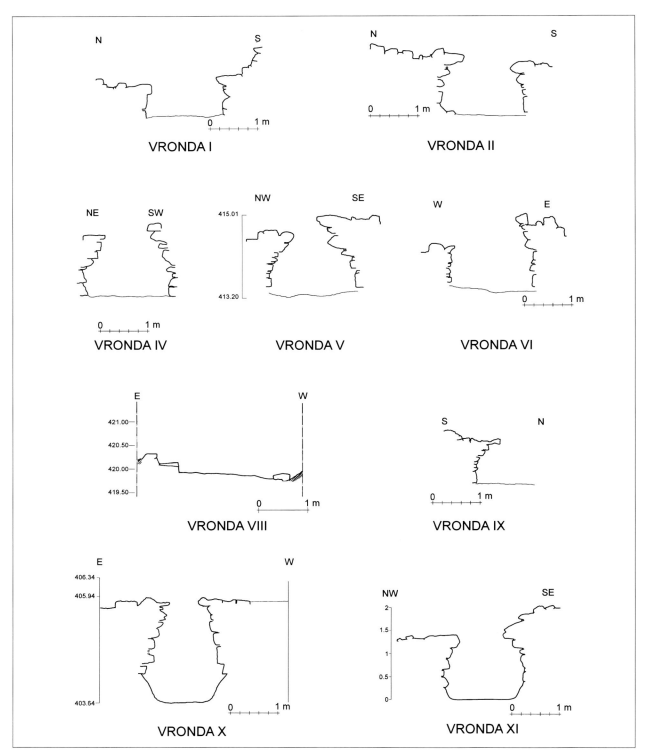

Figure 158. Sections of Vronda tholos tombs.

FIGURE 159

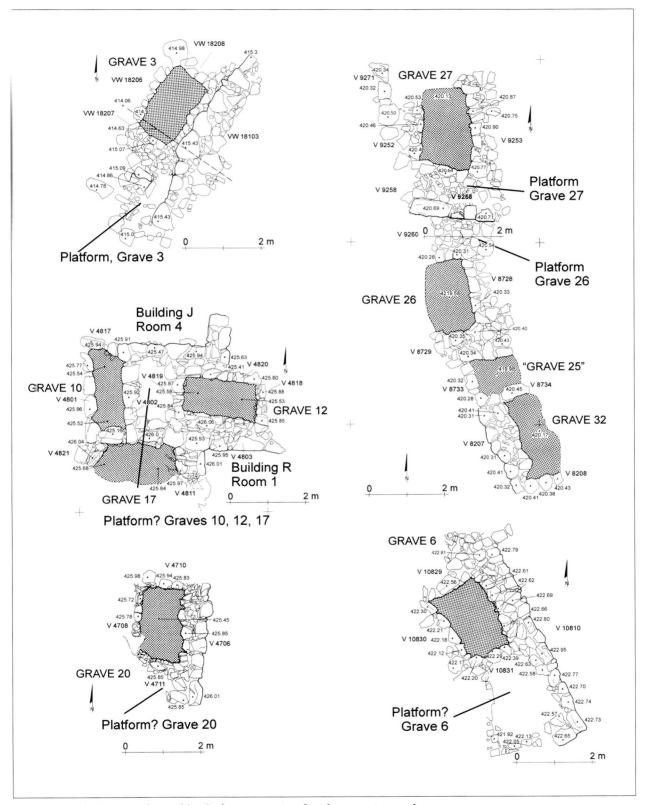

Figure 159. Platforms and possible platforms associated with cremation enclosures.

FIGURE 160

Figure 160. Decorated cups: (a) **IV P1**, (b) Type 1 (**GR3 P3**), (c) Type 2 (**GR3 P2**), (d) Type 3 (**GR1 P1**), (e) Type 4 (**GR12 P1**); monochrome cups: (f) **IX P29**, (g) **IX P31**, (h) Type 1 (**GR9 P55**), (i) Type 2a (**GR9 P18**), (j, k) Type 3a (**GR6 P13**, **GR36 P13**), (l, m) Type 3b (**GR9 P14**, **GR3 P7**), (n, o) Type 3c (**GR9 P15**, **GR26 P7**), (p) Type 3d (**GR21 P11**), (q) Type 4 (**GR30 P6**), (r) Type 5 (**GR9 P51**). Scale 1:4.

FIGURE 161

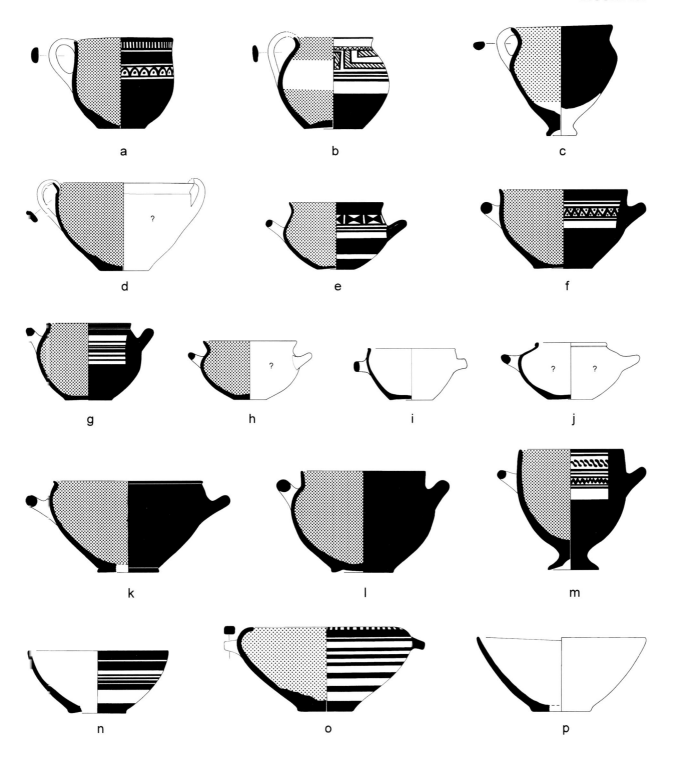

Figure 161. Mug-like cups: (a) Type 1 (**GR3 P1**), (b) Type 2 (**GR16 P3**); footed cup: (c) **IX P2**; kantharos: (d) **GR5 P11**; decorated skyphoi: (e) **GR12 P5**, (f) **GR19 P2**, (g) **GR19 P3**; monochrome skyphoi: (h) **GR26 P9**, (i) **GR26 P13**, (j) **GR26 P8**, (k) **GR4 P15**, (l) **GR30 P29**; stemmed skyphos: (m) **GR6 P3**; bowls: (n) **IX P5**, (o) **VII P1**, (p) **GR3 P20**. Scale 1:4.

FIGURE 162

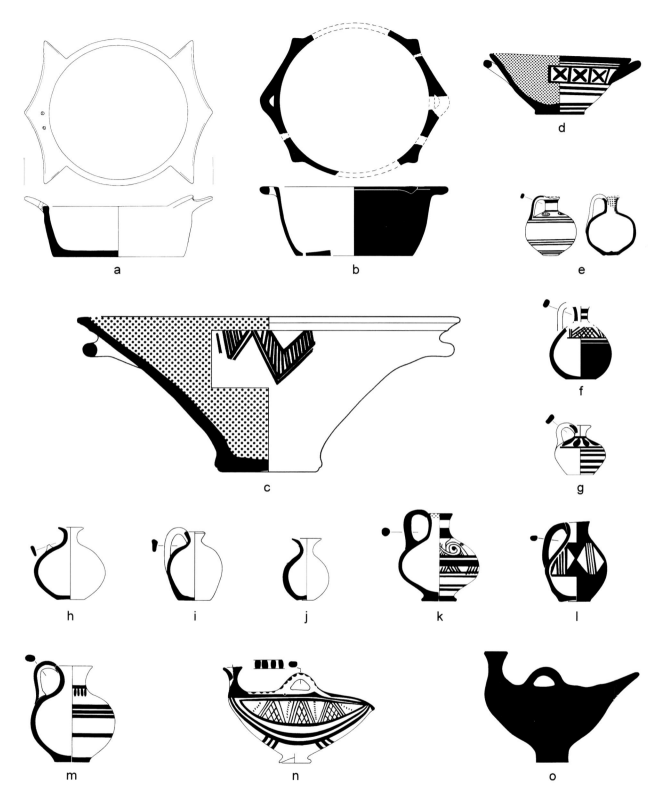

Figure 162. Tray: (a) **GR12 P27**; lekanis: (b) **GR32 P7**; kalathoi: (c) Type 1 (**GR12 P9**), (d) Type 2 (**GR36 P4**); decorated aryballoi: (e) with circles (**GR12 P13**), (f) crosshatched triangles (**GR30 P2**), (g) tongue pattern (**GR32 P1**); plain aryballoi: (h) Type 1 (**GR9 P31**), (i) Type 2 (**GR3 P15**), (j) Type 3 (**GR17 P7**); juglets: (k) **IV P3**, (l) **IX P12**, (m) **IX P13**; bird askoi: (n) **IV P7**, (o) **IX P53**. Scale 1:4.

FIGURE 163

Figure 163. Bell krater: (a) **GR12 P11**; krater: (b) **GR12 P12**; pedestaled kraters: (c) **GR27 P4**, (d) (**GR12 P41**); (ε) small krater: **GR4 P16**; (f) krater/basin: **GR6 P27**. Scale 1:6.

FIGURE 164

Figure 164. Stirrup jars: (a) **VIII P1**, (b) **IV P4**, (c) **IX P10**; lentoid flasks: (d) **II P1**, (e) **IV P8**; flask: (f) **GR3 P18**; lekythoi: (g) **IV P2**, (h) **GR17 P2**, (i) **GR36 P11**, (j) **GR4 P20**. Scale 1:4.

FIGURE 165

Figure 165. Jugs: (a) **IX P27**, (b) **IX P15**, (c) **VII P2**, (d) **GR6 P6**, (e) **GR28 P20**; wide-mouthed jugs: (f) **GR9 P6**, (g) **GR3 P4**; small oinochoai: (h) **IX P18**, (i) **IX P20**, (j) **IX P21**, (k) **GR12 P14**. Scale 1:4.

FIGURE 166

Figure 166. Large oinochoai: (a) **IX P22**, (b) **IX P49**, (c) **GR26 P23**; jug or oinochoe: (d) **GR9 P37**; hydria: (e) **GR26 P20**. Scale 1:4.

FIGURE 167

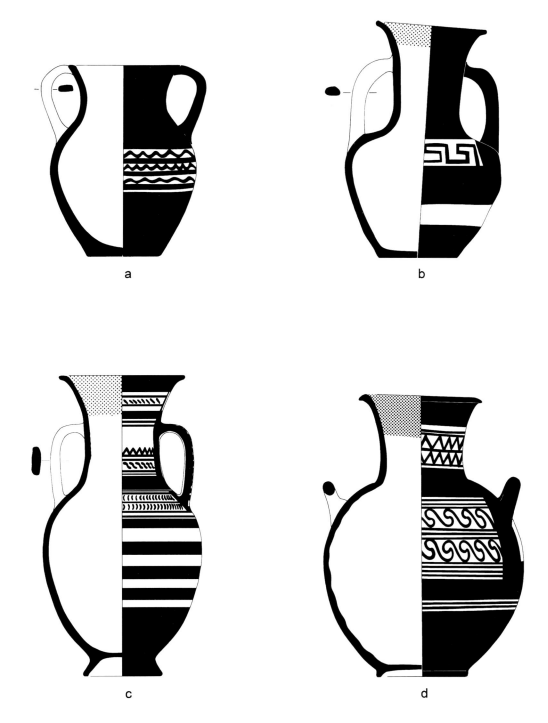

Figure 167. Small amphorae: (a) **IV P10**, (b) **IX P58**, (c) **GR16 P18**, (d) **GR28 P3**. Scale 1:4.

FIGURE 168

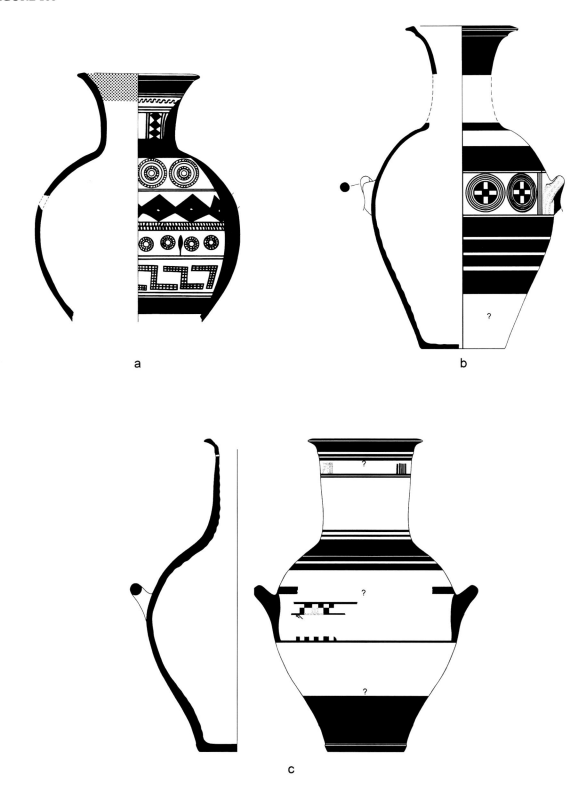

Figure 168. Large amphorae: (a) **GR9 P38**, (b) **GR9 P39**, (c) **GR20 P7**. Scale 1:8.

FIGURE 169

Figure 169. Small necked jars: (a) **IX P7**, (b) (**GR5 P2**), (c) (**GR3 P5**); large necked jars: (d) **IX P8**, (e) **IV P9**, (f) **VII P4**, (g) Type 1a (**GR5 P3**), (h) Type 1a (**GR28 P22**), (i) Type 1b baggy (**GR9 P36**), (j) Type 1b ovoid (**GR36 P9**), (k) Type 2 (**GR12 P19**). Scale 1:4.

FIGURE 170

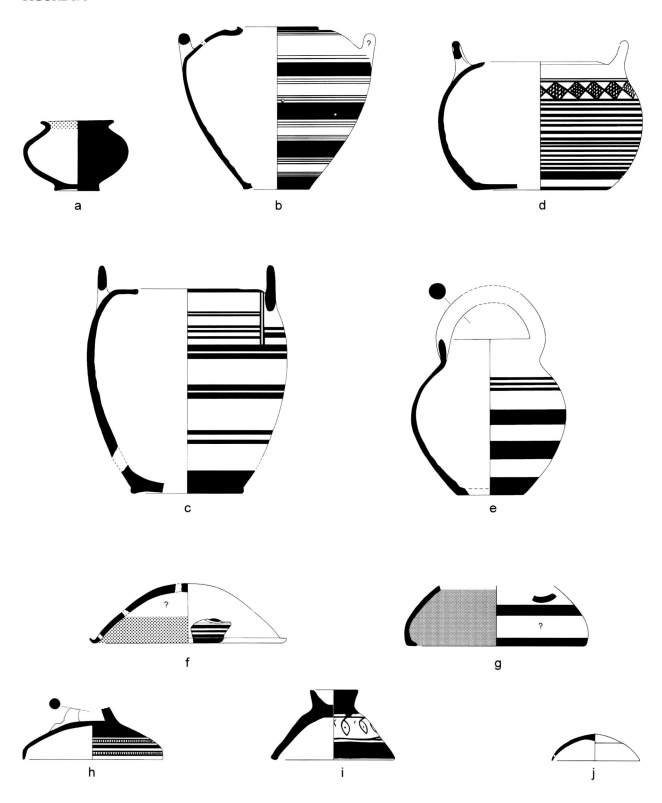

Figure 170. Pyxides: (a) **IX P45**, (b) **GR17 P4**, (c) **GR30 P28**, (d) **GR32 P2**; basket vase: (e) **GR9 P11**; lids: (f) **GR4 P24**, (g) **GR20 P4**, (h) **GR30 P3**, (i) **GR28 P19**, (j) **GR26 P17**. Scale 1:4.

FIGURE 171

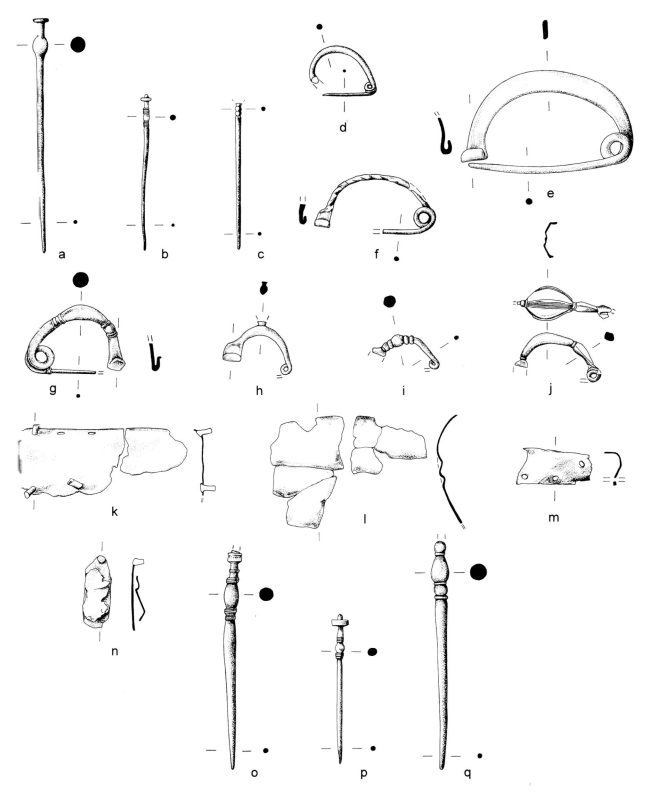

Figure 171. Bronze pins: (a) Type 1 (**GR12 M1**), (b) Type 2 (**GR4 M1**), (c) Type 3 (**GR3 M1**); bronze fibulae: (d) Type 1a (**GR26 M1**), (e) Type 1b (**GR1 M1**), (f) Type 1c (**GR20 M1**), (g) Type 2 (**GR9 M2**), (h) Type 3 (**GR28 M1**), (i) Type 4 (**GR23 M2**), (j) Type 5 (**GR30 M1**); bronze sheeting: (k) **GR9 M6**, (l) **GR30 M2**, (m) **GR17 M3**, (n) **GR20 M4**; iron pins: (o) Type 1 (**GR16 M2**), (p) Type 2 (**GR30 M3**), (q) Type 3 (**GR3 M3**). Scale 1:2.

FIGURE 172

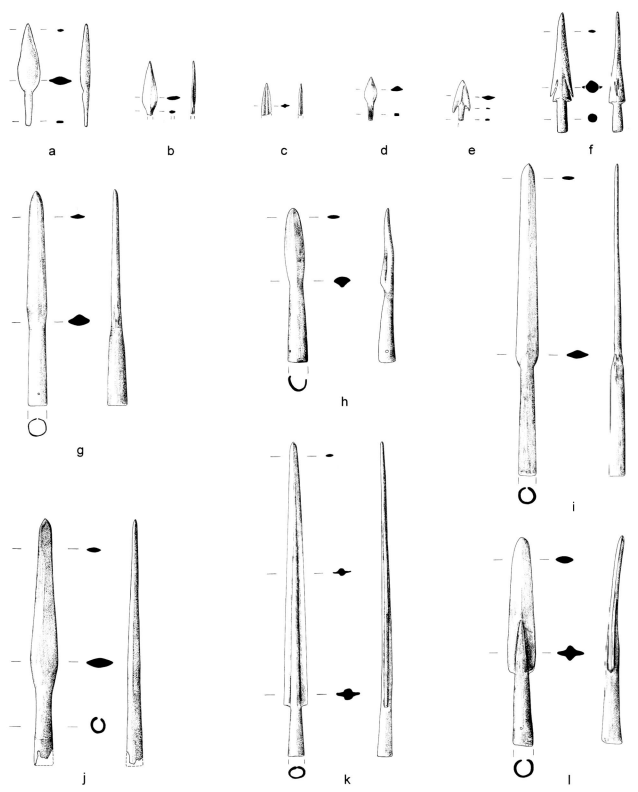

Figure 172. Iron arrowheads: (a) Type 1a (**GR12 M5**), (b) Type 1b (**GR12 M11**), (c) Type 1c (**GR12 M19**), (d) Type 2 (**GR1 M14**), (e) Type 3 (**GR1 M3**), (f) Type 4 (**GR12 M9**); iron spearheads: (g) Type 1a long (**GR16 M4**), (h) Type 1a short (**GR28 M3**), (i) Type 1b (**GR26 M3**), (j) Type 2 (**GR5 M2**), (k) Type 3 long (**GR9 M14**), (l) Type 4 (**GR9 M18**). Scale 1:4.

FIGURE 173

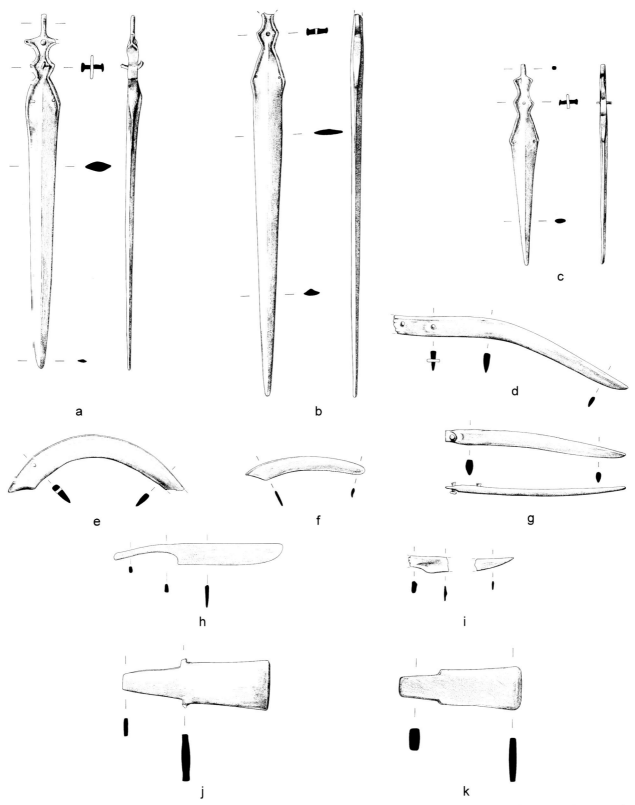

F gure 173. Iron dirks: (a) **GR9 M33**, (b) **GR9 M31**; iron dagger: (c) **GR9 M30**; iron knives: (d) Type 1 (**GR5 M7**), (e) Type 2a (**GR30 M12**), (f) Type 2b (**GR9 M38**), (g) Type 3 (**GR20 M9**), (h) Type 4 (**GR9 M35**), (i) Type 5 (**GR5 M9**); iron axes: (j) tanged (**GR6 M10**), (k) square shoulders (**GR9 M41**). Scale 1:4.

FIGURE 174

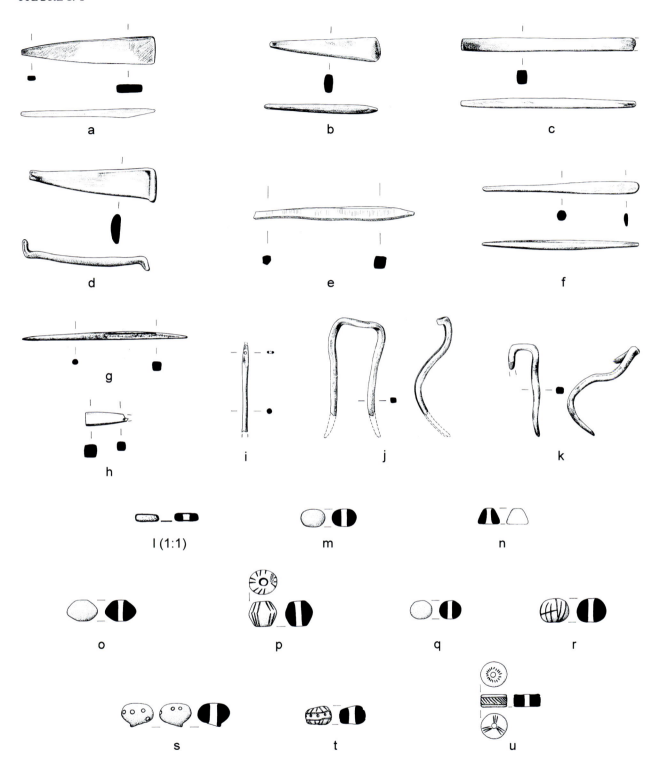

Figure 174. Iron chisels: (a) Type 1 with one bevel (**GR6 M11**), (b) Type 1 with two bevels (**GR12 M41**), (c) Type 2 (**GR28 M6**); iron tools: (d) scraper (**GR9 M43**), (e) file (**GR6 M15**), (f) spatulate tool (**GR12 M43**), (g) awl (**GR9 M47**), (h) punch (**GR6 M19**), (i) needle (**GR16 M3**), (j) fleshhook (**GR9 M55**), (k) fleshhook (**GR12 M45**); stone beads: (l) disk (**GR20 S1**), (m) rock crystal (**GR36 S1**), (n) conical (**GR9 S1**); terracotta beads: (o) biconical (**GR30 TC2**), (p) biconical incised (**GR3 TC1**), (q) globular (**GR36 TC2**), (r) incised globular (**GR30 TC1**), (s) impressed globular (**GR36 TC3**), (t) incised depressed globular (**GR12 TC1**), (u) incised disk (**GR26 TC1**). Scale 1:3 unless otherwise stated.

FIGURE 175

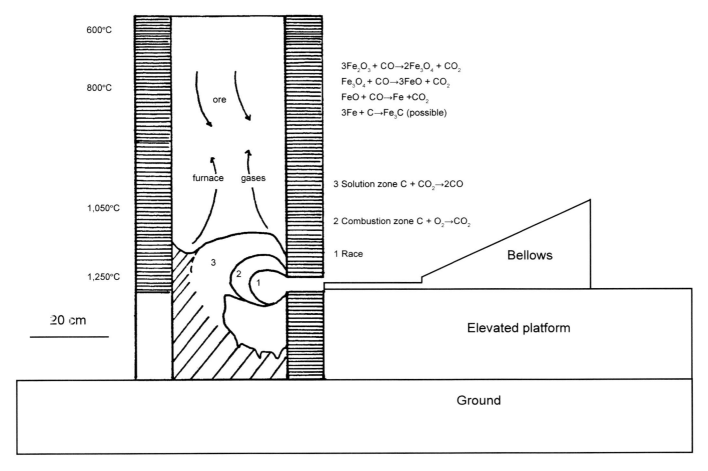

Figure 175. Schematic representation of a vertical section through the bloomery furnace showing the temperature scale (left) and different zones of heating with appropriate conditions within. The equations to the right show the gradual reduction of different iron oxides under the influence of carbon monoxide gas. In each case, carbon dioxide is formed. Bloomery iron making is about knowing how to empirically control the "right" ratio between the two gases. After Photos 1987, fig 3.4.1.

Plates

PLATE 1

Plate 1A. View of the Kavousi area from Pacheia Ammos; view from west. Photo K.T. Glowacki.

Plate 1B. View of Vronda from Azoria; view from northeast. Photo K.T. Glowacki.

PLATE 2

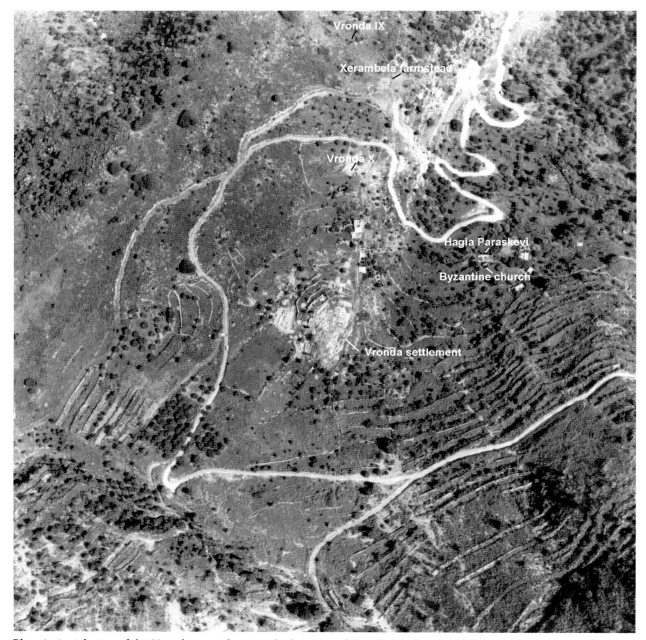

Plate 2. Aerial view of the Vronda area, showing the location of Vronda Tholos Tombs IX and X, the Xerambela farmstead, and the Byzantine church (north at top). Photo J. Wilson and E. Myers.

PLATE 3

Plate 3. Aerial view of the Vronda ridge (north at top). Photo J. Wilson and E. Myers.

PLATE 4

Plate 4A. Tomb I: top; view from southeast.

Plate 4B. Tomb I: stomion with blocking stones; view from west.

Plate 4C. Tomb I: stones piled over dromos; view from south.

PLATE 5

Plate 5A. Boyd's photograph of pottery from Tombs II, VII, and VIII (1901, pl. II).

Plate 5B. Tomb II: stomion; view from west.

PLATE 6

Plate 6A. Tomb II: stomion blocked with soil and stones; view from north-west.

Plate 6B. Tomb II: blocking stones in stomion; view from northwest.

Plate 6C. Tomb II: flat stones in pseudo-dromos; view from northwest.

PLATE 7

Plate 7A. Tomb II: stones piled over pseudo-dromos; view from north.

Plate 7B. Tomb II: lentoid flask (**II P1**).

Plate 7C. Boyd's photograph of pottery from Tomb IV (1901, pl. I).

PLATE 8

Plate 8A. Tomb IV: aerial view (north at top).

Plate 8B. Tomb IV: stomion and pseudo-dromos; view from northwest.

Plate 8C. Tomb IV: stones over pseudo-dromos; view from north.

PLATE 9

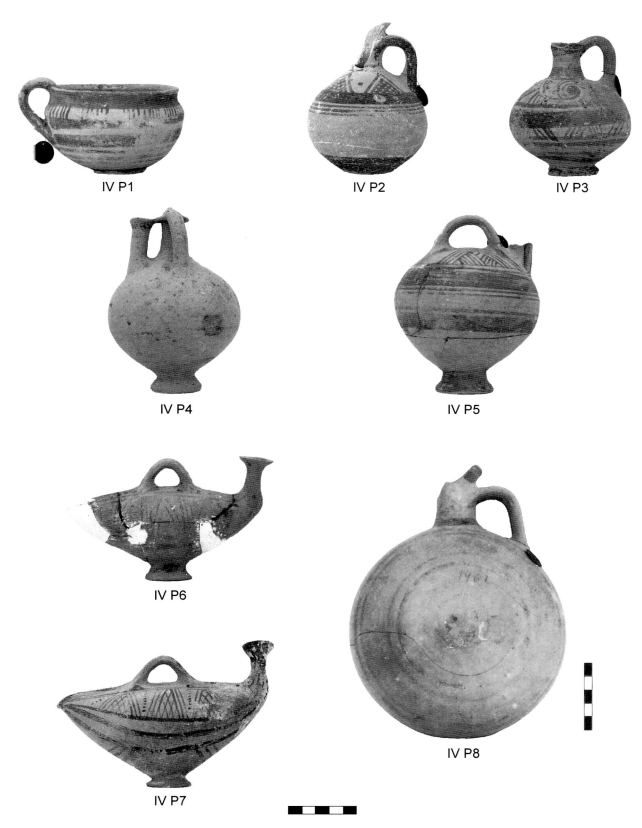

Plate 9. Tomb IV pottery: cup (**IV P1**), lekythos (**IV P2**), juglet (**IV P3**), stirrup jar (**IV P4**), askos (**IV P5**), bird askoi (**IV P6**, **IV P7**), and lentoid flask (**IV P8**).

PLATE 10

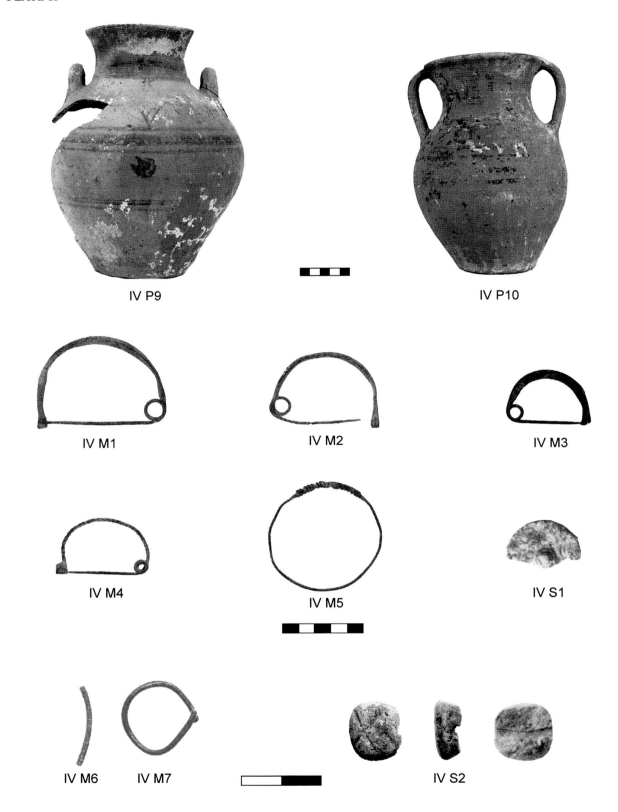

Plate 10. Tomb IV pottery and small finds: necked jar (**IV P9**), neck amphora (**IV P10**), bronze fibulae (**IV M1–IV M4**), bronze bracelet (**IV M5**), stone lid (**IV S1**; from area in front of tomb), bronze pin (**IV M6**), bronze ring (**IV M7**), and stone bead (**IV S2**; from Boyd's dump).

PLATE 11

Plate 11A. Tomb V: stomion and pseudo-dromos, cleaned; view from southwest.

Plate 11B. Tomb V: pithos (**V P3**).

Plate 11C. Tomb VI: stomion and pseudo-dromos, cleaned; view from southwest.

Plate 11D. Tomb VI: flat stones in pseudo-dromos; view from southwest.

PLATE 12

Plate 12A. Tomb VII: possible stomion; view from west.

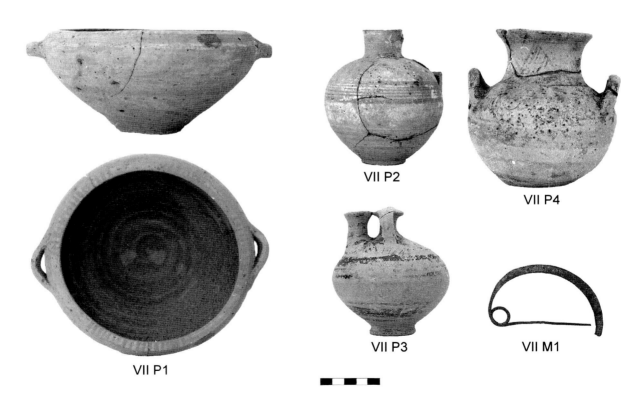

VII P1

VII P2

VII P4

VII P3

VII M1

Plate 12B. Tomb VII pottery and metal find: bowl (**VII P1**; exterior and interior), jug (**VII P2**), stirrup jar (**VII P3**), large necked jar (**VII P4**), and bronze fibula (**VII M1**).

PLATE 13

Plate 13A. Tomb VIII: aerial view (north at top).

Plate 13B. Tomb VIII: stomion with animal bones; view from north.

Plate 13C. Tomb VIII: stones over pseudo-dromos; view from southwest.

VIII M1   VIII P1   II-VII-VIII P1   II-VII-VIII P2

Plate 13D. Tomb VIII metal find and pottery: bronze pin (**VIII M1**) and stirrup jar (**VIII P1**); other pottery of uncertain provenience from Boyd's excavations: lentoid flask (**II-VII-VIII P1**) and oinochoe (**II-VII-VIII P2**).

PLATE 14

Plate 14A. Tomb IX: preserved corner; view from northwest.

IX P2

IX P4

IX P6

IX P7

IX P10

IX P11

IX P12

Plate 14B. Tomb IX pottery: footed cup (**IX P2**), footed two-handled cup (**IX P4**), bowl (**IX P6**), small necked jar (**IX P7**), stirrup jar (**IX P10**), lentoid flask (**IX P11**), and juglet (**IX P12**).

PLATE 15

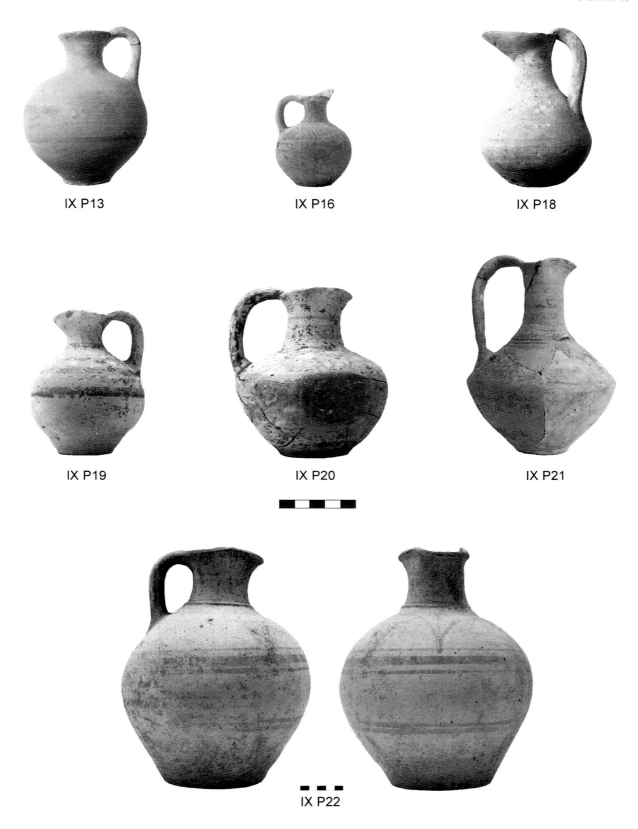

Plate 15. Tomb IX pottery: juglet (**IX P13**), small jug or oinochoe (**IX P16**), and oinochoai (**IX P18–IX P22** [two views]).

PLATE 16

IX P24

IX P27

IX P28

IX P29

IX P34

IX P42

IX P45

IX P50

IX P53

Plate 16. Tomb IX pottery: jug or oinochoe (**IX P24**), jug (**IX P27**), cups (**IX P28**, **IX P29**, **IX P50**), footed cup (**IX P34**), bowl (**IX P42**), pyxis (**IX P45**), and bird askos (**IX P53**).

PLATE 17

IX P58

IX P59

IX M1

IX M2　　IX M3　　IX M4　　IX M5　　IX M6　　IX M7

Plate 17. Tomb IX pottery and metal finds: neck amphora (**IX P58**), cup (**IX P59**), iron spearhead (**IX M1**), and iron knife fragments (**IX M2–IX M7**).

PLATE 18

Plate 18A. Tomb X; view from south.

Plate 18B. Tomb X: stomion; view from north.

Plate 18C. Tomb X: dog bones in interior pit.

PLATE 19

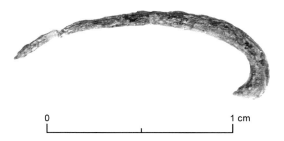

Plate 19A. Tomb X: bronze pin or fibula (**X M1**).

Plate 19B. Tomb XI: stomion and stones in pseudo-dromos; view from southeast.

Plate 19C. Tomb XI: top and interior; view from northeast.

PLATE 20

Plate 20A. Tomb XI: interior with stomion; view from northeast.

Plate 20B. Tomb XI: interior, showing wall construction; view from southeast.

Plate 20C. Pottery of uncertain provenience from Boyd's excavations in 1900: oinochoe or juglet (**Boyd P1**), stirrup jar (**Boyd P2**), krateriskos (**Boyd P3**), and juglet (**Boyd P4**).

PLATE 21

Plate 21A. Grave 1: northwest corner of enclosure after excavation; view from southeast.

Plate 21B. Grave 1: southwest extension, showing iron arrowheads on surface; view from southeast.

Plate 21C. Grave 1: southwest extension, close-up of iron arrowheads in situ.

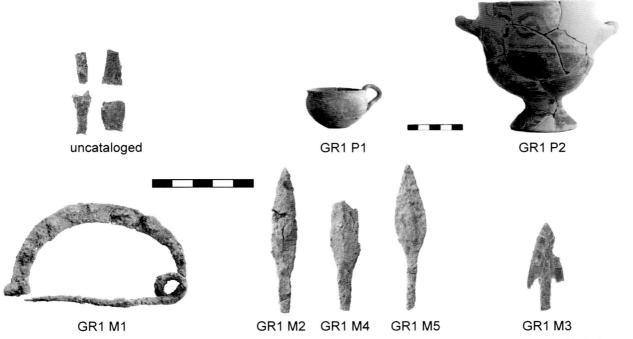

Plate 21D. Grave 1 finds: fragments of uncataloged arrowheads, cup (**GR1 P1**), skyphos (**GR1 P2**), bronze fibula (**GR1 M1**), and iron arrowheads (**GR1 M2–GR1 M5**). Photo **GR1 M3** C. Papanikolopoulos.

PLATE 22

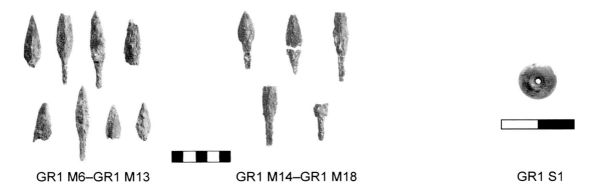

GR1 M6–GR1 M13   GR1 M14–GR1 M18   GR1 S1

Plate 22A. Grave 1 finds: iron arrowheads (**GR1 M6**–**GR1 M18**) and stone bead (**GR1 S1**).

Plate 22B. Grave 3: stone tumble over grave; view from south.

Plate 22C. Grave 3: stones within grave; view from southeast.

Plate 22D. Grave 3: cup (**GR3 P19**) and flask (**GR3 P18**) set in stones above grave.

Plate 22E. Grave 3: aerial view (north at top).

Plate 22F. Reconstructed crania from enclosure burials. Top row, left to right: Grave 12 Burial 5; Grave 17 Burial 1. Bottom row, left to right: Grave 21 Burial 4, 5, or 6; Grave 3 Burial 1; Grave 5 Burial 1.

PLATE 23

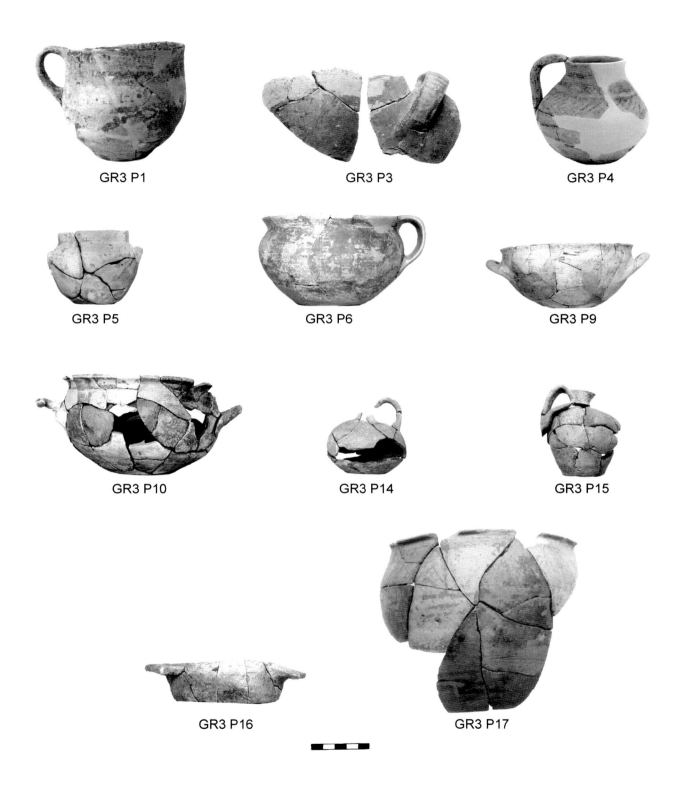

GR3 P1

GR3 P3

GR3 P4

GR3 P5

GR3 P6

GR3 P9

GR3 P10

GR3 P14

GR3 P15

GR3 P16

GR3 P17

Plate 23. Grave 3 pottery: cups (**GR3 P1**, **GR3 P3**, **GR3 P6**), wide-mouthed jug (**GR3 P4**), miniature necked jar (**GR3 P5**), skyphoi (**GR3 P9**, **GR3 P10**, **GR3 P17**), aryballoi (**GR3 P14**, **GR3 P15**), and tray (**GR3 P16**).

PLATE 24

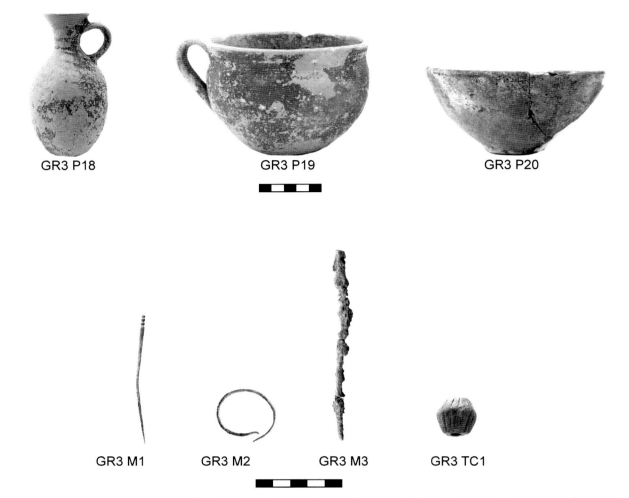

Plate 24A. Grave 3 pottery and small finds: flask (**GR3 P18**), cup (**GR3 P19**), bowl (**GR3 P20**), bronze pin (**GR3 M1**), bronze earring (**GR3 M2**), iron pin (**GR3 M3**), and terracotta bead (**GR3 TC**).

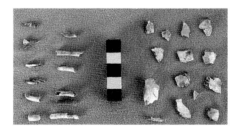

Plate 24B. Grave 4 Burial 2: bones of fetus.

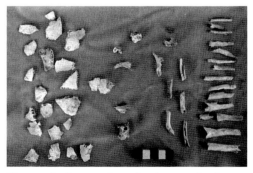

Plate 24C. Grave 4 Burial 3: bones of infant.

PLATE 25

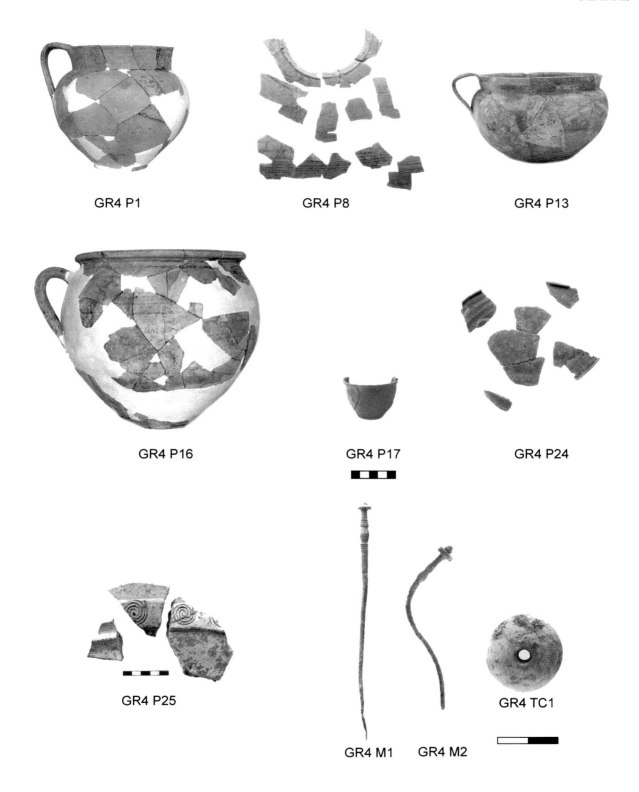

GR4 P1

GR4 P8

GR4 P13

GR4 P16

GR4 P17

GR4 P24

GR4 P25

GR4 M1

GR4 M2

GR4 TC1

Plate 25. Grave 4 pottery and small finds: cups (**GR4 P1**, **GR4 P13**, **GR4 P17**), pyxis (**GR4 P8**), krater (**GR4 P16**), lid (**GR4 P24**), pithos fragments (**GR4 P25**), bronze pins (**GR4 M1**, **GR4 M2**), and terracotta bead (**GR4 TC1**).

PLATE 26

Plate 26A. Grave 5 Burial 7 (inhumation); view from north.

Plate 26B. Grave 5: aerial view (north at top).

Plate 26C. Grave 5 after removal of burials; view from north.

Plate 26D. Grave 5 after removal of Burial 7; view from southeast.

Plate 26E. Area of Grave 5 showing stones before identification of grave; view from east.

Plate 26F. Grave 5 Burial 7: feet and legs in northeast corner.

PLATE 27

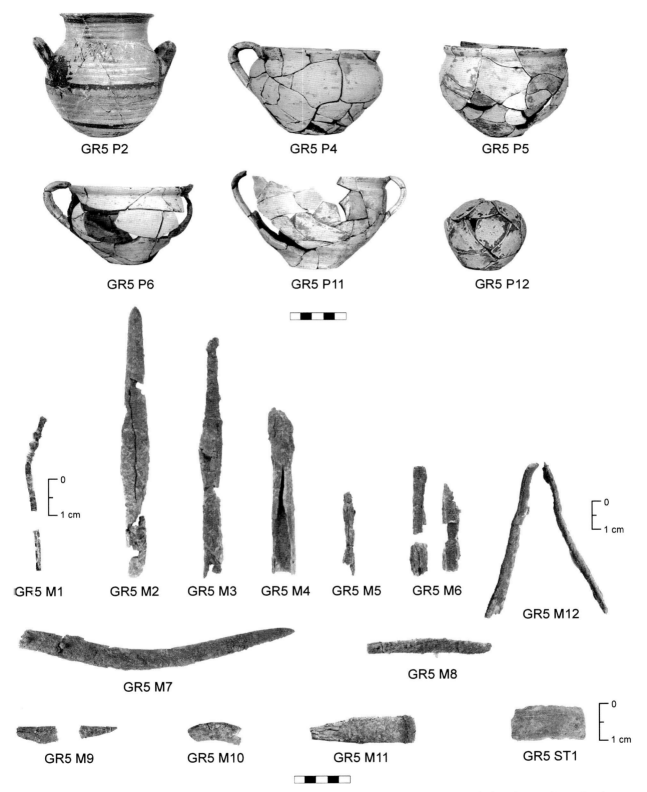

Plate 27. Grave 5 pottery and small finds: necked jar (**GR5 P2**), cups (**GR5 P4–GR5 P6**), kantharos (**GR5 P11**), aryballos (**GR5 P12**), bronze pin (**GR5 M1**), iron spearheads (**GR5 M2–GR5 M6**), iron knives (**GR5 M7–GR5 M9**), iron knife or sickle (**GR5 M10**), iron scraper (**GR5 M11**), iron tweezers (**GR5 M12**), and obsidian blade (**GR5 ST1**). Photo **GR5 M7** C. Papanikolopoulos.

PLATE 28

Plate 28A. Grave 6: hoard of iron tools at south end of enclosure; view from north.

Plate 28B. Grave 6; view from south.

Plate 28C. Grave 6: aerial view (north at top).

Plate 28D. Grave 6: stones within grave; view from southeast.

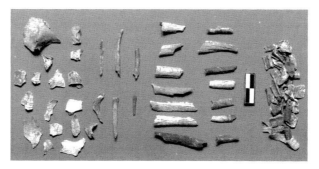

Plate 28E. Grave 6 Burial 2: bones of infant.

PLATE 29

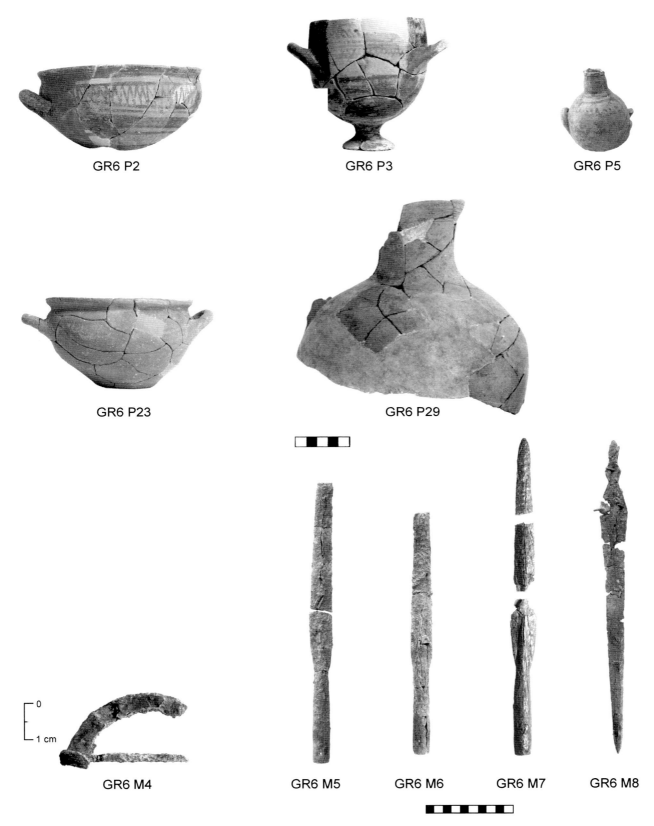

GR6 P2

GR6 P3

GR6 P5

GR6 P23

GR6 P29

GR6 M4

GR6 M5

GR6 M6

GR6 M7

GR6 M8

Plate 29. Grave 6 pottery and metal finds: skyphoi (**GR6 P2**, **GR6 P3**, **GR6 P23**), miniature amphora (**GR6 P5**), oino-choe (**GR6 P29**), iron fibula (**GR6 M4**), iron spearheads (**GR6 M5–GR6 M7**), and iron dagger/dirk (**GR6 M8**).

PLATE 30

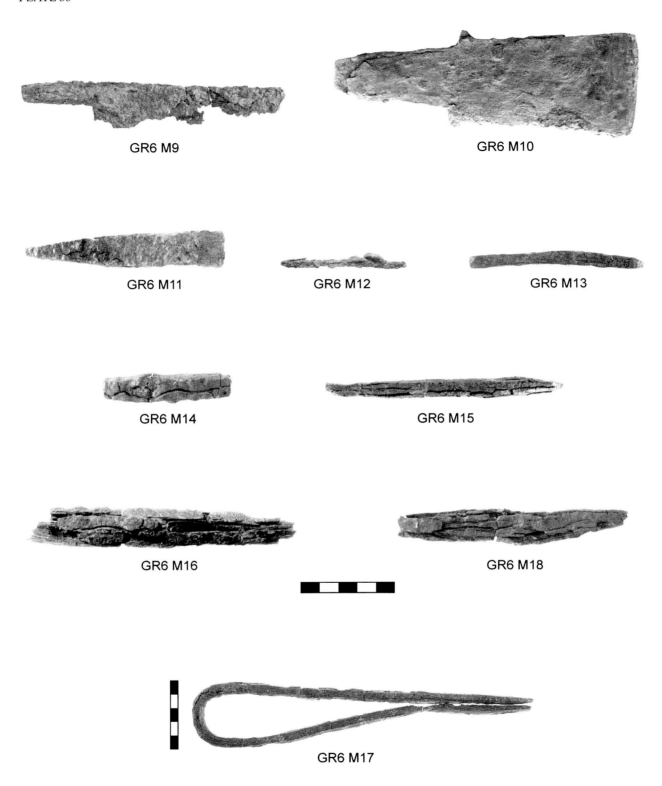

GR6 M9

GR6 M10

GR6 M11

GR6 M12

GR6 M13

GR6 M14

GR6 M15

GR6 M16

GR6 M18

GR6 M17

Plate 30. Grave 6 iron finds: knife (**GR6 M9**), axe-head (**GR6 M10**), chisel (**GR6 M11**), awl or chisel (**GR6 M12**), tools (**GR6 M13**, **GR6 M18**), punch or hammer (**GR6 M14**), files (**GR6 M15**, **GR6 M16**), and tongs (**GR6 M17**). Photos **GR6 M13**, **GR6 M17** C. Papanikolopoulos.

PLATE 31

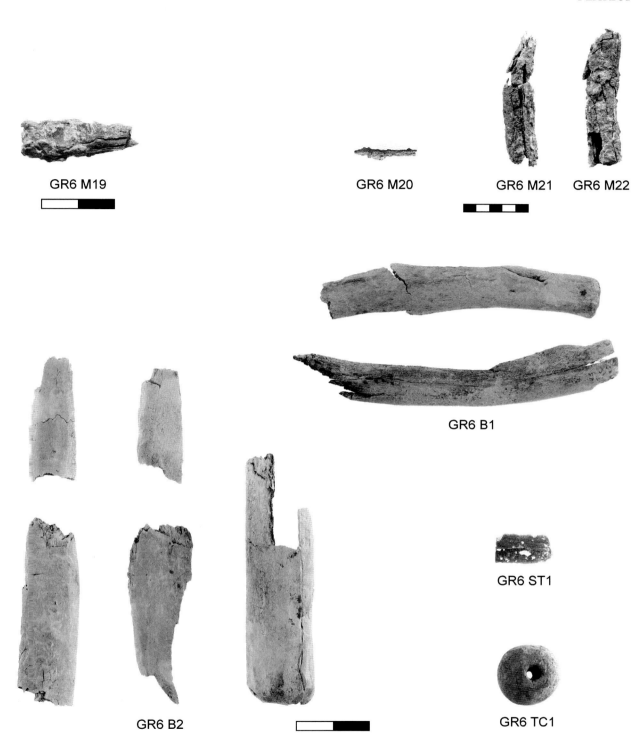

GR6 M19

GR6 M20 GR6 M21 GR6 M22

GR6 B1

GR6 B2

GR6 ST1

GR6 TC1

Plate 31. Grave 6 metal and other finds: iron tool (**GR6 M19**), iron awl(?) (**GR6 M20**), iron handles(?) (**GR6 M21**, **GR6 M22**), modified antlers (**GR6 B1**, **GR6 B2**), obsidian blade (**GR6 ST1**), and terracotta bead (**GR6 TC1**). Photos **GR6 B1** and **GR6 B2** C. Papanikolopoulos.

PLATE 32

Plate 32A. Grave 9: wall V 5303 on right; view from west.

Plate 32B. Grave 9; view from east.

Plate 32C. Grave 9: spears along west wall; view from east.

GR6 P2

GR6 P3

GR6 P4

GR6 P6

GR6 P9

Plate 32D. Grave 9 pottery: skyphoi (**GR9 P2**, **GR9 P3**), kalathos (**GR9 P4**), miniature jug (**GR9 P6**), and jug (**GR9 P9**).

PLATE 33

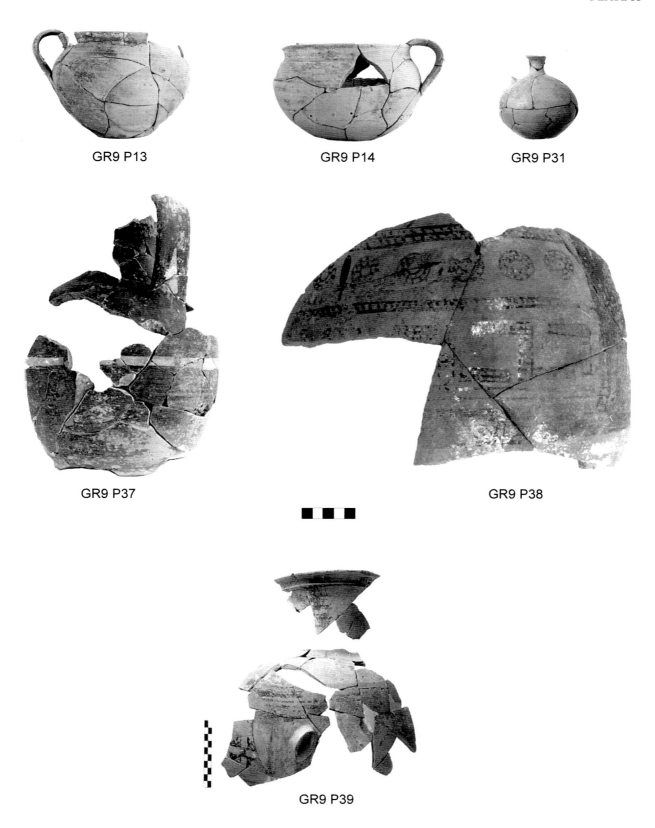

GR9 P13

GR9 P14

GR9 P31

GR9 P37

GR9 P38

GR9 P39

Plate 33. Grave 9 pottery: cups (**GR9 P13**, **GR9 P14**), aryballos (**GR9 P31**), jug (**GR9 P37**), and amphorae (**GR9 P38**, **GR9 P39**).

PLATE 34

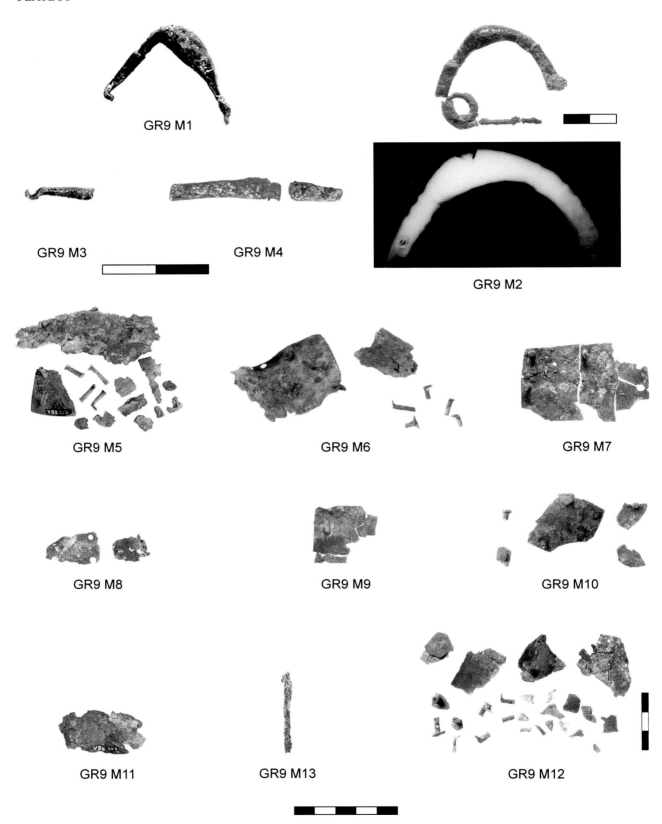

Plate 34. Grave 9 metal finds: bronze fibulae (**GR9 M1**, **GR9 M2** [X-ray view not to scale], **GR9 M3**), bronze awl/tool (**GR9 M4**), bronze sheeting fragment groups (**GR9 M5–GR9 M12**), and iron pin (**GR9 M13**). Photo **GR9 M2** K. Hall.

PLATE 35

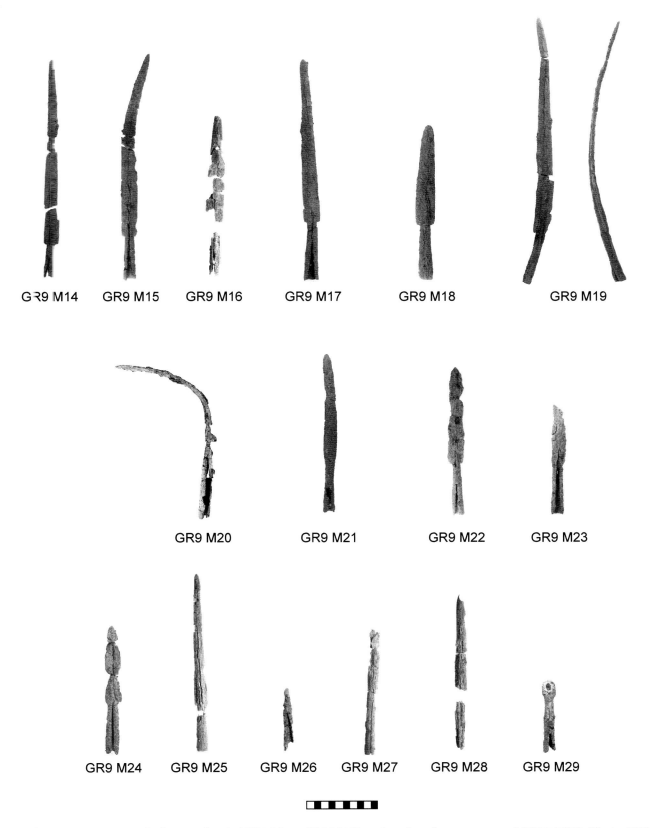

Plate 35. Grave 9 iron finds: spearheads (**GR9 M14–GR9 M28**), and socketed weapon or tool (**GR9 M29**). Photo **GR9 M21** C. Papanikolopoulos.

PLATE 36

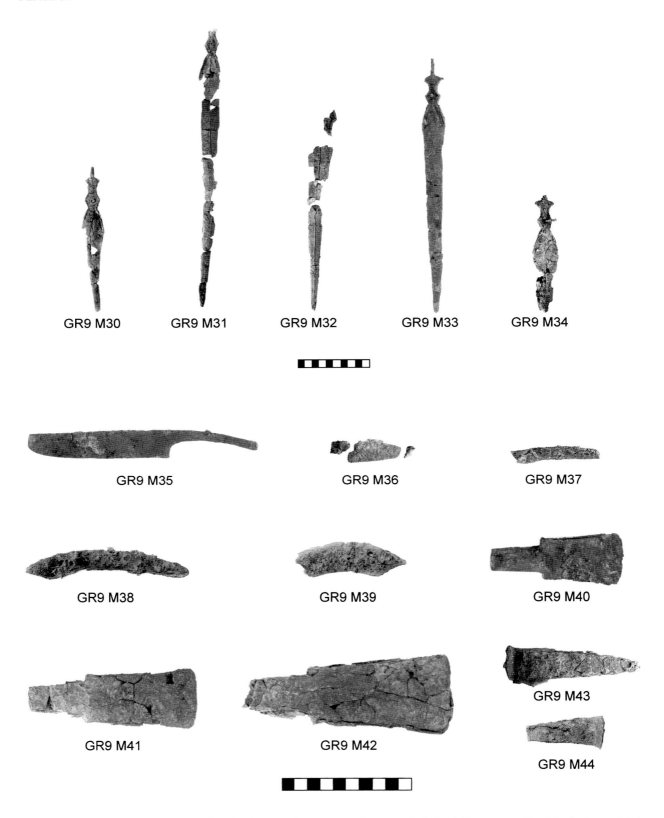

Plate 36. Grave 9 iron weapons and tools: daggers (**GR9 M30**, **GR9 M32**), dirks (**GR9 M31**, **GR9 M33**), dagger/dirk (**GR9 M34**), knives (**GR9 M35–GR9 M39**), axe-heads (**GR9 M40–GR9 M42**), and scrapers (**GR9 M43**, **GR9 M44**). Photo **GR9 M35** C. Papanikolopoulos.

PLATE 37

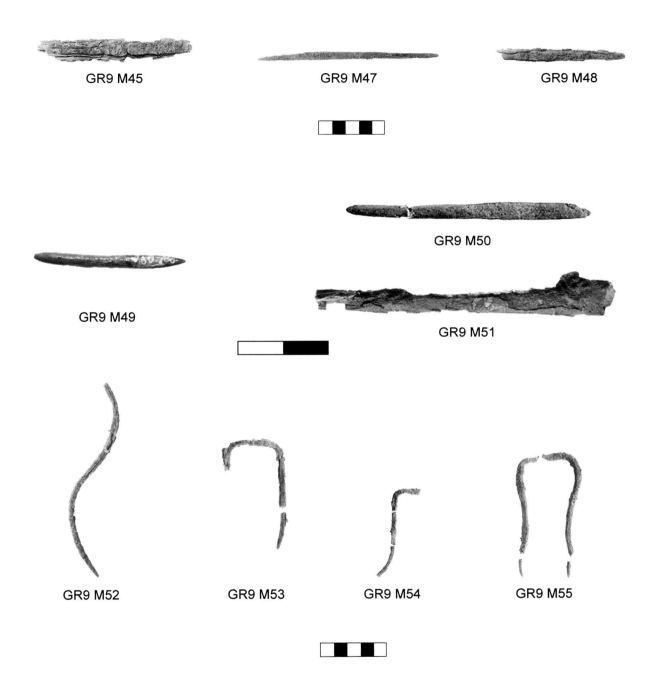

GR9 M45

GR9 M47

GR9 M48

GR9 M50

GR9 M49

GR9 M51

GR9 M52

GR9 M53

GR9 M54

GR9 M55

Plate 37. Grave 9 iron finds: chisel (**GR9 M45**), awls (**GR9 M47–GR9 M50**), tool (**GR9 M51**), and fleshhooks (**GR9 M52–GR9 M55**). Photo **GR9 M45** C. Papanikolopoulos.

PLATE 38

Plate 38A. Grave 10: pithos burial in south half; view from west.

Plate 38B. Grave 10: pithos burial in south half; view from south.

Plate 38C. Grave 10: after removal of pithos; view from south.

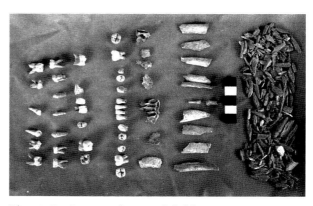

Plate 38D. Grave 10: bones of child.

Plate 38E. Grave 10: pithos **GR10 P1**.

Plate 38F. Grave 10: close-up of the decoration of pithos **GR10 P1**.

PLATE 39

Plate 39A. Grave 12: aerial view
(north at top).

Plate 39B. Grave 12, Burial 6: squatting facet on
distal left tibia.

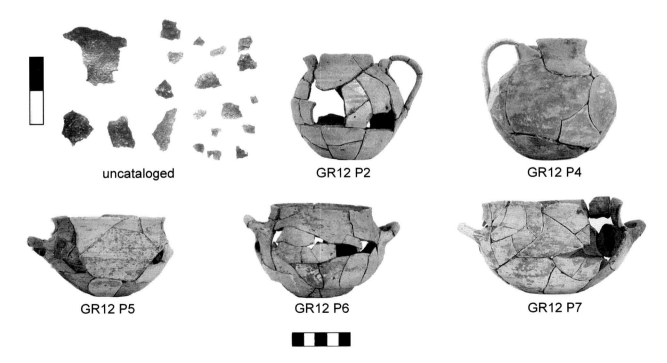

uncataloged   GR12 P2   GR12 P4

GR12 P5   GR12 P6   GR12 P7

Flate 39C. Grave 12 metal find and pottery: uncataloged bronze sheeting, cup (**GR12 P2**), wide-mouthed jug (**GR12 P4**), and skyphoi (**GR12 P5–GR12 P7**).

PLATE 40

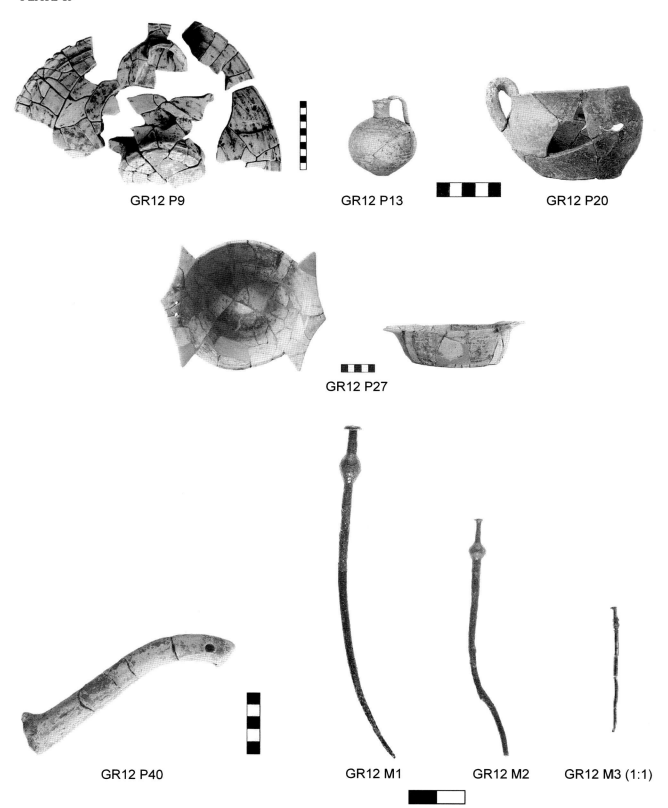

Plate 40. Grave 12 pottery and bronze finds: kalathos (**GR12 P9**), aryballos (**GR12 P13**), cup (**GR12 P20**), tray (**GR12 P27**), ladle or scuttle handle (**GR12 P40**), and bronze pins (**GR12 M1–GR12 M3**). Photos **GR12 M1**, **GR12 M2** C. Papanikolopoulos.

PLATE 41

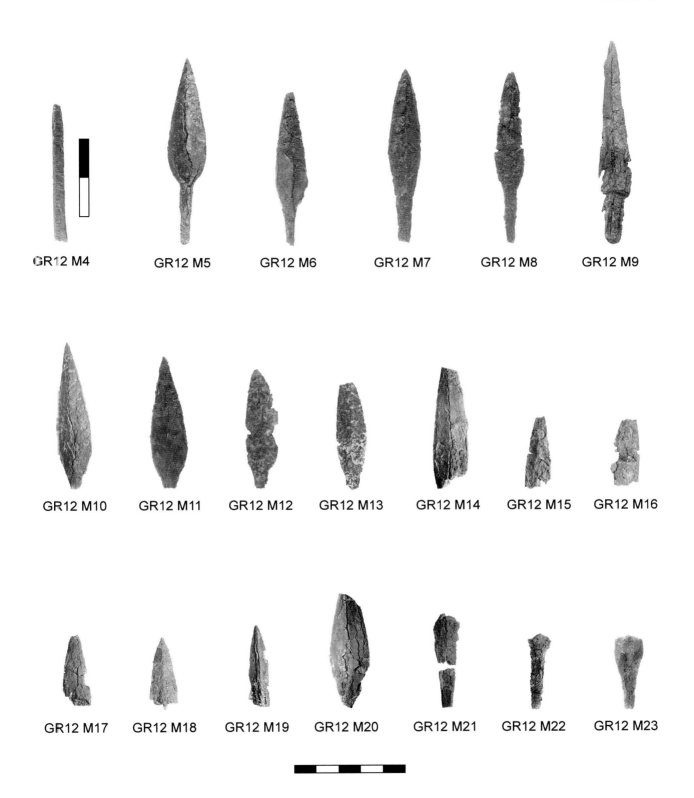

GR12 M4   GR12 M5   GR12 M6   GR12 M7   GR12 M8   GR12 M9

GR12 M10   GR12 M11   GR12 M12   GR12 M13   GR12 M14   GR12 M15   GR12 M16

GR12 M17   GR12 M18   GR12 M19   GR12 M20   GR12 M21   GR12 M22   GR12 M23

Plate 41. Grave 12 metal finds: bronze tool (**GR12 M4**) and iron arrowheads (**GR12 M5–GR12 M23**). Photo **GR12 M9**
C. Papanikolopoulos.

PLATE 42

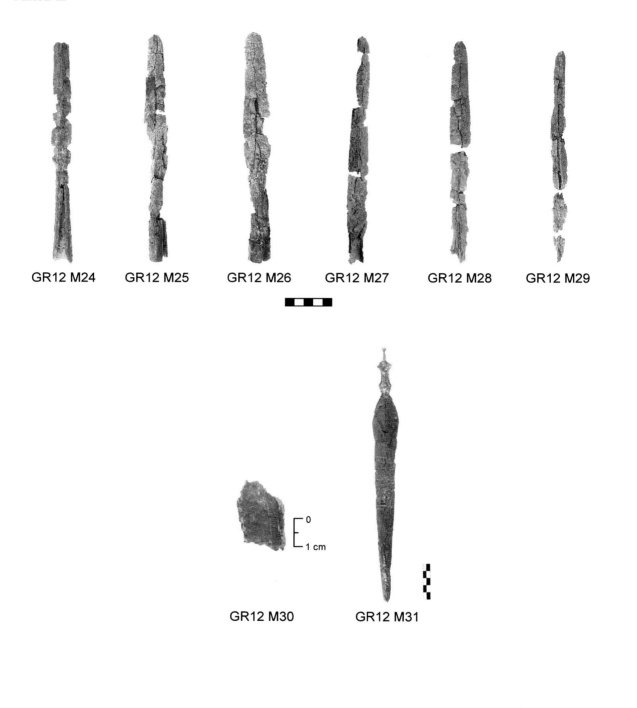

GR12 M24 GR12 M25 GR12 M26 GR12 M27 GR12 M28 GR12 M29

GR12 M30 GR12 M31

GR12 M32 GR12 M33 GR12 M34

Plate 42. Grave 12 iron finds: spearheads (**GR12 M24–GR12 M30**), dirk (**GR12 M31**), and knives (**GR12 M32–GR12 M34**).

PLATE 43

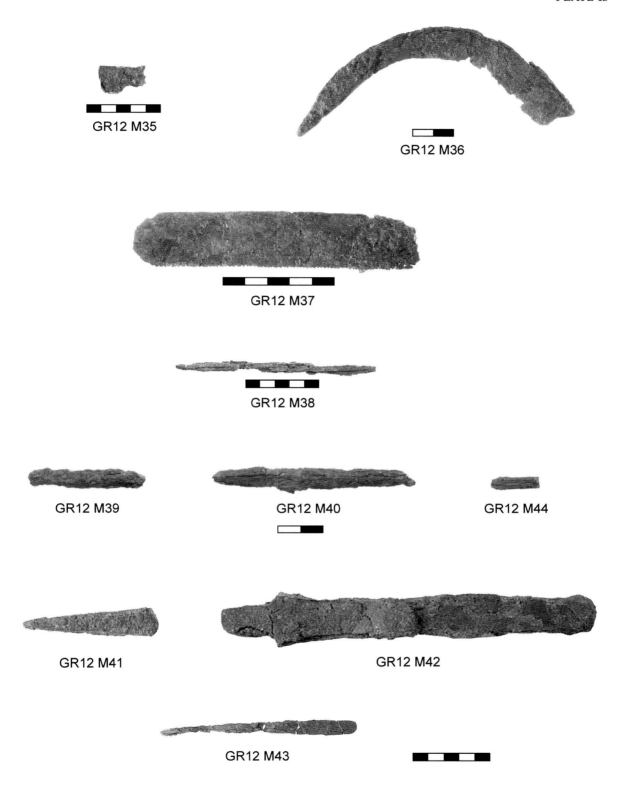

GR12 M35

GR12 M36

GR12 M37

GR12 M38

GR12 M39   GR12 M40   GR12 M44

GR12 M41   GR12 M42

GR12 M43

Plate 43. Grave 12 iron finds: knife (**GR12 M35**), sickle-shaped knife (**GR12 M36**), saw (**GR12 M37**), file (**GR12 M38**), awl or chisel (**GR12 M39**), chisels (**GR12 M40**, **GR12 M41**), tools (**GR12 M42**, **GR12 M44**), and spatulate tool (**GR12 M43**). Photo **GR12 M37** C. Papanikolopoulos.

PLATE 44

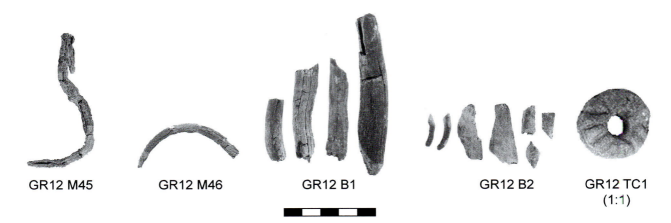

GR12 M45   GR12 M46   GR12 B1   GR12 B2   GR12 TC1
(1:1)

Plate 44A. Grave 12 finds: iron fleshhooks (**GR12 M45**, **GR12 M46**), modified antlers (**GR12 B1**, **GR12 B2**), and terracotta bead (**GR12 TC1**). Photos **GR12 B1**, **GR12 B2** C. Papanikolopoulos.

Plate 44B. Grave 15: circle of stones in doorway; view
from west.

Plate 44C. Grave 16: aerial view
(north at top).

Plate 44D. Grave 16: after excavation; view from southeast.

PLATE 45

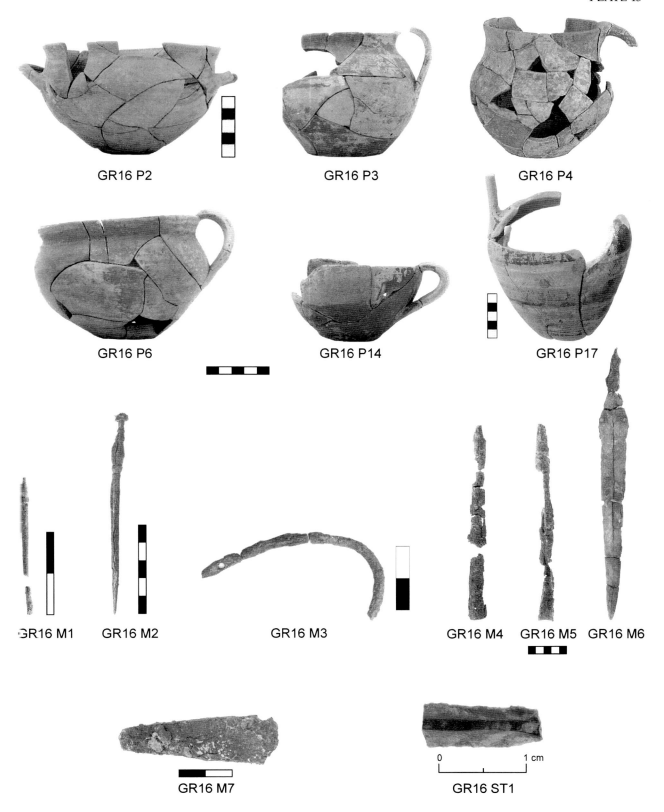

GR16 P2

GR16 P3

GR16 P4

GR16 P6

GR16 P14

GR16 P17

GR16 M1

GR16 M2

GR16 M3

GR16 M4

GR16 M5

GR16 M6

GR16 M7

0   1 cm

GR16 ST1

Plate 45. Grave 16 pottery and other finds: skyphos (**GR16 P2**), cups (**GR16 P3**, **GR16 P4**, **GR16 P6**, **GR16 P14**), amphora (**GR16 P17**), iron pins (**GR16 M1**, **GR16 M2**), iron needle (**GR16 M3**), iron spearheads (**GR16 M4**, **GR16 M5**), iron dirk (**GR16 M6**), iron chisel (**GR16 M7**), and obsidian blade (**GR16 ST1**). Photo **GR16 ST1** C. Papanikolopoulos.

PLATE 46

Plate 46A. Grave 17: view from south (Graves 10 and 12 in background).

Plate 46B. Grave 17: aerial view (also shows Graves 10 and 12; north at top). G. = Grave.

Plate 46C. Grave 17: view from west.

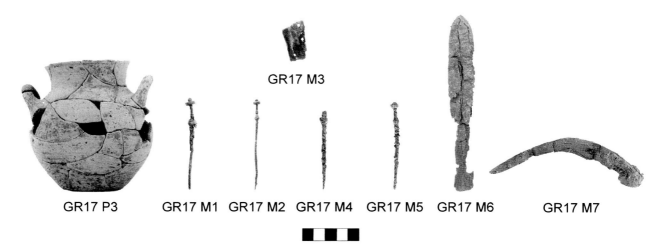

Plate 46D. Grave 17 pottery and metal finds: necked jar (**GR17 P3**), bronze pins (**GR17 M1**, **GR17 M2**), bronze sheeting (**GR17 M3**), iron pins (**GR17 M4**, **GR17 M5**), iron spearhead (**GR17 M6**), iron sickle-shaped knife (**GR17 M7**).

PLATE 47

Plate 47A. Grave 19: tree root growing through grave; view from north.

Plate 47B. Grave 20: aerial view (north at top).

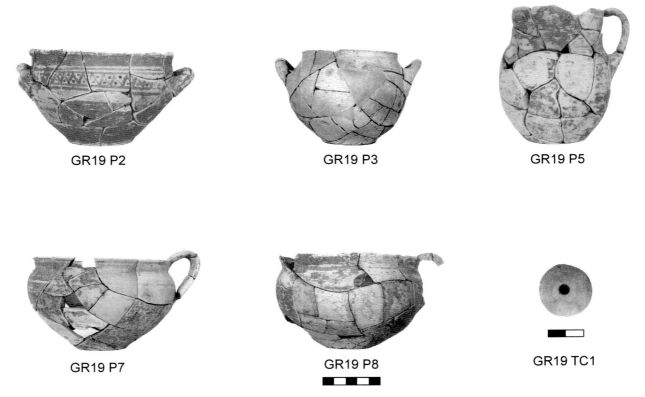

GR19 P2

GR19 P3

GR19 P5

GR19 P7

GR19 P8

GR19 TC1

Plate 47C. Grave 19 pottery and terracotta find: skyphoi (**GR19 P2**, **GR19 P3**), wide-mouthed jug (**GR19 P5**), cups (**GR19 P7**, **GR19 P8**), and terracotta bead (**GR19 TC1**).

PLATE 48

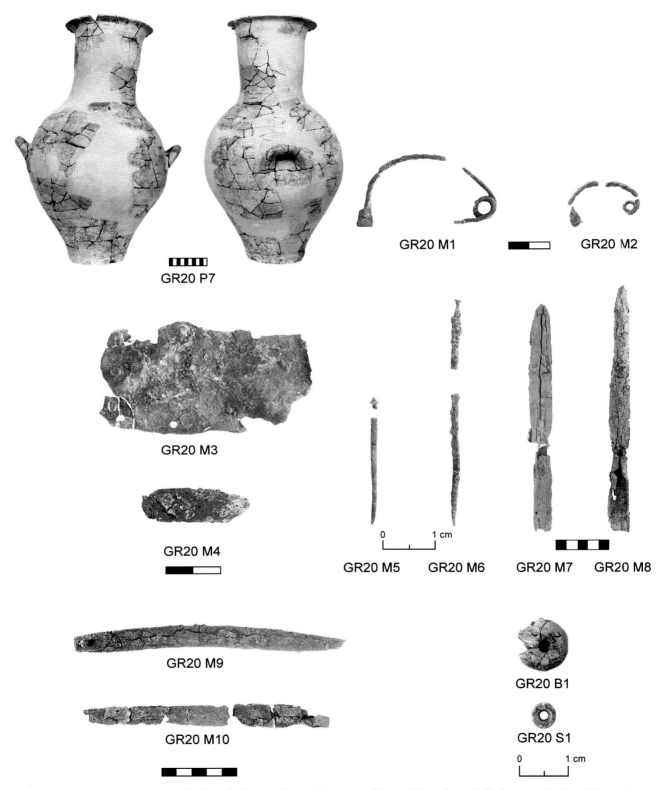

Plate 48. Grave 20 pottery and other finds: amphora (**GR20 P7** [front left, side right]), bronze fibulae (**GR20 M1**, **GR20 M2**), bronze sheeting (**GR20 M3**, **GR20 M4**), iron pins (**GR20 M5**, **GR20 M6**), iron spearheads (**GR20 M7**, **GR20 M8**), iron knives (**GR20 M9**, **GR20 M10**), bone or ivory bead (**GR20 B1**), and stone bead (**GR20 S1**). Photo **GR20 M9** C. Papanikolopoulos.

PLATE 49

Plate 49A. Grave 21: aerial view (north at top).

Plate 49B. Grave 21: top of grave showing rubble; view from south.

Plate 49C. Grave 21: top of cremation burials; view from south.

Plate 49D. Grave 21: pithos burial; view from southeast.

Plate 49E. Grave 21: pithos burial with objects inside; view from south.

Plate 49F. Grave 21: pithos burial after removal of contents; view from south.

PLATE 50

Plate 50A. Grave 21: bones of Burial 1.

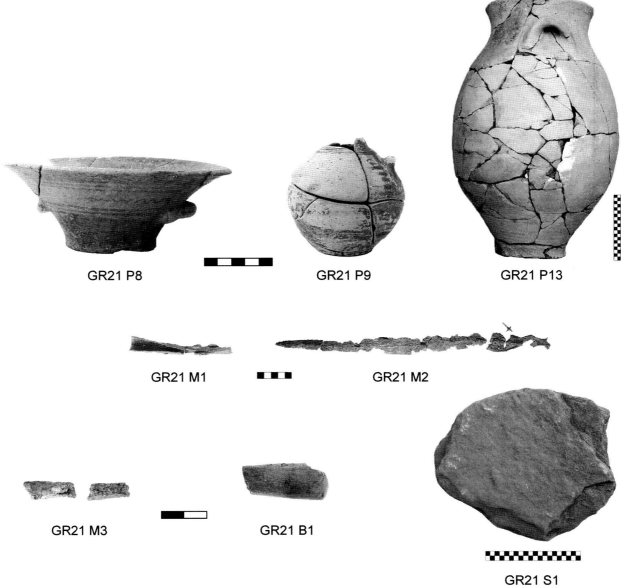

GR21 P8

GR21 P9

GR21 P13

GR21 M1

GR21 M2

GR21 M3

GR21 B1

GR21 S1

Plate 50B. Grave 21 pottery and other finds: kalathos (**GR21 P8**), oinochoe (**GR21 P9**), restored pithos (**GR21 P13**), iron spearhead (**GR21 M1**), iron dirk (**GR21 M2**), lead tubes (**GR21 M3**), modified deer antler (**GR21 B1**), and stone lid for pithos (**GR21 S1**).

PLATE 51

Plate 51A. Grave 23: view from north.

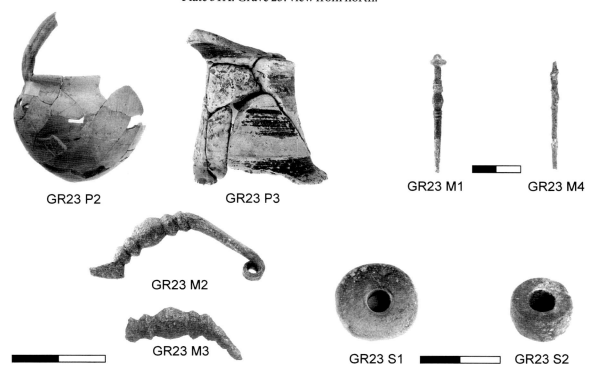

GR23 P2

GR23 P3

GR23 M1

GR23 M4

GR23 M2

GR23 M3

GR23 S1

GR23 S2

Plate 51B. Grave 23 pottery and other finds: basket vase (**GR23 P2**), stemmed krater (**GR23 P3**), bronze pin (**GR23 M1**), bronze fibulae (**GR23 M2**, **GR23 M3**), iron needle (**GR23 M4**), and stone beads (**GR23 S1**, **GR23 S2**).

PLATE 52

Plate 52A. Grave 26: aerial view (north at top).

Plate 52B. Grave 26: layer of stones separating the amphora burial from the lower burials; view from south.

Plate 52C. Grave 26: east wall and pit below at bottom of amphora burial; view from west.

Plate 52D. Grave 26: amphora burial; view from east.

Plate 52E. Grave 26: close-up of amphora burial from southeast.

PLATE 53

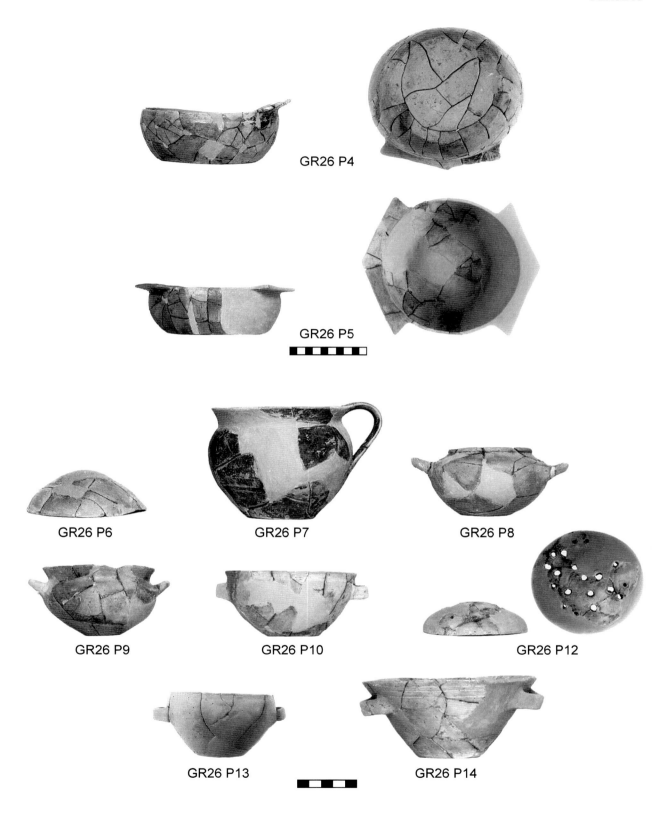

Plate 53. Grave 26 pottery: trays (**GR26 P4**, **GR26 P5**), lids (**GR26 P6**, **GR26 P12**), cup (**GR26 P7**), skyphoi (**GR26 P8**–**GR26 P10**, **GR26 P13**), and kalathos (**GR26 P14**). Photos C. Papanikolopoulos.

PLATE 54

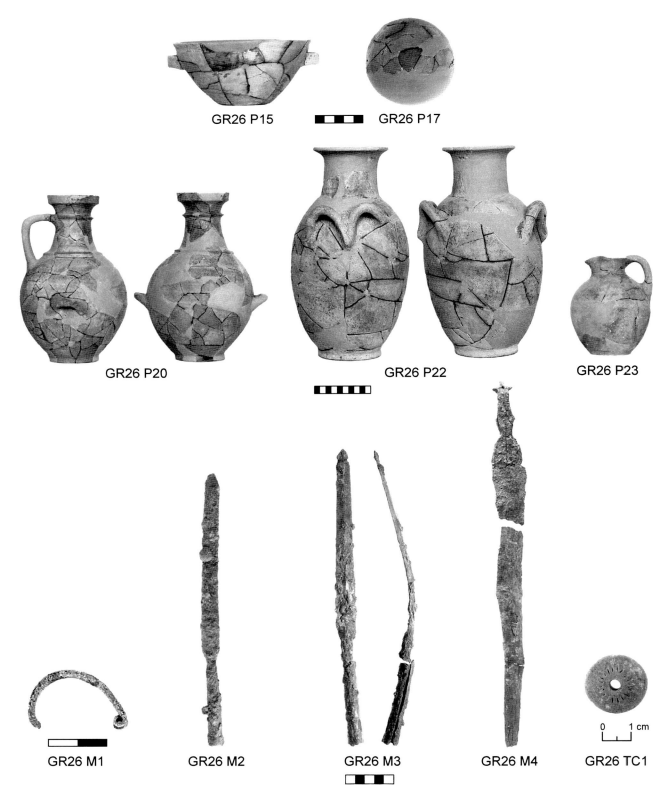

Plate 54. Grave 26 pottery and other finds: kalathos (**GR26 P15**), lid (**GR26 P17**), hydria (**GR26 P20**), amphora (**GR26 P22**), oinochoe (**GR26 P23**), bronze fibula (**GR26 M1**), iron spearheads (**GR26 M2**, **GR26 M3**), iron dirk (**GR26 M4**), and terracotta bead (**GR26 TC1**). Photos **GR26 P15**, **GR26 P17**, **GR26 P20**, **GR26 P22**, **GR26 P23** C. Papanikolopoulos.

PLATE 55

Plate 55A. Grave 27: aerial view (north at top).

Plate 55B. Grave 27: east wall (V 9253); view from west.

Plate 55C. Grave 27: south wall (V 9258) and platform; view from west.

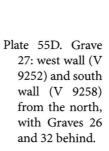

Plate 55D. Grave 27: west wall (V 9252) and south wall (V 9258) from the north, with Graves 26 and 32 behind.

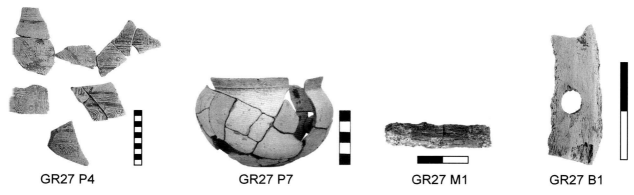

GR27 P4   GR27 P7   GR27 M1   GR27 B1

Plate 55E. Grave 27 pottery and other finds: fragments of krater (**GR27 P4**), cup (**GR27 P7**), iron tool (**GR27 M1**), and modified antler (**GR27 B1**). Photo **GR27 B1** C. Papanikolopoulos.

PLATE 56

Plate 56A. Grave 28: top of amphora Burial 6; view from west.

Plate 56B. Grave 28: amphora Burial 6; view from north-west.

Plate 56C. Grave 28: amphora Burials 6 and 7; view from west.

Plate 56D. Grave 28: aerial view (north at top).

Plate 56E. Grave 28: east wall VW 11015; view from west.

Plate 56F. Grave 28: tops of south and west walls, and sides of north and east walls; view from southwest.

PLATE 57

Plate 57A. Grave 28: deposit of cups in southeast corner and iron tool **GR28 M6**.

Plate 57B. Grave 28: Reconstructed group of Burials 6 and 7 with cup/lid **GR28 P19** on amphora **GR28 P3**, cup **GR28 P4** over necked jar **GR28 P22**, and stone lid **GR28 S1**.

GR28 P1   GR28 P2   GR28 P3

GR28 P4   GR28 P5

Plate 57C. Grave 28 pottery: skyphos (**GR28 P1**), jug (**GR28 P2**), amphora (**GR28 P3**), and cups (**GR28 P5**, **GR28 P4**).

PLATE 58

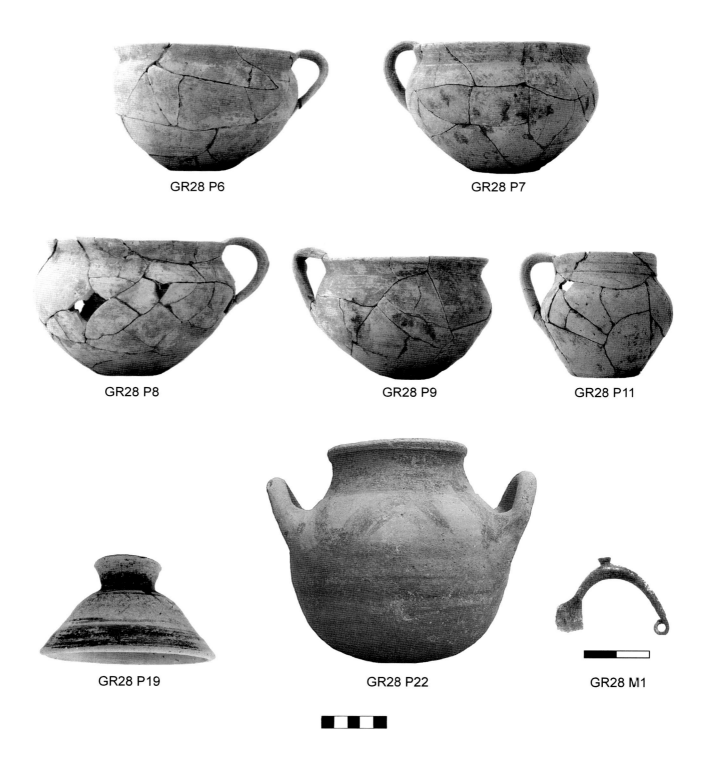

Plate 58. Grave 28 pottery and bronze find: cups (**GR28 P6**–**GR28 P9**), mug-like cup (**GR28 P11**), lid (**GR28 P19**), necked jar (**GR28 P22**), bronze fibula (**GR28 M1**).

PLATE 59

Plate 59A. Grave 28 iron objects: javelin heads (**GR28 M2**, **GR28 M3**), knife (**GR28 M4**), axe-head (**GR28 M5**), and tool (**GR28 M6**).

Plate 59B. Grave 29: lead button (**GR29 M1**).

Plate 59C. Grave 30: aerial view (north at top).

PLATE 60

Plate 60A. Grave 30: fractured left ulna of Burial 5.

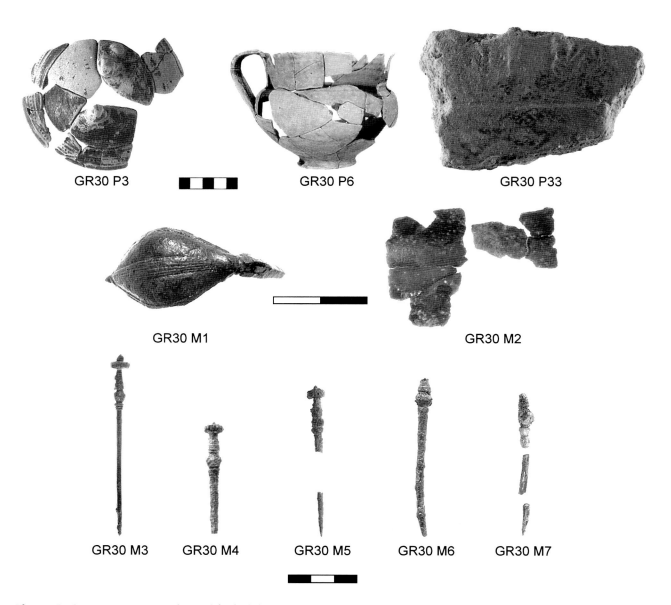

GR30 P3   GR30 P6   GR30 P33

GR30 M1   GR30 M2

GR30 M3   GR30 M4   GR30 M5   GR30 M6   GR30 M7

Plate 60B. Grave 30 pottery and metal finds: lid (**GR30 P3**), cup (**GR30 P6**), relief pithos fragment (**GR30 P33**), bronze fibula (**GR30 M1**), bronze sheeting (**GR30 M2**), and iron pins (**GR30 M3–GR30 M7**). Photos **GR30 P33** and **GR30 M3** C. Papanikolopoulos.

PLATE 61

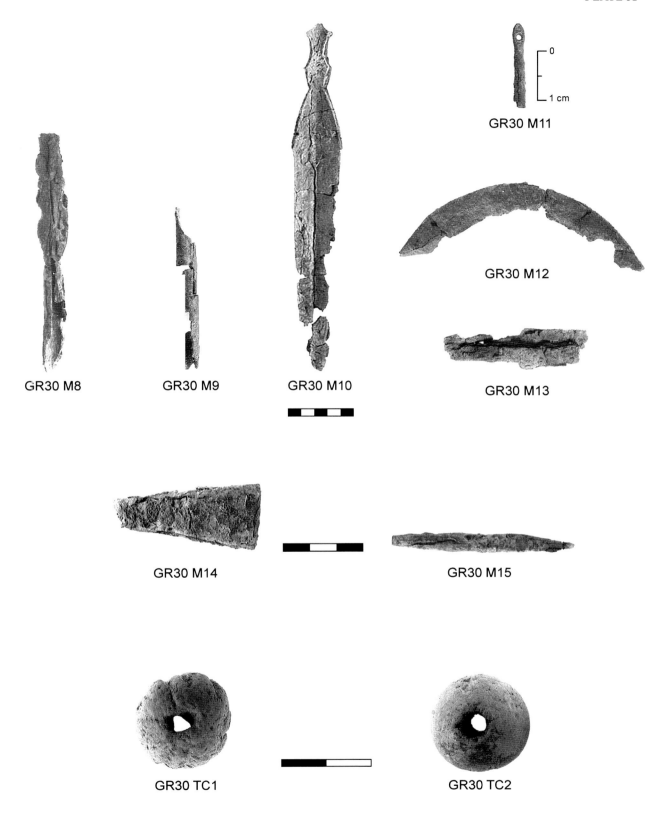

GR30 M11

GR30 M8

GR30 M9

GR30 M10

GR30 M12

GR30 M13

GR30 M14

GR30 M15

GR30 TC1

GR30 TC2

Plate 61. Grave 30 iron and terracotta finds: iron spearheads (**GR30 M8**, **GR30 M9**), dirk (**GR30 M10**), needle (**GR30 M11**), sickle-shaped knife (**GR30 M12**), axe head (**GR30 M13**), chisel (**GR30 M14**), and tool (**GR30 M15**); terracotta beads (**GR30 TC1**, **GR30 TC2**).

PLATE 62

Plate 62A. Grave 32: aerial view also showing Grave 25, in 1989 (north at top).

Plate 62B. Grave 32: aerial view also showing Grave 25, in 1990 (north at top).

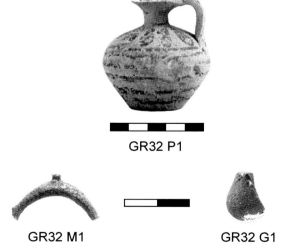

Plate 62C. Grave 32 finds: aryballos (**GR32 P1**), bronze fibula (**GR32 M1**), and glass bead (**GR32 G1**).

Plate 62D. Grave 34: view from east.

PLATE 63

Plate 63A. Grave 35: aerial view (north at top).

Plate 63B. Grave 36: aerial view (north at top).

Plate 63C. Grave 36: fracturing of stones in east wall; view from northwest.

GR36 P1   GR36 P2   GR36 P3

Plate 63D. Grave 36 pottery: skyphoi (**GR36 P1–GR36 P3**).

PLATE 64

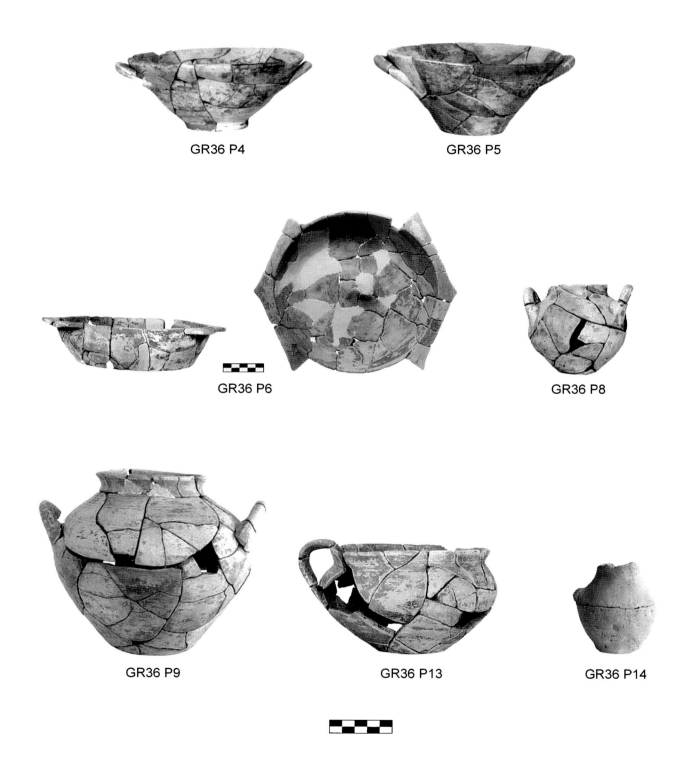

GR36 P4

GR36 P5

GR36 P6

GR36 P8

GR36 P9

GR36 P13

GR36 P14

Plate 64. Grave 36 pottery: kalathoi (**GR36 P4**, **GR36 P5**), tray with reflex lugs (**GR36 P6**), small necked jar (**GR36 P8**), necked jar (**GR36 P9**), cup (**GR36 P13**), and juglet (**GR36 P14**).

PLATE 65

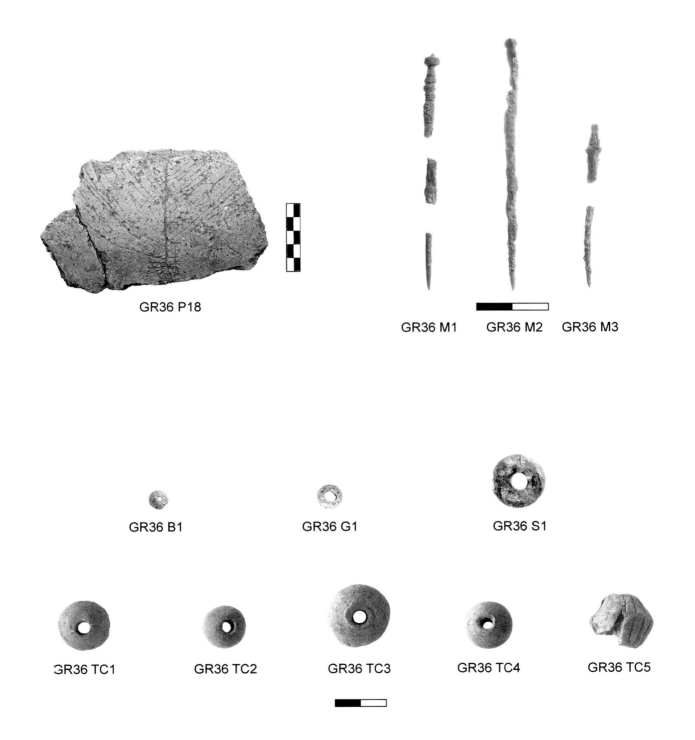

GR36 P18

GR36 M1   GR36 M2   GR36 M3

GR36 B1   GR36 G1   GR36 S1

GR36 TC1   GR36 TC2   GR36 TC3   GR36 TC4   GR36 TC5

Plate 65. Grave 36 finds: incised pithos sherd (**GR36 P18**), iron pins (**GR36 M1**–**GR36 M3**), bone or ivory bead (**GR36 B1**), glass bead (**GR36 G1**), rock crystal bead (**GR36 S1**), and terracotta beads (**GR36 TC1**–**GR36 TC5**).

PLATE 66

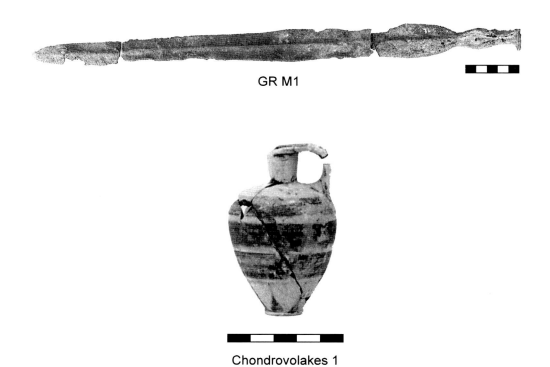

GR M1

Chondrovolakes 1

Plate 66A. Finds from Boyd's 1900 excavations: short iron sword (**GR M1**) and aryballos (**Chondrovolakes 1**).

Plate 66B. Grave 30: pelvis and vertebrae in anatomical position.

Plate 66C. Experimental pig cremation.

PLATE 67

Plate 67A. Grave 21, Burial 5: vertebral marginal osteo-phytes and facets with osteoarthritic pitting.

Plate 67B. Grave 9, Burial 5: linea aspera enthesopathy (muscle tear).

Plate 67C. Grave 6, Burial 1: ulna enthesopathy.

Plate 67D. Grave 30, Burial 5: fractured ulna, dorsal view.

Plate 67E. Grave 5, Burial 7: radius and ulna injury on inhumation.

Plate 67F. Grave 5, Burial 2 or 3: fractured zygomatic.

PLATE 68

Plate 68A. Grave 23, Burial 1: periosteal bone in infant tibia.

Plate 68B. Grave 19, Burial 4: dental abscess.

Plate 68C. Grave 3, Burial 1: hyperostosis frontalis interna.

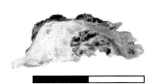

Plate 68D. Grave 5, Burial 4: infant sphenoid lytic lesion.

Plate 68E. Grave 24, Burial 1: hystiocytosis lesions on cranium.

Plate 68F. Grave 21, Burial 4 (left) and Burial 6 (right): crania with metopic sutures.

Plate 68G. Grave 12, Burial 4: suprameatal pit.

PLATE 69

Plate 69A. Grave 26: burned ovicaprid bones. Photo C. Papanikolopoulos.

Plate 69B. Grave 26: burned ovicaprid bones. Photo C. Papanikolopoulos.

Plate 69C. Grave 12: cervid metapodials. Photo C. Papanikolopoulos.

Plate 69D. Grave 10: pot stand for pithos burial; view from the south.

Plate 69E. Grave 21: pot stand for pithos burial; view from south.

Plate 69F. Vronda ridge; view from east. Photo K.T. Glowacki.

PLATE 70

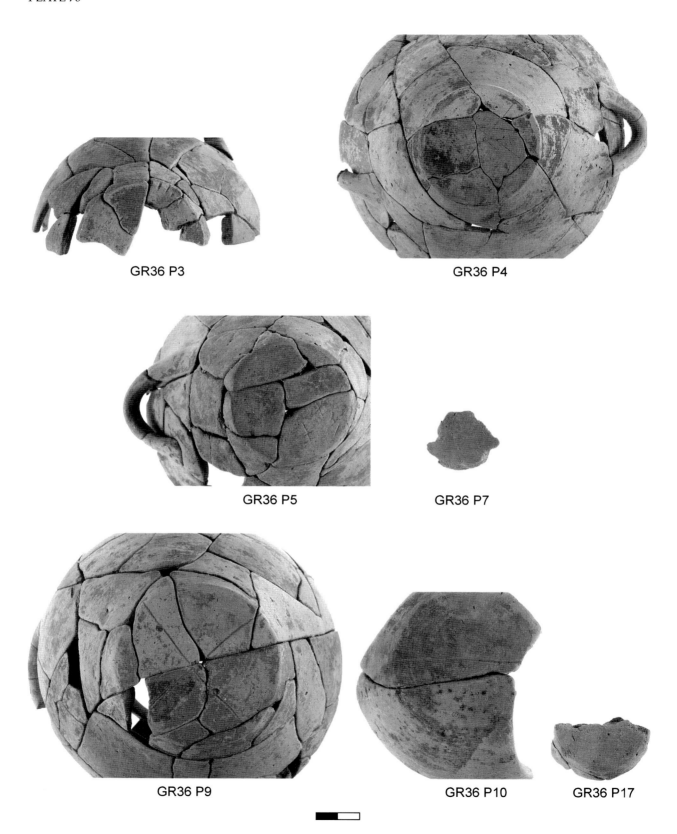

GR36 P3

GR36 P4

GR36 P5

GR36 P7

GR36 P9

GR36 P10

GR36 P17

Plate 70. Grave 36, pot marks (**GR36 P3–GR 36 P5**, **GR36 P7**, **GR36 P9**, **GR36 P10**, **GR36 P17**). Photos C. Papanikolopoulos.

PLATE 71

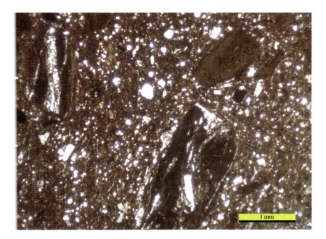

Plate 71A. Fabric Group 1, semi-coarse (KAV 15/17 [**GR9 P45**]), x25. Photomicrograph E. Nodarou.

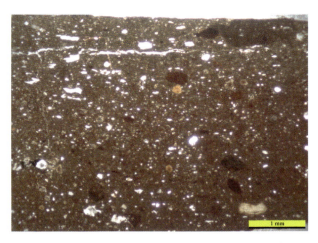

Plate 71B. Fabric Group 1, semi-fine (KAV 15/40 [**GR4 P16**]), x25. Photomicrograph E. Nodarou.

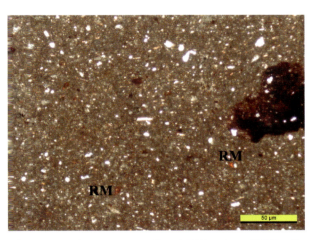

Plate 71C. Fabric Group 1, fine (KAV 15/102 [**IX P36**]), x50. Note the bright red minerals (RM) in the clay matrix. Photomicrograph E. Nodarou.

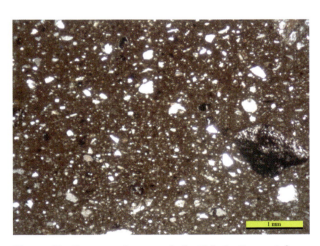

Plate 71D. Comparative sample for Fabric Group 1 from Papadiokampos (PDK 11/6), x25. Photomicrograph E. Nodarou.

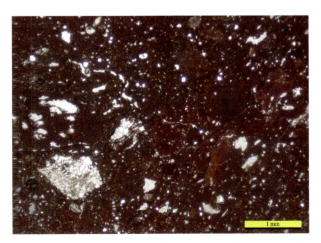

Plate 71E. Fabric Group 2 (KAV 15/77 [**GR28 P20**]), x25. Photomicrograph E. Nodarou.

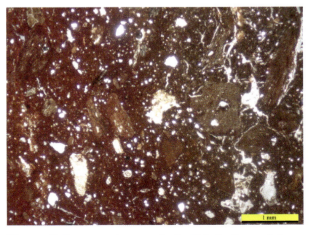

Plate 71F. Comparative sample for Fabric Group 2 from Papadiokampos (PDK 11/110), x25. Photomicrograph E. Nodarou.

PLATE 72

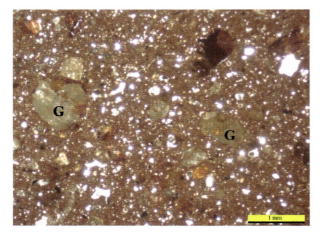

Plate 72A. Fabric Group 3 (KAV 15/24 [**GR9 P38**]), ×25. G = greenstone. Photomicrograph E. Nodarou.

Plate 72B. Clay sample from Chamaizi (CS 16/11), ×25. Note similarity with Fabric Groups 2 and 3. P = brown phyllite; G = greenstone. Photomicrograph E. Nodarou.

Plate 72C. Sample KAV 15/58 (**GR16 P22**), ×50. Photomicrograph E. Nodarou.

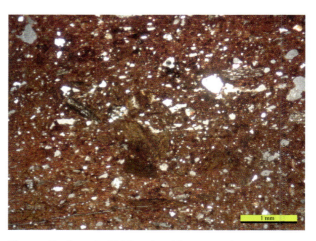

Plate 72D. Sample KAV 15/62 (**GR17 P11**), ×25. Photomicrograph E. Nodarou.

Plate 72E. Sample KAV 15/101 (**IX P9**), ×25. Photomicrograph E. Nodarou.

Plate 72F. Comparative sample for KAV 15/101 (**IX P9**) from Papadiokampos (PDK 11/172), ×50. Photomicrograph E. Nodarou.

PLATE 73

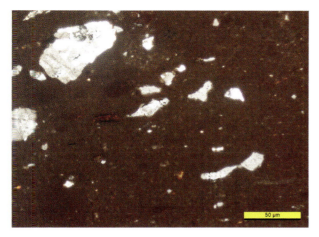

Plate 73A. Fabric Group 4 (KAV 15/57 [**GR12 P11**]), x50. Photomicrograph E. Nodarou.

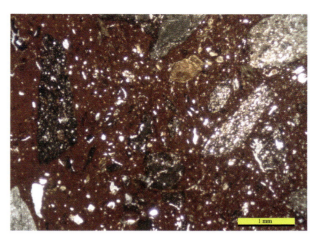

Plate 73B. Fabric Group 5 (KAV 15/29 [**GR6 P27**]), x25. Photomicrograph E. Nodarou.

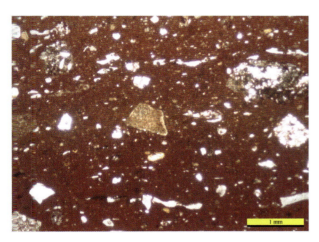

Plate 73C. Fabric Group 6 (KAV 15/83 [**GR30 P28**]), x25. Photomicrograph E. Nodarou.

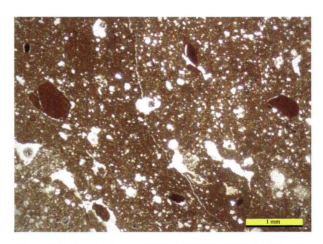

Plate 73D. Fabric Group 7 (KAV 15/45 [**GR1 P11**]), x25. Photomicrograph E. Nodarou.

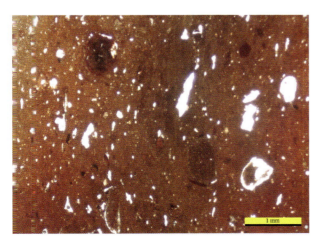

Plate 73E. Sample KAV 15/30 (**GR6 P28**), x25. Photomicrograph E. Nodarou.

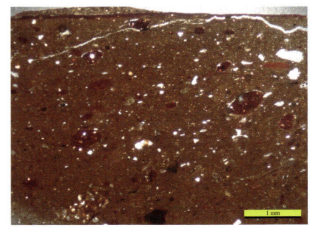

Plate 73F. Sample KAV 15/2 (**GR9 P18**), x25. Photomicrograph E. Nodarou.

PLATE 74

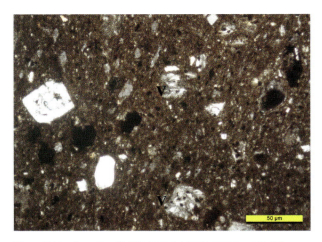

Plate 74A. Sample KAV 15/34 (**GR5 P15**), x50. Photomicrograph E. Nodarou.

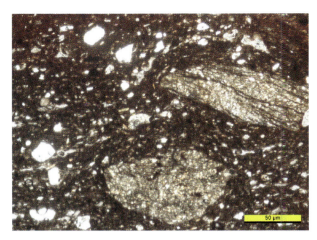

Plate 74B. Sample KAV 15/28 (**GR6 P22**), x50. Photomicrograph E. Nodarou.

Plate 74C. Sample KAV 15/64 (**GR19 P17**), x50. Photomicrograph E. Nodarou.

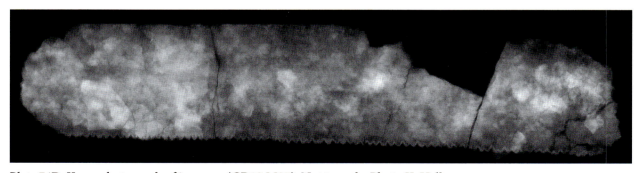

Plate 74D. X-ray photograph of iron saw (**GR12 M37**). Not to scale. Photo K. Hall.

PLATE 75

Plate 75A. Textile impression on spearhead **GR6 M6**. Photo K. Hall.

Plate 75B. View from Vronda summit looking north–northeast. Photo M. Eaby.

Plate 75C. View from Vronda west slope looking southwest–west across the northern isthmus of Ierapetra and the bay of Mirabello. Photo M. Eaby.

PLATE 76

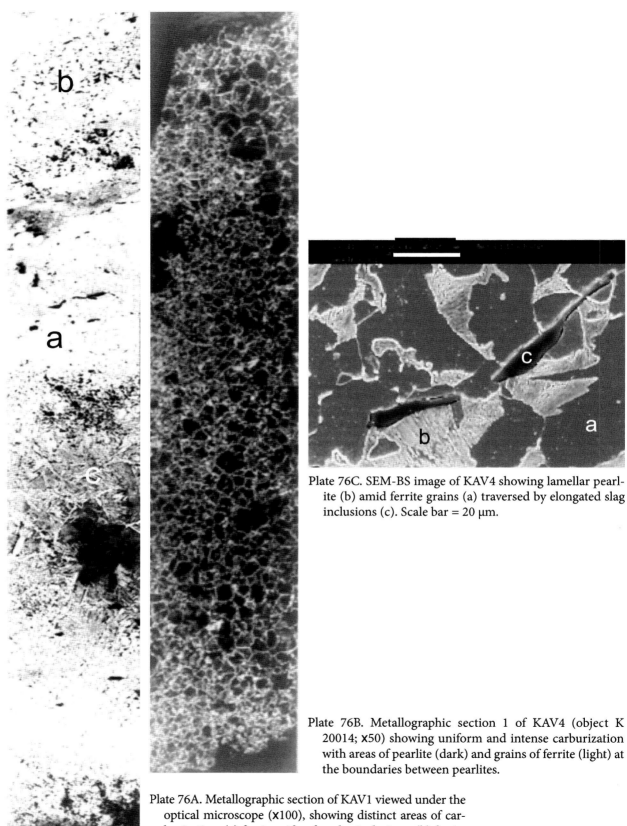

Plate 76C. SEM-BS image of KAV4 showing lamellar pearlite (b) amid ferrite grains (a) traversed by elongated slag inclusions (c). Scale bar = 20 μm.

Plate 76B. Metallographic section 1 of KAV4 (object K 20014; x50) showing uniform and intense carburization with areas of pearlite (dark) and grains of ferrite (light) at the boundaries between pearlites.

Plate 76A. Metallographic section of KAV1 viewed under the optical microscope (x100), showing distinct areas of carburization: (a) ferrite with a few slag inclusions, (b) ferrite with many slag inclusions, and (c) ferrite and pearlite.

PLATE 77

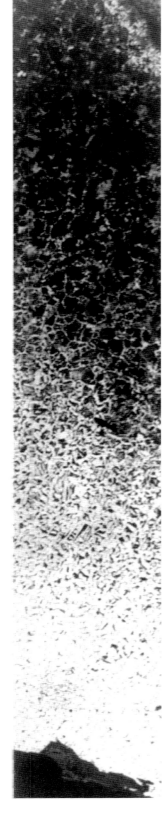

Plate 77A. Metallographic section 2 of KAV10 (object K 20014; x50) showing uneven carburization across the section with pearlite (dark) and grains of ferrite (light), and a gradual increase of carburization from the bottom to the top of the image.

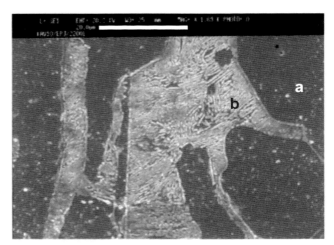

Plate 77B. SEM-BS image of KAV10 showing area of lamellar pearlite (b) with ferrite (a). Scale bar = 20 μm.

PLATE 78

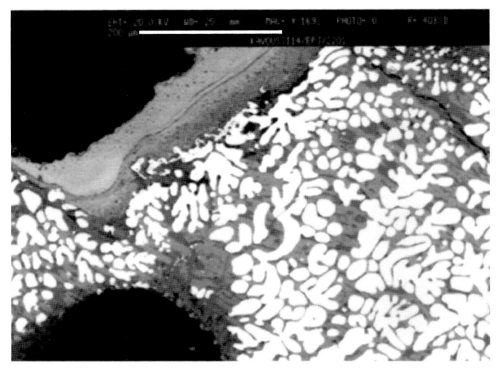

Plate 78A. SEM-BS image of KAV14 showing globular wustite (FeO, bright), needles of fay-alite (gray and appearing below wustite), and (weathered) interstitial glass (darker shade of gray). Scale bar = 100 μm.

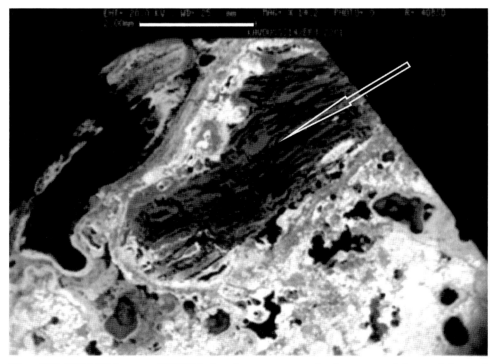

Plate 78B. SEM-BS image of KAV14 showing remnants of a fragment of charcoal (arrow) trapped within the matrix of partially reduced iron oxide. Scale bar = 2 mm.

PLATE 79

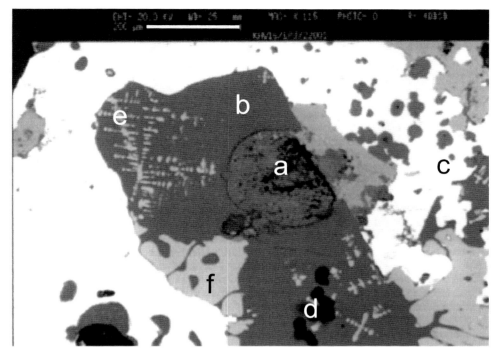

Plate 79A. SEM-BS image of KAV16 showing an unreacted iron ore inclusion (a) trapped within fayalite phase slag (b) and metallic iron (c); pores (d), dendrites of wustite (e), and globular iron oxide evolving from fine dendrites (f) are also visible. Scale bar = 200 μm.

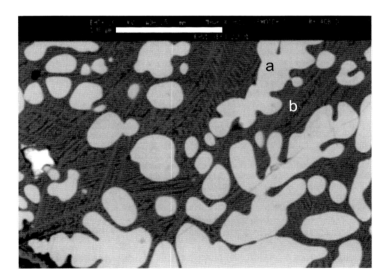

Plate 79B. SEM-BS image of KAV17 showing large dendrites of globular wustite (a) and fine dendrites of fayalite (b) growing out of interstitial glass (grayish black). The sequence by which the various phases will form depends on the localized conditions, with wustite forming first, followed by fayalite, and whatever Fe has not been "bound" by those two phases will remain in the glassy phase, the last to solidify. Scale bar = 100 μm.

PLATE 80

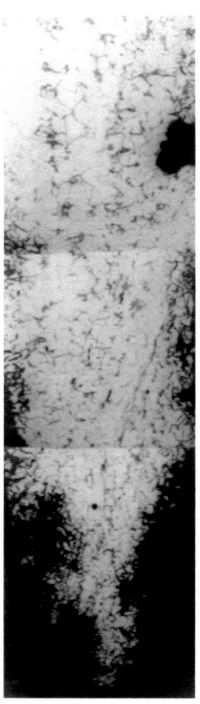

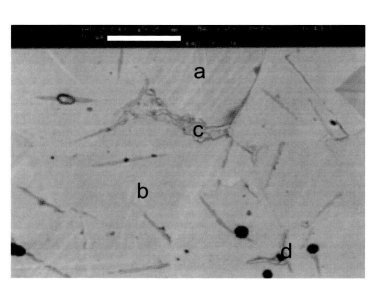

Plate 80A. SEM-BS image of KAV11 showing ferrite (a), fine and well-developed needles of iron nitride (b), cementite (c), and small slag inclusions (d). Scale bar = 50 μm.

Plate 80B. Metallographic section of KAV 26 (x50) showing ferrite with multiple slag inclusions following the line of working or hammering (composite of three images).

PLATE 81

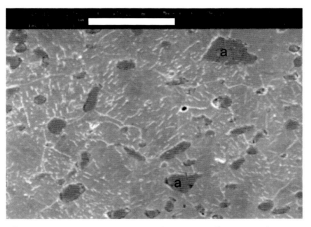

Plate 81B. SEM-BS image of KAV33 showing slag inclusions (a) of various sizes trapped within the ferrite matrix, with cementite growing within the grain boundaries. Scale bar = 100 μm.

Plate 81A. Metallographic section of KAV33 (x50) showing ferrite with multiple slag inclusions lining up along the line of working or hammering.

Plate 81C. Metallographic section of KAV35 (x50) showing ferrite matrix with many elongated slag inclusions drawn along direction of line of working.

PLATE 82

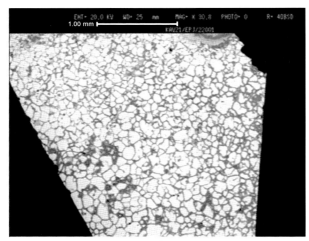

Plate 82A. SEM-BS image of KAV21 showing a section of the copper alloy consisting of tin bronze with lead inclusions. Intergranular growth of copper sulphide is shown in the dark areas around grain boundaries. Scale bar = 1 mm.

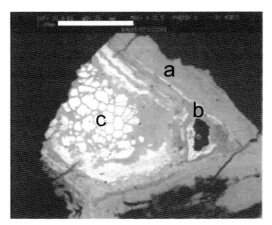

Plate 82B. SEM-BS image of upper section of KAV15 showing the metallic iron envelope having completely weathered to iron oxide (a), small islands of remaining low carbon iron (b), and angular grains of Cu-Sn alloy (c) separated by corrosion (light gray). Scale bar = 1 mm.

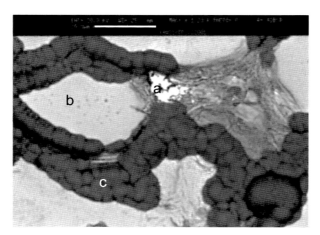

Plate 82C. SEM-BS image of KAV21 showing lead metal inclusion (a) at the grain boundaries of a copper-tin alloy (b), and with volume expanded (looking puffed up) and tin chloride corrosion growing at the grain boundaries (c). Scale bar = 20 μm.

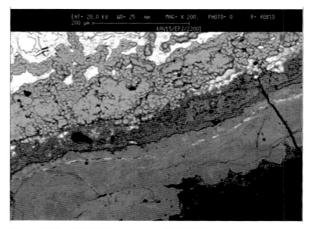

Plate 82D. SEM-BS image of KAV15 showing the interface between the copper alloy and iron part of the fibula. Scale bar = 200 μm.

PLATE 83

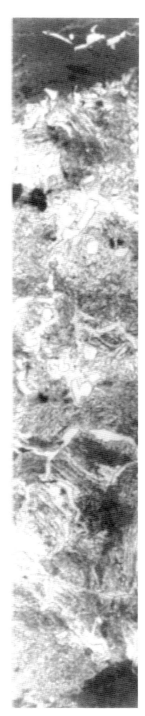

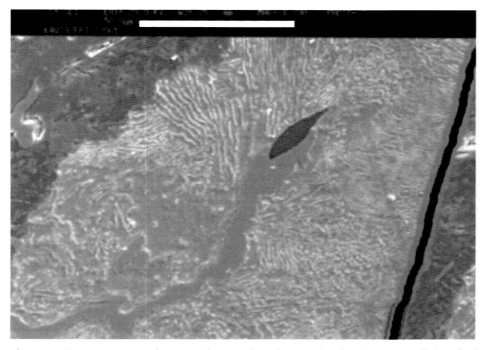

Plate 83A. Metallographic section of KAV29 (x50) showing a largely ferrite matrix with areas of angular pearlite.

Plate 83B. SEM-SE image of KAV29 showing lamellar pearlite (bright), a long "island" of ferrite (light gray), and a small teardrop-shaped slag inclusion near the center. Scale bar = 50 μm.